# Sipping from
## the Nile

# JEAN NAGGAR

# Sipping from the Nile

⚜

## My Exodus from Egypt

### A MEMOIR

*Jan. 2014*
*For Harriett,*
*Best wishes,*
*Jean Naggar.*

PUBLISHED BY

**amazon**encore ≶

Published by AmazonEncore
P.O. Box 400818
Las Vegas, NV 89140

ISBN-13: 9781612181417
ISBN-10: 1612181414

THESE PAGES ARE DEDICATED TO
THE PAST AND TO THE FUTURE

Thank you!

---

To the memory of my father, Guido Mosseri,
who always knew I would write.

To my mother, Joyce Smouha Mosseri, who supported
this project throughout and gave me her best stories.

To my children, Alan, David, and Jennifer,
and to my grandchildren, Ari, Justin, Gabriella,
Sarah, Anna, Yaniv, and Ben.

*For all of whom this book was written.*

To my husband, Serge Naggar,
who is essential to this story.

# Table of Contents

# Acknowledgements

I am deeply grateful for the time and support offered so generously by my family and friends. My profound thanks go to so many that I hardly know where to start.

My sister Susan read this memoir in all its iterations, steadfast and wise in her counsel and unfailing in her faith in the project.

My brother Jeff offered insights and anecdotes, lent me books, and read early material.

My children were always ready to help, commiserate, or rejoice. I deeply appreciate the gift beyond price of their time and valuable expertise. And thank you, Michael, for my title!

My cousins Dicky, Sylvia, Derrick, Judy, Brian, Hana, Gilly, Michael, Viviane, Gerry, Guy, Sandy, Suzanne, Helen, and Jackie, who shared so many of the experiences I describe, refrained from trying to impose their own memories on mine. All read the manuscript and shared wonderful additional information and anecdotes, some of which I was unfortunately not able to incorporate into this book. Thank you all. I could not have written it without your enthusiastic participation and the knowledge of your eagerness to share this with your children.

Particular appreciation goes to Viviane Bregman, who, despite an aversion to reading, read every word of several drafts along the way, and to my brother-in-law, Michel Danon, and my cousin Jackie Coen, whose caring and careful readings resulted in the correction of some inaccuracies. Bertie Bregman's early words of advice helped me to give shape to what I wanted to say. My school friend from the GPS offered invaluable help and connections in my search for early photos.

My friends Lynne Barasch, Firth Fabend, Benita Somerfield, Vivette Ancona, Betty Prashker, Sybil Steinberg, Wendy Weltz, Anne Engel, and Barbara Grossman had such unshakable faith in the viability of the project that it spurred me on when my spirits flagged and gave me the courage to pursue a readership beyond my family. Vicky Bijur went way beyond the call of friendship and duty in her advocacy and hard work for this book. She and Betty Prashker would not let me give up. No writer could have hoped for more steadfast, generous supporters.

Gratitude also to my office family for offering kind support at every turn and allowing me, every now and then, to switch roles and express my writerly angst to them; and to Maureen Baron and Susan Schwartz for their excellent suggestions.

My appreciation for the enthusiastic contribution of Mark Ferguson's expertise is boundless. I could not have put it all together without his help.

No words can fully express my deep gratitude to Fabrizio LaRocca for his kindness, creativity, and commitment to the project.

And thank you, Serge, for everything.

*A falouka on the Nile*

# PROLOGUE

*Sheets of rain* slashed down the steep sides of apartment buildings, instantly forming rivers that flowed toward the gutters and pooled along the sidewalk. It was a New York rain, violent and complete, pouring with sudden vigor from a leaden sky. The splayed skeletons of dead umbrellas lay beside mounds of garbage bags awaiting removal. The detritus of hundreds of peoples' lives clustered loosely in the glistening black bags, shifting and shuddering with the weight of the rain. Drenched and desperate I waved my arms at every cab in sight, all of them sporting "Off Duty" lights, the drivers hunched over the wheel, eyes staring straight ahead. I thought I had given myself plenty of time to get to my appointment at a Midtown publishing house, lulled into a false security by the gentle drizzle that had preceded this downpour. Now I was certainly going to be late.

I stood on the corner of Third Avenue and Seventy-Fifth Street. My office was close by. I glanced back, wondering if I should return and take refuge there, but I knew there was no way I could reach my author by phone to explain my delay. He was in town for the day and was counting on my presence at this meeting. I would have to find a way to get there. I clutched my umbrella, which tugged at my hand as the wind gusted, turning inside out and back, wrenching my arm and adding to my misery. My other arm went on pumping up and down, my sleeve dripping and my hand cold, as I grumbled under my breath. At last, miraculously, a cab stopped right in front of me. I clambered in, trailing water. Heaving a sigh of relief, I gave the Midtown address and sat back.

"A lot of rain," said the driver, peering at his streaked windshield. "This is a very bad rainstorm."

I agreed, but something about the cadences of his speech snagged my mind away from the moment. A stillness took hold of me. The present had become muted. The distant past stirred. Later, as we drew up in front of my destination, I asked tentatively, "Are you from Egypt?"

"Yes," said the driver without turning around, "I am Egyptian," his accent softening the hard *g* into a gentle slide of sound.

"I am from Egypt, too," I said, gathering my mortally wounded umbrella, my briefcase, and my gloves, and steeling myself for a dive into the protection of the glass-walled building to my right. There was silence as my cold hands fumbled in my briefcase for some change. The driver did not turn his head.

"Did you celebrate Ramadan?" he asked suddenly. I felt uncomfortable. The events of September 11th, the escalating suicide bombings in Israel, and the relentless rumblings and aftermath of war with Iraq invested the simple question with a weight beyond itself.

"No, I did not," I answered cautiously, and then, having been a New Yorker for many years, I added a little defiantly, "I am Jewish."

"I did not celebrate Ramadan either," he said, turning his head to look at me. "I am a Copt, a Christian." He added wistfully, "It is not a good time for Copts to be in Egypt anymore. So now I am here, in America. My family is in America."

I nodded, smiled, gave him a substantial tip, grabbed the receipt he held out to me, and headed for my meeting.

For the next three hours, the literary agent I have been for the past thirty years took over my thoughts and my energies. I worked to charm the wary, enhancing and facilitating the encounter between my author and his publisher, his editor, and his publicist. When balance was achieved at last, and smiles and handshakes had seen us on our way, the author and I stopped for a celebratory cup of coffee before he headed back to the bus to make his way to the airport, the edited manuscript weighing down his briefcase and his right arm.

Later, at home in my Manhattan apartment, I stood on my small sliver of terrace, hands on the metal balustrade, and gazed out at a jagged landscape of rooftops and windows, glancing down at the street gleaming below. All that was left of the rain was a soggy memory. The sky was still gray, but a few inches of clear blue had eased in here and there. I thought about my two small granddaughters, Sarah and Anna, cousins who would be visiting us together the following day, and wondered how I could occupy their busy minds and fingers, smiling to myself as I imagined their chatter and their intent faces. But somehow my thoughts kept returning to my cab driver and our brief conversation. I thought about how he had said "I am Egyptian," and I had said "I am from Egypt." I thought of another little girl and another terrace long ago. I remembered a photo. It was a black-and-white photo of a small girl in white pajamas, her dark hair rolled into a high curl on the top of her head above a solemn face with large, questioning, dark eyes. In the photo, she sits on a wooden horse on wheels on the expansive terrace outside her bedroom. How huge the balcony seemed then, bulwarked as it was by a massive stone balustrade, the heavy waters of the Nile glinting and rippling through the spaces between pillars. In the photo, the house, solid and permanent, towers above.

Memories are strange creatures. They hide in the shadows, lurk in the interstices of life, summoned by a smell, a sound, the expression on someone's face, the angle of a body, a turn in the road. Phantom passengers as we proceed along our lives, they brush a fleeting touch of the past against our urgent present.

As I stood and looked down at Seventy-Second Street in Manhattan remembering the little girl I had once been, I put my hand to my face, assaulted by a tactile memory of rubbing my cheek against the grainy stone of that balcony's wall in 1957. Trapped in the glare of a relentless Egyptian summer sun, I was leaning against the side of the house as if to absorb its solid warmth into my veins, tears blurring my view of the garden gate and the swirling Nile beyond. I could not believe that I would never see any of it again, that I was about to walk out of the red brick mansion my grandfather had built so many years ago to plunge into a future that had no framework, no guidelines, and no boundaries. It was terrifying. I was saying good-bye.

For two hundred years, my father, his father, and generations before them had spread roots in this ground. They had lived and loved, borne children, built houses and businesses, navigated among kings and princes, and prospered. This was their country.

✢ ✢ ✢

My grandfather, Joseph Mosseri, was born in Cairo in 1869, the year when the convoluted politics and finances attending the Suez Canal project culminated at last in the opening of the Suez Canal. Gazing contentedly from his windows at the changing and changeless surface of the great Nile River, he could hardly have imagined that a triumphant international event the year of his birth would disturb the deep roots his family had planted in Egyptian soil. This was his home. Nothing would change.

But in the summer of 1956 as the year began its descent into autumn, the winds of change gusted strongly, although to a girl sitting on a swing seat in the gardens of a fabled Swiss hotel, their portent was invisible. My mother, father, brother, sister, and I were accustomed to spending several weeks with my mother's parents and assorted aunts, uncles, and cousins at the Gstaad Palace Hotel to escape the fierce Egyptian heat as soon as the children were freed from school, then leaving for Europe, with three generations settling in for generous weeks of relaxation in mountain resorts, Villars, Crans, Chamonix, Gstaad, Wengen, St. Moritz, Interlaken, and others, where we revived in the indescribably clean, sweet-smelling mountain air and the company of family and friends. Later we would travel to European cities to absorb history and culture from monuments and museums, the rich cultural menu interspersed with the serious frivolity of shopping for change-of-season clothes.

The summer of 1956 was different.

A miasma of anxiety seemed to seep into every attempt at pleasure and relaxation. My brother, Jeff, and I still laughed and clowned our way through our tango lessons with the tall, ineffably elegant Mr. de Roy, but my parents and their friends looked more worried every day. They spent long hours reading the papers and huddling in groups around the vast, hushed lobby of the Palace Hotel, the men muttering anxiously over the stock tables in the *International Herald Tribune* or the *Wall Street Journal*, leaning back into large velvet armchairs, cups of after-lunch coffee balanced in their hands. I was distantly aware that something was wrong, but no one explained, and the unease I felt quickly disappeared as the tennis lessons and hikes, the dances and dinners, and the lazy mornings by the pool succeeded each other day after day.

✤ ✤ ✤

The uneasy August eventually drew to its close. As planned, we left Gstaad and moved on to London, to a red brick building in Victoria, minutes from Buckingham Palace, where my parents rented a "service flat" for a few weeks every year. In 1956, however, our arrival at St. James's Court did not herald my mother's and my yearly visit to the venerable Dickens & Jones department store to outfit me for a new year at boarding school. That year we were to see my brother Jeff off to his boarding school at Gresham's in Norfolk, and then return immediately to Cairo. We knew that my father's mother, Granny Mosseri, and my Aunt Helen had already settled into their daily routine and were looking forward to our return to the big house we all shared. My mother's family planned to stay longer in Europe, as they usually did.

When we left London for home, I was filled with a growing sense of excitement. My boarding school days were over at last. The strange summer that had seemed to float threateningly in a different universe had receded into the past without incident, and my disappointment at not having the possibility of attending Oxford or Cambridge was somewhat muted by the large envelope from the British Council awaiting me at home, in Cairo, containing confirmation of my acceptance into the university BA-abroad program. I had already received an enticing list of books to order for the courses. I had read the list so often that I almost knew it by heart. An addicted reader, I could hardly wait to go to the bookstore and put in my order knowing that the books were not in stock and would have to be sent from England. A few days after our return I attended the orientation and was impatient to start my first class the following week.

But no one went anywhere the week following our return. Nasser, Egypt's military dictator, nationalized the Suez Canal, bringing the armed forces of Britain and France posthaste to Egypt to protect international passage through the canal. Israeli forces began their march across the desert to join them. All planes scheduled to leave the country were grounded. Beyond the iron railings that surrounded our garden, we could hear muted gunfire, rifle shots, and the shouts of fierce, dense crowds demonstrating in the streets. Our home became our prison.

My sister, Susan, was eight. I was eighteen.

⚜ ⚜ ⚜

History—our family's and Egypt's alike—changed irrevocably that dazzling summer day as I stood on the stone terrace outside my bedroom and watched the world of my childhood ripple away, drowning in the heavy, grey waters of the Nile. Like a submerged Atlantis, it would shimmer faintly under the swell of life, invisible, untouchable, lost.

*Cairo*

# My Lost Egypt

*I knew* from earliest childhood that the world was a dangerous place, even though circumstances and my parents collaborated to shield me from that knowledge.

The walls of my nursery were painted to a rough finish, covered in a pink-tinged stucco that caught the sunlight pouring in from tall windows and transmuted it into a delicate filtered glow. My bed, snug against the left-hand wall, had a pink painted headboard with fuzzy lambs and bunnies frolicking in the center. In the next room, within earshot of a squeal, my Yugoslav nanny, Vera, slept among pale-blue furniture, guardian of the bathroom and the toy cupboard, an open door between us.

Nonetheless, from a young age I was convinced that monsters lurked under my bed at night, and that only by hugging the wall with my back to the room, my cheek and small body pressed up against the wall's rough cold, could I be safe.

Moreover it never occurred to me to discuss this with anyone. These were my monsters, and I had devised a way to keep them at bay. It was somehow clear to me, although I never articulated it even to myself, that my mother had many more fears than I, and that if I once opened the door to hers by telling her mine, my perfect world might permanently become a dark and fearsome place.

*At Mena House circa 1940*

Like all children, I accepted the family and circumstances that encompassed my childhood without wonder or question. An only child for close to five years, I thrived on the love and undivided attention of my parents, my grandmother with whom we lived, and my maiden aunt Helen, whose rooms adjoined the nursery wing which was home base for Vera and me. Although I was not aware of being lonely for companionship my own age, I created an imaginary friend I could see from my bedroom window way across the garden, a delicate child's face that never emerged out of shadow, peering through the dust of a distant window, as eager to establish contact as I was in my palatial home filled with the mysterious lives of many adults. I kept her very much to myself, and often spent time gazing at her from the terrace outside my bedroom, my mind filled with the life I imagined she led and the conversations I imagined us having.

The days of my early childhood seem pillowed in an abundance of time luminous with sunshine, time that nourished my consciousness with silence that was never silent, where birdsong and the hum of insects filled my senses and the grass winked white butterflies at the sky. In the garden that surrounded the majestic house that was home to me, I bent small legs to come even closer to the intricate maneuverings of ants and beetles finding their way among a forest of grasses. While Vera sat nearby, I wove tiny pink and white daisies that peppered the stubbly grass into patterns on the seat of a garden chair, near a trellised archway. That archway was like a secret cave, its sides thick with twigs and lush green leaves, smelling richly of humidity and earth. Fat, lazy bees buzzed and lumbered among flowers in dusty terra-cotta pots lining the gravel walkways.

Once, a black snake weaving its slithery way behind the pots caused grave consternation. The head gardener, his grubby white robe flapping as he ran, summoned the two chauffeurs from their somnolent stupor on chairs in front of the garage. His guttural alarm galvanized them, and suddenly there was a cacophony of voices, sticks beating a dull music on the baked earth pots, and finally, a shout of triumph as someone held up an incredibly long, ominous, flailing serpent. I, the small girl of the house, watched in horror, and was never to lose my fear of snakes. The black snake's skin hung for a long time on a nail in the garage. I averted my eyes whenever I ran past, and gave the flowerpots lining the walkways a very wide berth. The pots, I now knew, hid danger, despite the bold allure of their brilliant flowers. The snake, invisible, unknown, unimagined, had nonetheless been in my paradise all along.

Many years later, at some indeterminate moment in late childhood, I was practicing my violin in the mezzanine, the betwixt-and-between floor of the big house, when a stir outside caught my attention. Always happy for an excuse to stop practicing, I paused a moment and lowered my violin to gaze

*Violin practice on the bedroom terrace overlooking the Nile*

out of the window at the garden below. The reason lost in the mists of time, a snake catcher had been summoned to rid the house and garden of snakes. I watched, transfixed, as he seated himself cross-legged on the grass near the house, his white robe stark against the green. All I could see of his head was his thick white turban wound around a red embroidered skull cap as he began to play a thin pipe with a reedy sound. Suddenly, there they were, dozens of snakes slithering their way toward him from different directions, wriggling out of crevices in the wall, emerging from flower beds. Every now and then he would stop and insert them into one of several burlap sacks that lay beside him on the grass. The snakes were all different colors, large and small, and I wondered where this subterranean population had come from, and how I could have failed to know of their existence when they terrified me so. One of the house servants came out and paid the snake charmer his charge of so much per snake, and I found myself also wondering if his rich harvest could have been planted ahead of time, and whether the same assorted population of snakes would be let loose in the next household that called upon his services. I also wondered how many had not been seduced by his music and carried on their mysterious lives just out of my sight. I stepped carefully for a while after he came, and I never saw him again. The undulating burlap bags slung over his shoulders as he left returned in my nightmares in the years to come.

✦ ✦ ✦

As the passing years added inches to my height and peeled open my consciousness of a larger world, I no longer wove my patterns of tiny daisies into the seats of the garden chairs. Instead, tasting new freedoms, I rode a bicycle under a long pavilion of vines, the house scattered through the holes in the green like pieces of a puzzle I had yet to put together. I followed my father's eldest sister, Auntie Helen, and Aboudi the gardener through the narrow concentric circles of the rose garden, generous blooms perfuming the air, the heavy heads of the roses punctuating gray statuary with a brilliant display of reds, yellows, and pinks. The sight and scent of roses still sweeps me into the delight I felt then. Closer to the house, along massive stone walls, were beds of velvety purple and gold pansies, fragrant jasmine, and a turbulence of nasturtiums, luminescent orange in the bright sunlight. The roof of the garage, sloping gently up to the balustrade of the terrace outside the dining room, was sheer magnificence all summer. Tight matted profusions of deep-blue morning glory blossoms, tinged faintly with white at the borders of the petals, covered every inch. They paraded their beauty well into the afternoon and then closed up, leaving a sea of green to welcome the night.

Outside the graceful ironwork of the garden gates, I remained only dimly aware that a turbulent city teemed and heaved as political tensions proliferated and allegiances shifted the balance of power to respond to conflagrations that shook the world. To a small child, there was only beauty, and the occasional shadow that slithered under the bright bloom of the day.

Nothing could have seemed more peaceful, more permanent, than that garden of my childhood, cushioned in its rich profusion of palms, lawns, arbors, lemon trees, roses, and mango trees. The delicate wrought-iron tracery at its perimeters nonetheless allowed the eye to roam beyond the garden, across the broad street, past the moored houseboats to the sluggish silvery splendor of the Nile itself. In the far distance rose the golden Mokattam hills, the filigree spires of the Citadel piercing the clear blue Egyptian skies.

The Citadel, high above the city of Cairo, seemed like a delicate, magical castle, its elegant spires shimmering faintly in an early morning mist. Nonetheless its beauty hid a tale of merciless savagery. I learned later of the treachery of Prince Muhammed Ali, who overthrew the Mameluks in 1811. Power-hungry descendants of non-Arab slaves used as soldiers in the early Middle Ages, the Mameluks went on to dominate and rule Egypt as sultans for decades, vying for power with the Ottoman Turks and maintaining feudal power under Turkish rule even after their military defeat by Napoleonic forces. Muhammed Ali, however, put an end to that. Legend has it that he invited the most powerful Mameluks to a banquet in the Citadel in 1881 and then ambushed and slaughtered all of them but one. A Mameluk named Hasan is said to have leaped out of a window over the precipice on his

*The Citadel, Cairo*

horse and escaped to freedom. In the magical castle of my child-hood imaginings, some one thousand Mameluks were killed that day, and in subsequent days some three thousand more were slaughtered in the streets, permanently putting an end to Mam-eluk dominance.

Unaware of any of this as a child, I dreamed my dreams and roamed around my garden, familiar with every one of the squat palms that punctuated its interior, their innocent flat fronds ending in wicked black needlepoints. I stretched my neck to gaze upward at the tall, gawky palms whose distant heads swayed gently with the breeze. I knew each of the big old mango trees that offered shade. Every year, at the time of the mango harvest, a white-robed Arab took up residence in the garden together with his black-robed wives and sisters and flocks of grubby barefoot children. They had bought the fruit of our trees, which they collected in large rope baskets, shimmying up the trees, a rope around their waists, working silently and fast until the trees were bare of the heavy, sweet-smelling fruit. I watched this intrusion into my ordered world with interest. I knew that my father loved mangoes, preferring the longer Hindis with their smooth dark skin and firm orange flesh to the stringy fruit with bright yellow flesh that grew in our garden. When mangoes were in season, he sliced and peeled one every day after lunch with concentrated precision, dipping his fingers in a silver fingerbowl where a single rose petal floated and offering pieces of the succulent fruit to my mother and to me.

Set in the center of the garden, the opaque waters of the river Nile visible from many of its windows and terraces, my grandfather's house reflected the graciousness of generations of prosperity and security. Nonetheless his ancestors had seen their share of displacement and challenge. Expelled from their ancestral homes in just such a situation of stability, they had been prosperous merchants living lives of ease and influence in Toledo, Spain. That stability came to an abrupt end in 1492, shattered and scattered by the infamous Spanish Inquisition. Some fled to the Ottoman Empire and others to Livorno, where they made use of their skills and contacts in the gentle Tuscan sunshine of a more welcoming Italy. Over time, they set about laboriously reconstructing their lives by trading across the Mediterranean to the ports and cities of the Middle East; one branch of the family, led by the first Nessim Mosseri that history has given us, decided to set up home in Cairo, Egypt, in 1750. Liking the climate and the country, he and his descendants took root there, swiftly becoming influential journalists, bankers, and financiers, leaders in the multilingual, multicultural, thriving Jewish community in Cairo.

I took for granted the majesty of my surroundings as much as I did the rich variety of people, generations, and languages that flowed about me in those early years. The house was my world, and the nursery rooms upstairs were my kingdom. Downstairs, spacious reception rooms leading around a large center hall were defined by wall-to-wall sliding doors most often left open, golden light filtering through filmy voile panels that shielded the furnishings from the violence of the Egyptian sun and billowed out from French doors leading to ample stone terraces. The front door was imposing, framed in wrought-iron tracery around panels of thick, opaque bubbled glass. A substantial lantern of iron curlicues hung from an iron chain, marking the center of the ceiling above the marble floor of the foyer, its etched glass panels throwing light against creamy walls.

To one side of the entrance foyer was the paneled library, where, from the vantage point of their portraits on the wall, my great-grandparents Nessim and Elena surveyed the leather-bound encyclopedias and gold-tooled volumes of the classical literature of many cultures clustered on the shelves below them, sheltered from dust by glass doors crisscrossed with metal. An ancient radio dominated a cabinet by the door.

A little girl accustomed to smiles and attention from the adults who surrounded me, I often sat on the sagging leather couch in the library and stared up at Elena's portrait, wondering why she gazed back without the hint of a smile, knowing that her commanding presence in our house must have meaning for me, but unsure how to go about finding it. In her portrait, Elena stares out almost defiantly, dominating the cumbersome frame that surrounds her, her heavy face dark and stern, her iron-gray hair piled into a disciplined Victorian roll above her face. She sits there impatiently, certain of her validity in the time and place she inhabits, the fur of her fox stole luxuriant and silver, each hair separated and tipped by light. She is a woman of character, a woman of substance. She knows little of the struggles of her forebears and nothing of the upheavals that lie ahead for her descendants. Egypt is where she defines herself, and where she wields a regal hold on the cosmopolitan society that surrounds her. Devout, imperious, strong, and assured, she is widowed young, but she will send her sons to schools in distant England and on to university at Oxford and Cambridge, and marry her daughters to men of her choosing. From the center of the community she dominates, she will reach out to touch the world.

The two portraits of my great-grandparents were separated by two gigantic Chinese vases and surrounded by dim lighting reflecting against the polished wood of the library cabinets and walls. The wire-and-glass doors of the bookcases and rich gold-lettered spines of rows upon rows of well-thumbed leather-bound books alternated with the worn brown leather of the couch and armchairs. It was a room that seemed to hold the wisdom of the ages and to transcend time and place. Dark. Quiet. A room where I often sought refuge in childhood and as I was growing up.

An arresting painting hung at right angles to the portraits of Elena and Nessim, above the leather couch to the left of the library door. It was an oval oil painting by the nineteenth-century Italian painter Gioia of a woman sitting on a chair reading an open book, her face absorbed and meditative, light glinting on the ripples of her long, golden hair and delicate features. I loved that painting when I was a little girl. I loved to sit on the couch, twist my small self around, and gaze up at it, enthralled.

Across the foyer from the library, a door with mirrored panels on the outside opened into a traditional Arab sitting room.

*The Arab sitting room*

A spectacular Venetian glass chandelier glinting like a graceful waterfall of carved ice was the focus of its richly ornamented ceiling. Its walls were painted in classical Arab style with ornamental Arabic lettering and intricate geometric patterns in a mosaic of dark blue and burgundy. Low seating with striped upholstery and rare wood tables and cabinets inlaid with delicate patterns of ivory and mother-of-pearl completed the illusion of being transported to another time and place.

✦ ✦ ✦

Within the generous confines of the house, many languages mingled in my ear and in my consciousness from my earliest days, streaming into one flowing river of communication. My father and his mother and sisters were as comfortable conversing in any of three languages—Italian, English, or French—and switched without noticing from one to the other when the phrase they needed eluded them in the language they had initially used or when someone more comfortable in a different language joined the conversation. Vera, my nanny, and Marietta, my grandmother's personal maid, communicated with each other in their native Yugoslav and spoke French or Italian to all of us. Although my Mosseri grandfather's first language was Arabic, the Mosseri families had retained a powerful sense of identity with their Italo-Spanish roots and spoke mainly Italian among themselves until the advent of my father's generation. By then, Arabic had receded to a language used mainly in the household, spoken to interact with the staff. My father's cultured Egyptian friends and business acquaintances were as comfortably multilingual as he was, and indeed considered the English or French languages and cultures as profoundly theirs as their native tongue.

I considered my own life perfectly usual and ordinary, since it was usual and ordinary to me, but I did notice with some surprise that not everyone we knew had their own synagogue in the garden. Following a tradition begun by his father, my grandfather Joseph had built a small synagogue into the far left corner of our garden. My mother, father, aunt, grandmother, brother, sister, and I attended Sabbath services there every Saturday, walking through a vine-covered walkway at the back of the house. Up a narrow flight of stairs there was a tiny ladies' balcony where I sat with the women of the family and the occasional neighbor who dropped by for services and later joined us at the house for the Sabbath meal. I liked having such a good overview of the proceedings and found my grandmother's whispered Hebrew a mysterious and comforting incantation as she sounded out her prayers to herself reading from her tiny, worn, black prayer book.

There was never a shortage of men from the less affluent Jewish quarters to assemble weekly in our little synagogue for *minyan*. The early death of my father's older brother Nessim at the age of thirty-three had precipitated my grandfather's death, which came six months later, and had left my father with a household of women. So a motley group of men came out to Giza from the Haret El Yahud, otherwise known as the Quarter, to make up the required quorum for religious services.

Maurice, a small tubby fellow, officious and ubiquitous on the Sabbath and on holidays, stood out from the gaggle of assorted individuals he led for *minyan*, his dark European suit loose-fitting, a *tarbush* on his head. Others also wore the red conical *fez* with its swinging black tassel, a remnant of the Ottoman influence in Egypt. For years, as a child, I puzzled over how the Saturday *minyan* could be Jewish, as they muttered and prayed in an Arab-accented Hebrew, bowed, swayed, and shouted responses, some in flowing white robes and red *tarbushes*, the harsh sound of the guttural Arabic linking them to the outside world as they left after services in a flutter of white cloth and clamor.

The king had once wanted to name Grandpa Mosseri his finance minister. My grandfather refused. The title of Bey was conferred on him, nonetheless, and a street close to the house was named for him. But while the Mosseri family along with other prominent and influential Jewish families in Egypt steered their course among princes, they were also heavily involved in the foundation and financing of Jewish schools, hospitals, old peoples' homes, and orphanages. Auntie Helen worked and supervised in the hospitals and orphanages, giving freely of her love, intelligence, and organizational skills, while Auntie Mary worked with the elderly, a tradition that her daughters have continued with caring and compassion throughout their lives in other countries. Impoverished young women were taught fine embroidery skills in the Jewish schools, and beautifully handmade linens and lingerie were regularly purchased from them by the elite from all the various international communities, enabling them to bring some financial independence into their lives and their marriages. Brides from the Quarter were sometimes married in our little family synagogue, and I remember fine wedding banquets and wedding feasts prepared for them and served by the house staff on the lawn near the synagogue.

Skipping about the upstairs hall later in the day at the close of the Sabbath, playing hopscotch by myself on the white marble floor tiles that surrounded the carpeted area, I watched Maurice bringing my grandmother and my aunt the greens to smell for a "green" week ahead, as he bustled importantly through the huge, dark upstairs hall where they sat and drank tea, and where a stained-glass skylight shot ruby and emerald patterns of light onto the floor in the center.

The days streamed past with the leisurely flow of a mature river secure within its borders, thick, deep, and immutable. The punctuation of the weekly Sabbath and the drama of Jewish holidays braided seamlessly into the seasonal turning of the calendar. The fierce heat of summer encased everything in its fiery embrace, but the house always offered refuge. Wide white marble steps leading to the front terrace and the front door glittered and threw back the heat into small sandaled feet as I raced up the steps, past stone urns trailing flowers and vines, past the huge wrought-iron-and-glass front door, past the dark surprise of the entrance, to sink into the cool and the silence of the big house.

✦ ✦ ✦

From my earliest days, Auntie Helen was an integral part of my life. Her rooms were adjacent to the blue day nursery and the pink night nursery. Only recently, I realized that those rooms must once have belonged to her brother, Nessim. She never spoke of it or of him.

*Auntie Helen*

In contrast to my own childhood, when I was the only child in a household of assorted adults, Auntie Helen's childhood was spent in her grandparents' multi-generational family residence in the bustling center of Cairo, where she and her younger sister Mary had a turbulent pool of cousins to play with, the most mischievous among them wilting under the stern eye of their grandmother, Elena, whose unsmiling portrait hung in the library and for whom Auntie Helen was named.

From when I could walk, I wandered into the dark cave of her room, the upholstery of the bed and its alcove covered in a burgundy fabric, the walls of the room paneled in a light wood. My mother, terrified of losing control over the one element of the household that was hers, strictly forbade such visits, since my aunt had little patience for rules not of her own devising and had been known to ignore my mother's admonitions regarding food and behavior. In Auntie Helen's room, which seemed all the more exotic and delicious for being forbidden, wide-lattice wooden shutters closed against the heat or opened onto a small balcony overlooking the garage roof and its profusion of morning glory. A crystal chandelier hung from the ceiling. The faceted pieces danced and gleamed in the brilliant sunlight that filtered through the shutters, tinkling gently in the afternoon breeze when the window was open. The room smelled faintly of the rose water that both my aunt and my grandmother used as a skin freshener. To one side, a small dressing room opened into her bathroom, its narrow perimeters bordered with shelves on which sat ornate silver bowls and tumblers, alternating with spilled face powder dusty pink in color, my aunt's ruffled nightwear hanging on a hook by the bath adding a note of unexpected whimsy.

She had large, dark eyes that emphasized her strength and intelligence, and she wore her thick black hair in a braid down her back when she was in her room or rolled severely into a bun anchored by huge black hairpins. She was forever taking one out, tightening the roll at the back of her head with it, and poking it determinedly back into place.

My father's two sisters, Helen and Mary, were born thirteen months apart and were the best of friends, although quite different in physique and in temperament. Auntie Helen, the eldest, had contracted polio when she was two years old. As a result, and despite every effort of my grandparents, who took her to specialists around the world, she always limped and used a cane with a tortoiseshell handle. Her left leg remained appreciably shorter than her right, and as a child I was fascinated by the wooden contraption that she wore on her left foot before lacing it into her shoe. From the uneven thud and drag of her footsteps I could always tell when she was approaching my room and looked forward eagerly to her visits.

Bookcases and photographs lined her walls. I was particularly intrigued by a photo of my two aunts, impossibly young and giggly, dressed in their uniforms of VADs (Voluntary Aid Department) during the First World War. Beside it stood another photo, this one of Auntie Helen by herself in her crisp, starched uniform. She rose to the rank of colonel in the Red Cross in the Second World War, during which she worked tirelessly for children in the hospitals, rolled bandages in her spare time, and offered the hospitality of our home to the many Jewish soldiers who came through Cairo with the British armed forces.

Two strong women, my aunt and my grandmother were often at daggers drawn. My father was sometimes the peacemaker when his sister's pent-up emotions got the better of her and her raised voice echoed around the big house as she vented her irritations at her mild-mannered mother. Although she often exasperated him, he loved and respected her and always turned to her for advice regarding business matters; sadly, it seemed that her role in the world would offer her neither the burden of responsibility nor the satisfaction of success.

As I grew older and ventured more confidently into my aunt's sanctuary, I came to realize that her world encompassed larger horizons than the placid social life I saw her lead with my grandmother. I had listened eagerly as she told me about her travels to exotic places. I had gasped in wonder when she described her voyage to Finland in her youth, where she took saunas and rolled naked in the snow. But I later discovered that Abba Eban had dined at our house, that she corresponded with Golda Meir, and that she collaborated with the fledgling Zionist movement to help create the State of Israel. A woman of forceful intelligence, she had few outlets for her vibrant interest in the politics of the day and the business of the hour. Never one to opt for discretion, she voiced loud and decided views and participated in clandestine activities that disturbed the air and made my parents uneasy, nervous that she would bring the forces of evil down upon them and their young family if the Egyptian government ever caught wind of her interests.

Certainly, the formation of the State of Israel changed the dynamic between Arab and Jew in the Middle East. It became a polarizing magnet, leading to huge rifts in the standing social structure, cutting through generations of tradition and peaceable interaction. While most Jews worldwide rejoiced that Jews would at last have a homeland, those in Arab countries cast a wary eye at the chasm that was opening beside them, threatening irrevocably their safety and their way of life. While I thought of my aunt as a fascinating person, I had no concept of the seismic shift that

*Auntie Helen's bedroom*

her activities were helping to produce in the internal psychological geography of the Arab countries, which were never again to accept their Jewish neighbors as brothers. With the creation of the State of Israel, militant Islam was granted a voice and a cause. Beneath the innocent fabric of our daily lives, darkness stirred and raised the ghosts of the past, faint indeterminate shades flickering just beyond consciousness.

Despite the understanding that her efforts could permanently undermine the way of life she had always known, Auntie Helen, accompanied by her distinctive cane, traveled alone again and again to Suez and Ismailia after the end of the Second World War to supervise and expedite the loading of Jews emigrating to Palestine onto makeshift boats in the dead of night. Her indisputable difficulty walking and the misgivings of her nearest and dearest made no difference. I knew nothing of all this. I was five years old and had a new baby brother by then, and he brought the only seismic change in life as I knew it.

As I grew up and learned the wonders of reading and the possibility of entering worlds of the imagination created by others, Auntie Helen discovered my interest in writing and gave me her old Olympus typewriter. Later, she opened her bookshelves to me, and I entered the worlds of Sholem Alechem and Arthur Koestler, dark realms of persecution and passion.

She never married. As in any close-knit community, people were always gossiping and speculating, murmuring that men were afraid of her strength and spirit, or that she thought no one was good enough for her. Perhaps, they muttered, she considered her short leg such a handicap that anyone asking to marry her would only be interested in capturing control of her fortune and would not be marrying her for herself, and consequently she preferred to remain single. As I grew up and my knowledge of the world deepened, it seemed to me that in that restrictive society she simply never found her match, for despite a manner that was often acerbic and always opinionated, Auntie Helen had a heart of gold.

✦ ✦ ✦

Auntie Helen came into her own in the household in the spring as the Passover holiday approached. Heralded weeks ahead by her marshaling of the troops, she directed the total upheaval of the household. Floors and walls were scrubbed down under her eagle eye. The house servants took down books from shelves, dusted them, their pages fluttered to tease out the last speck of dust, and replaced them on newly polished wood. Leaning on her cane and shouting instructions, she watched as the huge carpet that covered much of the marble floor of the vast downstairs hall was rolled up in a symphony of guttural cries. An army of white-robed, red-turbaned servants heaved in unison and carried it out to the lawn, where it was unrolled and beaten with flat wicker beaters until clouds of dust lingered in the still air of a hot, sunny day. With more shouting and confusion as Auntie Helen waved her cane in frustration, the men rolled the carpet up again, heaved it onto their strong shoulders, and replaced it in the hall where tall tapestry chairs and huge Chinese urns with potted palms marked each corner.

As the Passover holiday approached, the drama and disruption around us amplified, turning our ordered environment into a war zone. Sounds took on a hollow quality and echoed throughout the house, ricocheting off the walls. Everything vibrated to Auntie Helen's loud cries of distress at my grandmother's interpolations as she and my aunt disagreed loudly and volubly on method and ritual, arguments between the staff almost coming to blows as tempers flared in the tense atmosphere.

Finally, the kitchen was dismantled and scrubbed and closed for the duration of the holiday while a second large kitchen in the basement, used only for the eight days of Passover every year, was opened and readied. I was usually forbidden from exploring the dark mysteries of the sprawling basement under the house, but as Passover approached, one or another of the adults would take me down with them into the musty underbelly of our home. A few dangling lightbulbs gave off meager lighting, and my senses tingled as I watched where I trod, wary of dangers I knew and those I imagined. It was easy to stumble on forgotten artifacts half-buried in dust, and I was aware that snakes could hide where darkness reigned, so I clutched the hand that brought me and shivered. I was also beginning to be aware that many things lurked outside my emotional field of vision casting lengthening shadows into the golden permanence I believed was mine forever.

As we walked among the detritus of years on the hard-packed earth, a heavy smell of mildew in our nostrils, discarded shards of my father's and his brother's childhood and youth lay all about us, barnacled under years of dust: my father's armies of lead soldiers; an elaborate crimson and gilt bar complete with seating and lavishly decorated with paintings of fat cherubs, their luminous flesh gray with grime, where he and his friends had gathered when he was a young man; broken painted wagons; and mounds of papers and books that seemed to rustle and shudder in the shadows.

The basement kitchen, however, directly below the main kitchen of the house, was pristine. We climbed the stairs to the upstairs pantry where Ali, the head *suffragie* (majordomo), was directing two of the younger servants who staggered under the weight of a large water-filled cauldron that they lifted to the table. My aunt added three stones, and when the water finally came to a boil, she solemnly pronounced the blessing, beginning the *aghallah*, the ritual sterilization of metal utensils to ready them for Passover use. From my vantage point on a wooden stool, I watched the steam rise and listened to the clang of metal utensils from every room in the house as the clean ones piled up on the table. Auntie Helen, together with the cook, stirred the silver and metal objects three times in the boiling water, after which they plunged them into a pot of cold water, dried them, and stored them in the basement kitchen, ready for the week ahead. I remember our silver baby cups disappearing from the nursery then reappearing, gleaming and purified, at the start of the holiday. The cook, Osta Mohammed, always gaunt and temperamental, became even more emaciated as the holiday approached and as his theater of operation transferred itself inexorably downstairs into the nether regions of the house.

In the midst of the yearly Passover upheaval, my mother once appeared at the door of the small room where my brother and I were having a Hebrew lesson under the solemn tutelage of my father's old Hebrew teacher, Maitre Dabila, sounds of chaos and the movement of heavy furniture wafting into the room behind her. Laughing as we winced at the noise, she declared that it was all very well for our ancestors to insist on such rigors of cleanliness and housekeeping since all they had to do was to move a tent to a clean patch of sand. We children thought her comment uproariously funny, but Maitre Dabila pursed his lips and was not amused.

Just before the holiday began, cupboards were eased open, holding complete place settings for sixty people or more, entire services of delicate gold-bordered dishes with my great-grandfather's monogrammed initials in flowing gold letters on each. Similar dishes used the rest of the year were locked away with ceremony for the duration of the holiday. Monogrammed crystal goblets and ruby-colored cut crystal wine glasses side by side with matching emerald green ones sparkled in readiness for the coming Seder nights. The intertwined initials of Nessim and Elena were everywhere. Despite the many achievements of his short life, my great-grandfather's irreverent descendants were to remember him most because every conceivable object that has come down to us from his day—silver, crystal, porcelain, and linen—has his monogram elegantly incorporated as part of its design.

Making a mockery of all this human activity, the occasional *hamseen*, a hot desert wind, blew fine particles of sand from deep in the desert into every nook and cranny as it had done from time immemorial in spring and summer, stinging the eyes and the skin, often immediately following the tremendous effort of cleaning the big house from top to bottom for the Passover holiday. Nature established its dominion over the efforts of humans to tame their environment, and there was nothing we could do about it.

As the holiday drew close, the intensity of preparations increased. Racks with flat golden Passover cakes appeared as if by magic, all the more delicious for being a one-week-a-year delicacy. Tables were set up in the small pantry next to the dining room, and everyone sat down to help with the ritual cleaning of the rice, which emerged quite dirty from the large burlap sacks in which it was stored. We had to sift through each mound of rice with great care and pass it along to the next person until, in accordance with Sephardic tradition, it had been cleaned three successive times, and the result stored in new bags set out for Passover use.

Ritual required the presence of a shoulder of lamb, complete with knucklebone, on the Seder table. Auntie Helen, who was responsible for ordering the food, had great difficulty every year securing the two shoulders she needed from the butcher for the two Seder nights. It was a perilous process, and she could not risk failure. So one year, convinced that she had solved the problem, she ordered an entire lamb from the kosher butcher.

"Look what that *Ibn el kelb*—that son of a dog—did to me!" she wailed when it arrived, reduced to the ultimate Arabic insult in her despair, her face a mask of tragedy while my father tried to stifle his laughter. "He has ruined our holiday." The butcher had sent the lamb minus the two shoulders, and only the full force of her most strident fury produced the meat she needed in time for the holiday.

The next year she decided to go one step further and circumvent the problem. Some weeks before the holiday, a sheep took up residence in the garden. Intrigued, Jeff and I fed it *berseem*, bunches of parsley that it seemed to enjoy, and we spent time playing with it every day.

My mother grew increasingly apprehensive as the day of doom approached. Afraid of the irreparable damage that the truth might inflict on the delicate psyches of her offspring, she carefully instructed all the house staff, my father, my grandmother, and my aunt that no one should make the connection for us between the pet that had mysteriously disappeared and the tender brown roasted shoulders of lamb that would soon be set out on the Seder tables.

The night after the sheep's disappearance from the garden, Vera, in despair, summoned my mother to our bedroom long after bedtime. "I don't know what has happened to the children," she declared. "I can't get them to listen. You need to come at once and help me to calm them down."

My mother followed her back to the room and found Jeff and me jumping happily on our beds on either side of the room, shouting something to each other that convulsed us with giggles. With mounting distress, she listened to what we were shouting. "*Fen il harouf?*" (where is the sheep?) one of us would say, and the other would respond in sepulchral tones, "*Fil talaga!*" (in the icebox), a response that set off hysterical laughter again.

So much for our delicate sensibilities.

The one person she had forgotten to caution was Aboudi, the gardener, who had grinned wickedly as he responded to our surprise at finding the sheep gone from the garden.

While my aunt busied herself berating the butcher, wielding her cane in the air for emphasis, shouting orders to all and sundry, and supervising the scouring of every object in the house, and my grandmother retreated to her rooms, emerging to attempt to rein in the chaos as the holiday approached, my mother was spared all responsibility for the running of the household during the Passover upheavals as she was the rest of the year. The youngest woman in the house by quite some years, she fitted into her husband's household as best she could, steering an uneasy course around the territorial domination of her opinionated elders.

Deprived of so many outlets for her creative energies, she therefore focused her needs and her energies on her children. We were in her control, we provided the anchor she needed for her love, and we were the beneficiaries of her constant attention to our care and nurture. The intensity of that loving attention was sometimes overwhelming, particularly in my early childhood, when I alone was its recipient.

My mother herself was a person unburdened by any awareness of shades of gray in the matter of life. There was the way her family did things, and there was everything else, which must have made it particularly difficult for her to navigate a household so different from her own. Her teeming childhood of noisy, jostling brothers and sisters and her British boarding school experience had given her no frame of reference for the life into which her marriage catapulted her. She adored my father, but he was away at work all day. His mother and sister, two older women, had held sway in the house for many years before my mother came to live there as a young bride, and they saw no need for her participation. Strong, somber women still wrapped in the shreds of their losses, they ran their household as they always had. My mother must have longed for the fun and ebullience of her own home and for the power to create her own environment for herself and her young family. It is ironic that the very sounds and smells that filled the days of my childhood with reassurance must have been a constant reminder to her that she was in an alien environment.

As the holiday approached, the long arduous preparation for our famous family *haroseth*, the traditional Passover jam used for the Seder, began with a visit to Auntie Helen's storeroom, a windowless room kept cool, dark, and locked, and to which she alone held the key. I loved tagging along when she pushed open the storeroom door and went inside. It was a small room but filled with an overwhelming array of sacks bulging with different kinds of beans, nuts, flour, sugar, rice, and a multitude of spices, emitting a symphony of assorted smells I can still summon into memory at will. Large glass jars squatted on the shelves, stacked to the ceiling, each filled to the brim with pickles and dried fruit, syrups and jams. With the door closed on the cacophony of cleaning still going on outside, the room was silent, mysterious in the dim yellow light of one dangling electric bulb. It was a treasure chamber, and she plundered it relentlessly in readiness for the coming event. Plump dates were pitted, raisins were added, and the fruit was then thoroughly washed in seven successive clean waters, where the peel was gradually rubbed off the dates and discarded. Then it went into large pots, where it simmered for twenty-four hours. She added sugar and vinegar, and while the date and raisin mixture reduced into a heavy syrupy sweetness, my aunt and her helpers cracked hazelnuts, walnuts, and almonds and pounded them into tiny pieces, to be added in large quantities at the end, making for a mouthwatering, soul-satisfying, thick, rich, reddish-brown *haroseth*, symbolizing the mud used by the slaves in Egypt to make bricks. No mud could have tasted so heavenly, nor has any *haroseth* since.

⚜ ⚜ ⚜

To a small child most often relegated upstairs to the quiet simplicity of nursery meals, the Seder table was an extraordinary wonder to behold. In the massive dining room with its heavy mahogany sideboard, broad carved chairs with leather seats were aligned edge to edge around the beautiful mahogany table extended to its fullest, hidden under heavy, opulently hand-embroidered linens immaculately ironed. Huge, ornate silver candelabra and appointments glittered down the center of the table, enhanced by arrangements of fresh flowers from the garden. Lights above caught in the multicolored crystal of the glasses, flashed on the gold rims and curling monograms of the plates, enlivened the greens of the bitter herbs, the rich brown of the roasted shoulder of lamb, the mottled flat expanses of the handmade *matzohs*.

*The dining room*

When we were very small, we crept with awe into the dining room to admire the table and then clambered up the long flights of stairs to our own domain, where my father celebrated a less burdensome Seder for our benefit before repairing downstairs to officiate at a table that usually held forty or more. By the end of the second Seder night he had often completely lost his voice.

When we were considered old enough to behave with some decorum, we too were allowed to sit at the table downstairs, our *Haggadas* open, the chatter swelling like ocean waves around us as my father tried to keep order and proceed with the prayers. The relatives and guests ate, talked, and shrieked with laughter in a medley of voices and languages, and then talked even louder, through my father trying to be heard as he sang the *Birkat ha Mazon*, the Grace after Meals, his voice fading into the high ceiling, rising and falling with the lovely Sephardic melodies, and then embarking faintly but with gusto into the traditional songs that rounded out the evening.

By the time we got to the songs, it became a matter of honor to match my exhausted father round for round, playing games with each other and with him as we sang faster and faster and tried to show with our loyal participation how little we appreciated the noisy social banter around us. The sweetness of his voice and the warmth of his presence have continued to echo down the years, and I miss them now that he is gone.

Along with the other special foods that appeared during the week of Passover, Granny Mosseri made special jams every year—sweet, creamy, grated almond and coconut served to guests in silver containers with a long-handled silver spoon and a tall glass of iced water. We had them every day of the holiday for dessert. But it was Auntie Helen, despite everything else she had to organize, who found the time to make *narring*, the best jam of all: half-inch-long rolls of pure delight, made of thick, chewy orange rinds soaked and cooked to a sticky perfection in a rich golden syrup. She made it from a particular kind of small, bitter orange that only put in an appearance in January; while distantly related to marmalade, *narring* offered an altogether different taste experience.

Shielded from the future by the wondrous cloak of the present and caught up in the immediacy of childhood, the story itself of the mighty exodus from Egypt held no actual relevance for me. It did not seem strange to be celebrating a departure, an exodus from Egypt while sitting at a table in our home in Cairo. I never made the connection. What did freedom mean in the context of my world? I accepted the tale the *Haggadah* told as merely a fairy tale of a different kind. The Prince found Cinderella in one story and the Jews escaped Pharaoh in another. There were always trials and quests in the fairy tales my mother read to me, and Cinderella's glittering ball seemed more real to me than slaves making bricks out of mud and straw. To a small girl, Passover meant ritual and song, a best dress to wear and delicious food to eat, a week when bread was replaced with unusual foods and a tantalizing glimpse into the sophisticated world of adults. But an ominous message I never suspected lay concealed in the metaphor of the ritual we observed and the sumptuous appointments around us, waiting to cast its shadow to blot out the light.

❧ ❧ ❧

*Family portrait in the Piazza San Marco, Venice, Italy, 1939*

# EARLY YEARS

*Although I* spent most of my early childhood in the house in Cairo, I was born in Alexandria, in my Smouha grandparents' house by the Mediterranean, on a chilly winter afternoon, the last Sunday of Hanouka. I was born at 3:30 in the afternoon of December 5, 1937, and my poor mother and I struggled mightily through a particularly long and painful labor to begin forging our separate ways in the world. My mother's parents had prepared a birthing room for their daughter at the top of the stairs across the landing from their bedroom. Because my parents lived in Cairo, one of my mother's brothers and his wife had vacated their bedroom for the occasion, so I arrived into a lovely space with pale painted walls awash with Mediterranean light and the soft sounds of the distant sea lapping against the sea wall beyond the Corniche road. My Smouha grandparents' bedroom faced the gardens, the pergola, the tennis courts, and at the opposite end of the garden, the utilitarian block of flats they had added to the property for two of their married children.

That December of 1937, my mother's waters had broken in Cairo three days earlier, but with the magnificent insouciance of the under-informed, having no idea what this might mean, she insisted on keeping to her schedule and going to her parents to have the baby in Alexandria, over Granny Mosseri's frantic protests. My parents took the train, which meandered its way along the Nile Delta toward Alexandria, stopping at little towns and villages along the way.

By the time they reached Sidi Gaber, the Alexandria train station, my Smouha grandparents were beside themselves with worry. The train was some forty-five minutes late, and they were sure it had been stopped in some less-than-sanitary Arab village for their new grandchild to be born.

Three days later on a sleepy Saturday, I had still not made my grand entrance into the world. Granny and Grandpa Smouha and assorted young people from the household piled into cars and left for the center of town to go to the movies. My mother, always eager and energetic, wanted to go, too, but this time reason prevailed. She stayed at home and she and my father played a game of Ping-Pong to pass the time. Intensely competitive in everything she attempted, she always played to win. He was good, too, but she and I must have made a powerful team, for despite the discomfort of her late pregnancy, that game was the only time she ever defeated him.

I was a breech baby, with a large bruise where it didn't show and an unblemished face. I weighed six pounds at birth and was nineteen inches long. When I finally arrived, my mother listened anxiously for the first cry. After what must have seemed an interminable wait, a frail squeal was heard, and my mother gave a sigh of relief and sank back against the pillows. It had been an arduous labor, and with her red hair dark with sweat, she rested against the cool linens and closed her eyes. In the sudden stillness of the room, my grandmother, the doctor, and the starched British nurse/midwife continued to murmur to each other in hushed tones and to fuss over the baby. Suddenly, there was a lusty yell, and everyone sighed in relief. My mother opened her eyes and sat up in alarm. "Wasn't it all right before?" she asked anxiously.

All too soon for my mother, it was time to return to Cairo, but an eager Mosseri grandmother and Auntie Helen awaited the arrival of the new baby, and my father had responsibilities and had to return to his work, so the three of us left for Cairo and our new life as a family.

✤ ✤ ✤

As I grew out of babyhood, I was often ill with colds and bronchitis, and living in a multi-generational household brought both rewards and trials. As I lay in my bed feeling sorry for myself, Granny Mosseri and Auntie Helen paid state visits, holding my hand, sitting silently, and keeping me company. Sometimes we played cards. Marietta, wrinkled and brown as a walnut, her vivid blue eyes smiling through the folds of her aged face, shuffled in and out of our rooms bringing hot chamomile tea or a blue metal funnel in a basin filled with steaming water for inhaling. She had witnessed my father's birth and he could do no wrong in her eyes. By extension, she adored his children. She had come to Egypt from Trieste as a young woman to be my grandmother's personal maid. Whispered information was that she was an unwed mother who'd had a son later killed in a war. I had no idea what any of this might have meant in the context of her own life. I knew what she meant in the context of mine. She was Marietta, and her shuffling footsteps and reassuring presence stitched together much of my childhood. Vera, my gentle Yugoslav nanny, gave me sponge baths to take down the fever, while my mother took my temperature, put fragrant cool wet handkerchiefs soaked in Eau de Cologne on my burning forehead, and dispensed sympathy and medication.

Vera also dispensed less pleasant treatments with remorseless fervor. My very memory shudders when I think of the antiflogistin treatment which was considered the preferred solution to respiratory infections that had gone to the chest. I hated it. Bronchitis invariably meant this thick gray concoction in a round metal container, exuding a sharp metallic smell. Marietta usually brought it from the upstairs pantry in a basin of boiling water with a cloth over it to keep it hot while she carried it down the long corridor to my room. To the accompaniment of my groans and squirms, Vera or my mother spread it quickly and thickly on clean linen and placed it on my chest. I had to hold the poultice in place, whimpering mournfully, and then they helped me to roll over very carefully without disturbing the front, while a second poultice of the same substance was slapped onto my back. Desperate shouts that it was too hot were ignored by my normally tender and caring mother and nanny. I dreaded the feel of the goo on my skin, knowing that it would have pilled into nasty little gray balls all over my bed by morning. I lay trapped into immobility by my disgust, glaring up at them as they moved solicitously about the room, hardly daring to breathe for fear of making an even worse and more uncomfortable mess.

A form of cupping called *ventouse* was an alternate treatment. A tray bearing a number of small, heated, down-turned glass jars on a clean cloth was ceremoniously carried in. I had to lie on my stomach, and the hot jars were placed on my back, left for a few minutes to form a vacuum, and then removed, leaving a series of raised red circles all over my back. This was intended to draw out the mucus from the bronchial tubes, and although less unpleasant than the antiflogistin, it was no fun at all. It was an incredible relief when my chest was massaged with warmed camphorated oil to supplement the less pleasant treatments.

*Granny Mosseri with five granddaughters: (left to right) Colette, Jackie, Suzanne, Helen, and Jean on her knees*

For intestinal ills, Granny Mosseri made her own special remedy that was stored in dark green, dusty, long-necked bottles topped with a piece of rag and a cork, and kept in the vast, cool basement of the house. It was made with fermented fennel and had a spiky, prickly taste. When one bottle was empty, a new one was brought up from the cellar and ceremoniously uncorked. Granny Mosseri's *Eau de Fenouil* was famously effective and put a stop to everything short of dysentery. The recipe has been lost, but the memory of the distinctive taste lingers on.

Whether or not these treatments actually worked, I did survive double pneumonia and any number of childhood illnesses, coaxed out of fevers as much by the loving care that surrounded me as by the treatments themselves.

The Cairo summer brought a plague of voracious mosquitoes and consequently a filmy white netting over my bed every night to prevent the bites. As evening approached, unaware as we all were then of the dangers of DDT, the young upstairs servant, Sadik, earnest and skinny in his gleaming white robe and red *tarbush*, hurried through the rooms with a Flit gun, a metal cylinder filled with DDT sporting a piston with a red wooden handle, pushing the piston in and out and releasing a pungent mist everywhere. The wooden feet of our beds were placed in a shallow saucer of water to protect us at night from the legions of tiny black ants whose bites stung and left angry red welts on the skin.

Food was a constant source of anxiety to my vigilant mother. I did not eat a raw salad for the first twelve years of my life, and we drank only boiled milk, as the milk was not pasteurized. I watched with some envy as Marietta brought my grandmother and aunt saucers of thick unpasteurized cream sprinkled with sugar some winter afternoons as they sat in the chilly upstairs hall together, drinking tea. The bony *gamousas* to whom we owed our milk were scrawny buffalo who munched on sparse vegetation outside mud huts in villages along the Nile. They were sometimes attached to a *shadduf*, a pulley, and we could see them as we drove past, trudging in tired circles in a cloud of dust to draw up water from a well to irrigate the fields, hoarse shouts and the swirl of dusty robes urging them on.

✦ ✦ ✦

Before I was five, before the arrival of my two siblings, I was a painfully shy little girl, safe in my own world, knowing how to protect myself from its hidden demons. But when I was ushered out of the magic haven of my home to attend one of the magnificent children's parties to which we were often invited, I lost my bearings and floated in a frightening world where anything might happen. Time after time, I wiggled in frustration as Vera and my mother carefully curled my hair, dampening it with water and pinning it up with metal twists sheathed in brown fabric. As soon as my hair was dry, they unwound the twists and released the bouncing ringlets that nature had never intended me to have.

The two young women ignored my tearful face as I was carefully eased into one of my freshly ironed party dresses. My mother, a skilled needlewoman, made many of my dresses, taking great pride in the exquisitely smocked bodices. Fluffing the skirt out, she twirled me about, beaming with delight as she prepared to send her freshly curled and polished little daughter out into the world.

"I won't know anyone!" I wailed, to deaf ears.

"You'll have a lovely time!" my mother assured me as she tucked us into the back of the car.

As soon as our snub-nosed black Ford drew up at the gates of a strange house, we could hear sounds of music chatter and merriment spilling from the house ahead, and I pulled back frantically as Vera tugged me toward the door. I knew the challenges that awaited my four-year-old self. I knew I would get pushed about by bigger kids and would never find an empty chair when the music stopped in Musical Chairs. I knew no one would want me and my bouncing ringlets as partner to hold hands and dance through the arch of arms for Oranges and Lemons. I knew I would never understand the clues in the treasure hunt and my team would fail to win the prize because of me. Inside my starched, perfectly attired self, a faint voice mewed in misery, unheard and unattended as we moved inexorably into the lights and laughter.

Terrified that I might lose Vera in the crowd, I hid behind her skirts, advancing gingerly, clutching at her as she tried to maneuver the gift she carried in one hand while prying me from my hiding place with the other. We headed for the lady of the house, who stood near the door dispensing wide red kisses, her head *suffragie* hovering in the background to take our coats and relieve us of our festive package. I found the flawlessly coiffed and dressed women stunningly sophisticated and alarming as I peered at them from behind Vera's skirts. They leaned down and admired my dress exclaiming over my mother's workmanship as I shrank back from their large, vividly lipsticked mouths and loud voices, from the jangle of their jewelry and their shrieks of laughter. I pulled away as they patted my head with hands tipped with long red nails and waved us into the house toward the heart of the event. I was used to a more muted world, where the lights were dimmer and my quiet nursery life revolved around my unspoken needs.

Possibly some of my anxiety came from the fact that many of the adults at the parties had known my father since grade school and seemed to have an ease of communication with his past and his world that I did not possess. I loved my father dearly, but his world seemed a larger, more dangerous world than my mother's, for while my mother feared most things, my father seemed to fear none. He left the house daily to venture into realms of which I had no understanding and where I suspected that dangers dogged his every step.

Since I arrived in the world in December of 1937, my early years held the muffled drumbeat of escalating events in Europe as the uneasy peace between the wars crashed into the powerful currents that became World War II. An unidentifiable miasma of discomfort permeated the seeming stability of the colonial era and spread to poison the consciousness of Jews everywhere. Something had cast a shadow on my sunlit world. I sensed its presence, but no one told me what it was.

Adults often assume that if they take care not to discuss frightening situations with young children they will protect them from fear, neglecting to acknowledge that children are tuned in to different channels. Whispers and concerned looks, the relief sensed in a long hug, the radio suddenly switched from news to music, all these signals and many more are unfailingly internalized, misinterpreted, and tucked into the subconscious of small children. Without the anchor of acceptable explanation and communication, their fears billow out into threatening unidentifiable shapes, stirring hidden levels of anxiety.

I was more at ease in the protected nursery world in which my mother had so carefully cocooned me, a more domestic world that seemed to have me at its center. Intuitively, I sensed her own wariness toward those who had known her husband far longer than she had. I was too young to realize that his old friends shut her out with their reminiscences and their laughter, that she even felt alienated in the big beautiful house in which she lived with her mother-in-law and sister-in-law, older women whose losses hovered in the air, dark as the clothes they wore.

At the children's parties, my mother's and my unspoken insecurities notwithstanding, Vera and I would continue to move into the reception rooms of the house. Noise and merriment, color and movement flared stronger and stronger as we walked along. Invariably, these parties were enormous, elaborate, anchored to reality by a long table groaning under the weight of huge platters of delicate delicious sandwiches, a multitude of cakes, and crystal glasses at every child's place filled with the brilliant colors of jellies, orange, yellow, red, and green. Every household outdid itself and strove to outdo the others. Each cook was a superb pastry chef and reveled in these opportunities to show off his skills.

I sat stiffly with the other children on little gilt chairs, while nannies and mothers and stately white-gowned *suffragies,* their heads covered with red *tarbushes,* hovered in the background, making sure that everyone behaved with decorum and had enough to eat and enough lemonade to drink. Vera stood beside me, chatting to the nannies on either side. Some parents dropped their children off or stayed in another sitting room, but the nannies were always there, running the show. They reigned supreme. They set the rules, organized the games, disciplined the rowdy, and comforted the stricken. Swiss, French, German, and British, they had their own pecking order, German and British voices predominating. Some were brisk and competent in starched uniforms, others rotund and comforting, their hair pulled into respectable greying buns, their eyes on their charges. Vera did not fit the mold. She was young and cheerful, with bright blue eyes that glowed and sparkled. I loved her almost as much as I loved my mother and my father. I never asked myself how she fitted into the nanny hierarchy. She was my refuge and my companion, strict disciplinarian and loving playmate.

But small as I was, it did not escape my notice that even the awesome figures of the parents shrank to human size when confronted by a glance of blazing disapproval from one of the other nannies, most of whom lived out their years, famous and despotic, among the wealthy households they helped to shape. As their charges grew up, the nannies migrated from palace to mansion to estate, leaving their cultural imprint on the children of princes and those of the multicultural leaders of Egyptian society.

There were games organized before and after tea. There was always Musical Chairs, and true to my shame, I was always out first. There was a game that involved a circle of children sitting on the floor, while one child ran around the circle singing, "*I sent a letter to my love and on my way I lost it, somebody has picked it up and put it in his pocket. It isn't you, it isn't you, it isn't you, it's* YOU." On that word, the handkerchief was dropped behind one of the children, who then picked it up and continued the game. I lived in dread that the handkerchief would materialize behind my back. We played Oranges and Lemons, London Bridge Is Falling Down, and Blind Man's Bluff, and sometimes everyone danced the conga, snaking through huge bedrooms and magnificent formal rooms dotted with fine antiques, upstairs and downstairs, in a motley assortment of adults and children. The parents giving the party often had separate bridge tables for the adult guests set up in one of the sitting rooms, and a hush hung over the tables as the adults sat ramrod straight, with solemn faces, intently perusing the cards. We were not encouraged to pay those rooms a visit. Rather we were shepherded into another room, where a *"gala gala"* man, a sinewy white-gowned Arab conjurer, held us in thrall as he made rabbits and doves appear from hats and pulled endless streams of knotted handkerchiefs from his sleeve, purple and orange, blue, green, yellow, and red, striped and polka-dotted, on and on and on, while we all squealed and jumped up and down in excitement and disbelief, I along with the rest, my fears forgotten.

✦ ✦ ✦

Many of the children's parties were fancy-dress extravaganzas to which children of all ages were invited, regardless of the age of the child for whom the party was given. Madame Marika, our family's dressmaker, a soft-spoken Greek woman married to an Italian, was often to be found in the lofty mezzanine center room of our house in Cairo, where the light poured in from a high arched window. Her three daughters were named for flowers: Rosetta,

Violetta, and Marguerita. Their musical names enchanted me like whiffs of exotic perfume and invested Madame Marika with a romantic aura she could scarcely have imagined as she sat on the hard white couch surrounded by multicolored bobbins of thread and fabric, the hum of her old treadle Singer sewing machine echoing faintly through the house. She worked alone, shielded from the rest of the household by spectacular stained-glass arched doors that echoed the window's generous size and shed their jeweled splendor down the wide marble staircase that led to the downstairs hall.

*The mezzanine*

Looking down into her face from my small height as she knelt to pin up a hem, I was aware of a slightly greasy sheen to her skin under the heavy makeup she wore. Her warm brown eyes were large and seemed sad, and her voice was a gentle arpeggio of sibilances, as the words spun from her like silk, often cascading through a mouth filled with the pins she was about to use on a hem or a waist. She stood me on a table while she and my mother made me twirl slowly in the hot room, and together they pored over the perfect drop of the hem with all the concentration of artists at work. I felt fidgety, tired, and faint, but twirl I did until they were satisfied that the hem was perfectly round and perfectly aligned from every angle.

Given the challenge of a fancy-dress party, Madame Marika was a miracle worker. The assembly of a costume was considered serious business. It was taken as a family challenge and elicited, at least in my household, lengthy conferences with Madame Marika and both my parents, and forays into my grandmother's boxes of beads and silk veils, bone corsets, sparkling jewels, and gold cloth. She opened her treasure trove of old, battered boxes and watched us as we plunged our hands into her past, exclaiming and admiring, while memories of her girlhood brought a wistful look to her eyes.

There were no prizes for best costume. The glory was in the infinite amounts of time and imagination that went into creating a wonderful moment of superbly crafted fantasy for each child. We have photos of me as a little Dutch girl, with a real lace cap and real wooden clogs ordered from Holland; a Persian princess, swathed in veils and wearing a row of gold coins across my forehead; and a Victorian girl, twirling my grandmother's delicate lace and ivory parasol, with real Belgian lace bordering my pantaloons and my grandmother's girlhood corset digging into my body. Aged twelve and slim, I was appalled to realize that her waist, when she was married, was smaller than mine.

*Jean in a Dutch girl costume*

✦ ✦ ✦

I used to visit my Mosseri grandmother, Jeanne, in the suite of rooms that made up her private apartment. They took up the southeast corner of the house and shared the large stone terrace with our rooms, although in the nineteen years I lived in the house with her, I never saw or heard her step through the French doors that opened onto the terrace.

Granny Mosseri's boudoir had a wall covered in fading sepia photographs and ivory miniatures of her family, her sisters, her children, her grandchildren, and the many friends she and my grandfather had made when they traveled throughout the world. Some were tattered or faded almost beyond recognition, but there they stayed on Granny's wall, pinned haphazardly to the dusty rose-colored brocaded wall-covering, zigzagging among the prayer books and dusty diaries, the neatly labeled boxes and hat boxes on the shelves, creating a dizzying mosaic of love that she bathed in every day as she dressed.

I stared in fascination at the many photographs of my unknown grandfather scattered about the place. Too small to understand that she might have welcomed the opportunity to talk to me about him, I respected her silence on the subject and confined myself to solemn study of the images on her wall. I saw a kindly, portly man with an air of authority about him. Beetling silver brows and a mustache gave him a distinct aura of Victorian prosperity and respectability, while a lurking twinkle I discerned in his eye made me think of my father with his mischievous take on life and wicked sense of humor.

The year 1869, when my grandfather was born, saw the birth of another event that was also to have a profound influence on my life. It was the year of the official inauguration of the Suez Canal.

The port of Suez, east of Cairo across a hundred-mile stretch of desert, had been inhabited since Roman times and had long been a portal to the Mediterranean, but in the nineteenth century the Suez Canal came into being. Brainchild of Ferdinand de Lesseps and considered one of the outstanding engineering achievements of the century, it opened a direct passage between the Mediterranean and the Indian Ocean, producing a vital connecting link between the colonial forces of the Western world and the vast riches of the Far East and India. Conceived in a welter of debt, ambition, and national politics, it took fifteen years to build and came to symbolize trade, prosperity, and the continuation of a colonial presence knitting together East and West. The khedive of Egypt commissioned the composer Verdi to create an opera in honor of this momentous event, and he produced the magnificent opera *Aida*—although he ran late, and opening night failed to coincide with the inauguration.

However, portentous as the completion of the Suez Canal was to be, to Elena and Nessim Mosseri, filled with youth and faith in their shared future in 1869, the historic inauguration of the Suez Canal undoubtedly paled in significance beside the birth of their son and heir, my grandfather, Joseph. They could not know how profound an impact international events surrounding the canal would later have on their descendants.

Joseph was the eldest of eleven, an only child for ten long years during which his mother must have wondered if she would ever conceive again. Imperious daughter of the prominent Cattaui family, she cannot have taken this failure lightly. Family legend has it that a visiting holy man arrived at her door one day, insisting on being heard. When she reluctantly answered his summons, he told her she would have many more children providing she spent a night in prayer on the slab of the Maimonides synagogue and that she gave his own name, Eli, to her next child. He promptly vanished from the annals of family history and no anecdote has come down the generations to confirm that regal Elena spent a night on the slab in the Maimonides synagogue, but the indisputable fact remains that when my grandfather was ten, Elena gave birth to a second son, Eli, and went on to produce Esther, Regina, Jacques, Maurice, Vicky, Donald, Lionel, Felix, and Emil, eight sons and three daughters in rapid succession, and to bequeath her extraordinary, dark Cattaui eyes to generations to come.

The Suez Canal had even less significance for me than it had for Nessim and Elena Mosseri, even though I was a small girl growing up so many years later in the house that Joseph Mosseri built on the banks of the Nile, standing in the seemingly vast space of her grandmother's bedroom and trying to make sense of a world that was gradually revealing itself as something outside and beyond the boundaries of my physical being.

To my child's eye, the two towering single beds in Granny Mosseri's bedroom—buttressed imposingly by gleaming brass frames and knobs, always immaculately made up with mountains of pillows and soft snowy linens, placed against opposite walls separated by the entire width of the room—were part of the mystique of my absent grandfather. They also hinted at the lost and utterly unimaginable youth of a kindly, absentminded grandmother with sad, deep-set eyes, a succession of black or gray clothes, and iron-gray hair pulled back and anchored by disobedient black hairpins which sprang out unbidden to be found often in her wake.

My father used to tell a tale that unlocked, for one moment, the door to their youth. His father had never held my grandmother to a budget, or asked her for an accounting of her expenditures. Nonetheless, with the laborious meticulousness of a serious-minded young girl only recently released from the schoolroom, she sat every night, her long, dark hair braided down her back, poring anxiously over the accounts of the day until she had balanced her account book. One night she simply could not get the columns to balance. I imagine my grandfather saying, "Jeanne, leave that now. It's late. Come to bed." I imagine him patient and portly, in a voluminous nightgown, sitting and smiling in the magnificent white and brass bed that was not my grandmother's. I imagine her consternation, "I can't go to sleep until I see where I've gone wrong!" I imagine that he said, "Bring it here. Let me take a look." She must have handed over the small black leather-covered account book, page open, date clear at the top in her large looping handwriting, expenses down to the last *piaster* listed there. I imagine the twinkle in my grandfather's eye turning into a shout of laughter. The more bewildered she looked, the louder he chuckled. At last he was able to get the words out to explain. "No wonder you couldn't balance it," he must have exclaimed, "You added in the date!"

After my grandmother's death at eighty-three, her children came upon dozens of small black leather notebooks, where night after night, year after year, she had faithfully recorded her every expense, long after her husband and eldest son had died, long after the high white bed on the opposite wall from her own had stood empty and unwrinkled, year after lonely year.

⚜ ⚜ ⚜

Although I could not have put words to it then, I knew that my Granny Mosseri was a sociable, hospitable lady who loved to spend time with friends. She loved to travel and learn new skills and crafts everywhere she went. She loved to gossip and to shop. She took great pride in entertaining and welcoming guests to her home.

Every Saturday afternoon of my early childhood, she and my aunt Helen entertained their friends for tea and games of bridge or canasta. She was "at home," and she called the friends who came every Saturday afternoon, some of whom she could remember from the convent school where she went to elementary school, *mes petites amies*. I could hear the hum of their voices all the way upstairs as I waited impatiently to be dressed in my best and then made my way carefully down one wing of the long marble staircases, and then down the central staircase, my small hand reaching up to clutch the polished brass banister. The stairs must have seemed an endless challenge for small legs, because I often dreamed of placing a hand on the banister and magically floating all the way down, sometimes flying above the big hall and the adults in the dining room before returning to rest in my bed.

The servants hurried to and from the sitting room, which was filled with card tables, a heavily laden buffet table lining one wall. On this were displayed my grandmother's massive monogrammed silver tea set and her delicate porcelain cups, hand-painted with exotic birds and flowers, with their matching saucers and tea plates with gold rims. There were several cakes for which our Osta Mohammed was renowned. I particularly remember his round coconut cake, covered with large, snowy flakes of coconut, its light sponge layers separated by a thin filler of cream, and the entire cake rich with a wonderful syrup that suffused every layer. There were my Auntie Helen's famous *Baba Au Rhum*, as well as the ubiquitous *kaak*, crunchy circles of pastry brushed with egg and scattered sesame seeds; cheese *sambouseks*, semicircular pastries filled with a salty mixture of white cheese and crushed mint and brushed with egg and sesame seeds; sticky almond *madeleines*; twisted cheese straws; and melting *menenas* made of crumbly short pastry stuffed with a paste of dates and nuts and sprinkled generously with powdered sugar. Auntie Helen's *menenas* were renowned and said to be the lightest and most mouthwatering anywhere. Miniature *petits fours* as colorful and intricate as jewels as well as tiny sandwich rolls and finger rolls, cut in half, spread with rich fillings and arranged tastefully on silver platters, were ordered from Groppi, the famous Swiss *patissier* who had his tearooms in the center of town.

One of my grandmother's friends was a slight, small-boned woman with a shock of wiry gray hair standing out from her face. She saw herself in contrast to the other ladies, who were generally of generous, not to say majestic proportions, and since she didn't play bridge, she was in the habit of perching herself winsomely on the arms of chairs and fluttering from table to table to observe the bridge players, punctuating her travels around the room with exclamations in a little girl voice and the occasional high-pitched giggle. One Saturday, seeing a small antique table empty of ornaments near where she wanted to be, she pulled it over and sat on it. The delicate table splintered in a resounding crash, sending its startled occupant to the floor. There were gasps and cries of consternation as the bridge players rose from their seats and gathered about the scene of the accident. The lady got to her feet, shaken but unhurt.

My grandmother, who had momentarily been out of the room directing kitchen traffic, heard the crash and came sailing heroically into the sitting room. Determined to be the perfect hostess, she waved her arms dismissively, announcing to all that it did not matter one iota, no one was to worry, her eyes drawn to her shattered antique table in pieces on the floor. My mother, instantly sizing up the situation, tried to get her attention: "Mother," she muttered, steering her mother-in-law into a corner, "Mother, everyone is concerned about the lady, not about your table."

The Saturday visitors, busy with their chatter and their cards, nonetheless found time for frequent forays to the tea table and were also plied with delicacies by the attentive *suffragies* and urged to eat by my grandmother and my aunt. Most of the ladies were widows. They dressed in black or gray, their hair was gray or white, and few of them wore more than a dusting of powder on their faces. They seemed profoundly ancient to this small girl as I made the rounds politely, my eyes dazzled by the splendors on the buffet table. The ladies exclaimed at the sight of me, pinched my cheeks, and as I winced away from their fingers whispered quite audibly to each other that it was such a shame that Guido's daughter had not inherited her mother's gorgeous red hair. One of the more regal ladies who attended these Saturday afternoon events on a regular basis was a neighbor and distant cousin of Granny Mosseri's, Marguerite Aghion Sapriel, dressed always in black, her blue-tinted hair rolled up at the back, culminating in deep waves to frame her face. She lived a stone's throw away from us in a big house with her daughter and son-in-law, Denise and Gaston Naggar, and two young grandsons who later attended the same grade school as I did, the GPS, Gezira Preparatory School.

Granny Mosseri's Saturday tea parties also frequently welcomed a fashionably dressed lady, her elegant black dresses and vivid makeup standing out from the more discreet apparel of the other ladies. She was Madame Mahmoud, a Frenchwoman married to an Egyptian Pasha. Enormously wealthy, Mahmoud Khalil owned a magnificent collection of French impressionist paintings and sculptures, which were subsequently left to the Egyptian government and are now housed in the Mahmoud Khalil

*Granny Mosseri*

Museum in Giza. Consequently, Madame Mahmoud, carefully made up and elegant, gave herself airs and held herself somewhat aloof from the other ladies, although she was always glad for the company, partaking generously of the delicious food. Her beautiful villa was a few houses down the Nile road (then called *Sharia Farouk*) from ours, number 88.

I can remember walking along the pavement outside our iron railings and beyond with my father after an infrequent rainstorm, imbued with the importance of having him all to myself. I was still an only child, so I must have been three or four years old. The houseboats lined up on the other side of the road swayed gently with the movement of the Nile waters. I jumped the puddles with more abandon than decorous walks with Vera allowed and held tightly to my father's hand as he pointed out the Mahmoud house, and then the Castro house where other friends of ours lived. I was terrified of passing that particular garden because they owned an enormous slavering Great Dane, black as pitch, who hurled himself at the garden railings as soon as a whiff of our arrival stirred his nostrils, barking thunderously and towering above the small girl that I was, his large jaws open to display huge pointed teeth as he stood on his hind legs and bayed his warnings. I was never quite convinced that he could not reach us, despite my father's amused assurances to the contrary. The Castro family had named their dog Hamlet, an excellent name for a princely Great Dane, but the servants all called him "Omelet," which had quite a different ring to it, and despairing of retrieving his dignity, the family changed his name to Rajah. After the Suez crisis, the Castro house was taken over by the Egyptian government and later became the residence of President Anwar Sadat and his wife.

The daughter of Marguerite and Charles Castro, Yolanda (Bunny) Sherriff, had married an American and was living in New York with her husband and children. Many years later, sometime after the assassination of Anwar Sadat, his widow, Mrs. Sadat, was giving a lecture in New York City which Yolanda Sherriff attended. Impressed by the woman, Yolanda made her way to the podium to congratulate Mrs. Sadat on her excellent speech. They began to exchange pleasantries, and as Yolanda was about to leave, Mrs. Sadat, not aware of the irony, turned to her with the comment, "But you must come back to Egypt to visit and to show it to your children," adding the traditional Egyptian courtesy, *beti betak*, "My house is your house." Which indeed it was.

✤ ✤ ✤

*The house Joseph Mosseri built*

Granny Mosseri had entered the world as Jeanne Aghion. Her family, also survivors of the inquisition in Spain, had fled to Amsterdam, where they flourished and multiplied greatly before seeking and finding a home in Egypt. Fun-loving and pious, the Aghions were known for having serious-minded, beautiful daughters. Consequently they married into every prominent family in Egyptian Jewish society, casting a widespread Aghion heritage that can be found by scratching the surface of many relatives and acquaintances from Egypt. Once we could read, we children were vastly amused to find an entry in the Jewish Encyclopedia for a Van Aglion, a maverick who became notorious for following the false Messiah, Shabbatai Zvi. Upon having discovered the entry in one of the many volumes of the encyclopedia that filled shelves in the library, we often turned to his picture and teased Granny that we could identify the recognizable deep-set Aghion eyes she herself shared with the rest of her family.

*Jeanne Aghion portrait*

*Joseph Mosseri portrait*

As an article my cousin Ester Coen discovered in the *Papyrus* journal attests, my grandparents' wedding in 1894 was a grandiose affair. Joseph Mosseri was then twenty-five years old. His handsome blue-eyed father had died at the age of forty-three, and he was helping his mother to raise a houseful of turbulent younger siblings. His bride was nineteen.

*The wedding took place in Cairo [on March 20, 1894] between Miss Jeanne Aghion and Mr. Joseph Mosseri, son of the well-known banker. The splendor and magnificence of the luxurious sitting rooms, the guests milling about in their gorgeous outfits, the twin orchestras, one a military band and the other a regular orchestra, playing delightful music, the gardens lit up with multicolored lights from Venetian lanterns, and the fireworks raining their golden splendor into the mild evening air...To be faithful to the event, our description would strain credulity. We will therefore limit ourselves to saying that the loveliest of our Alexandrian ladies lent their presence to an event that will long be remembered in the annals of Egyptian society.*

Jeanne and Joseph started out their married life in the capacious family mansion my great-grandfather Nessim had built twelve years earlier, when he carefully selected a site outside the main city of Cairo. Run with an iron hand by his wife, Elena, the household teemed with Grandpa Mosseri's younger brothers and sisters, and my shy young grandmother undoubtedly chafed under her stern mother-in-law's eagle eye.

Two of her sisters, Emma and Gabrielle, had also made brilliant marriages, to Sir Vita Harari and Baron Jacques de Menasce respectively. When the Sultana of Egypt appointed ladies-in-waiting from different prominent communities, my grandmother Jeanne became the lady-in-waiting representing the Jewish community, succeeding her sister Lady Emma

*Jeanne Aghion in her wedding dress*

Harari, when the latter relinquished her position owing to the unwelcome attentions of one of the royal princes. As lady-in-waiting, much bejeweled and in great elegance, my grandmother attended royal functions at the Egyptian Court for many years.

But urban development spread rapidly around the house in the Avenue Fouad, which soon found itself in the bustling commercial center of Cairo, and my grandfather, seeking the space and privacy his father had once thought to preserve, moved his growing family out of the Mosseri family home and built a gracious Italianate villa on the road that led to the pyramids. It was an imposing mansion built of red brick, accented with cream-colored stone and white marble, its stately façade facing the river Nile, the red-tiled roof of the small pergola to the left of the roof dominating the Giza landscape. There they raised a family of two girls, Helen and Mary, a son, Nessim, and eight years later a late-life child, my father, Guido, who was to have three children of his own.

⚜ ⚜ ⚜

*Villa Smouha, Alexandria*

# World War II

*My parents*, together with most in their social milieu, were in the habit of taking a respite from the intense Cairo summer heat by vacationing in Europe. But shortly after I put in an appearance in their lives, World War II had begun in earnest and summer vacations in Europe were no longer an option. My summers as a small child were therefore spent in Alexandria in my Smouha grandparents' house. I have little memory of war in those early summers. The deep blue Mediterranean and the novelty of sandy beaches overwhelmed my senses and filled my small person with delight, while the drumbeat of approaching danger must have become more and more insistent to the adults who surrounded me.

My parents and I often went to the beach at Sidi Bishr, where Granny and Grandpa Smouha had a cabin and where two of my mother's younger sisters, Peggy and Edna, frequently joined us, later with their husbands, Cesar Setton and Jacques Adda. The cabin, one in a long row of cabins curved along the beach, was comfortable and had all amenities necessary for a delightful beach experience. Granny Smouha's cook prepared splendid picnic lunches, which we ate laced with the salt air, ravenous after our exertions in the water and the sand.

Once again, I was the sole child in the company of indulgent adults. My father and my two uncles constructed elaborate sand castles under my bedazzled eyes. I learned the delight of sinking toes into wet sand and rejoiced in the tactile pleasure and triumph of digging a moat deep enough to reach water. The Mediterranean at Sidi Bishr was tamed within a wide semicircular bay ringed with beaches of fine golden sand, shielded from the more violent moods of the sea by a barrier of tumbled rocks, beyond which the white-capped breakers charged and roared. There was a barnacled wooden raft anchored between the beach and the barrier, creaking and swaying on its thick rope, slimy with seaweed. My father and uncles raced each other out to the raft and sat there soaking up the sunshine and keeping an eye on the comings and goings on the beach.

My father was in his early thirties then, my mother in her mid-twenties. My father taught me to swim at Sidi Bishr. I can still remember the feel of his strong hand under my stomach, balancing me in the salt water, and his voice urging me to paddle with my arms and legs, and I remember my terror that somehow my head, which always felt too far from his hand and too heavy, would pull me from the safety of his presence and sink me, coughing and spluttering, before he could pull me up. He encouraged and instructed, and one day, judging that I was ready, he launched me toward my uncle's open arms, and—reaching one of the many small independences that pepper childhood—I swam.

My parents, filled with the optimism of youth and sublimely unaware of the magnitude of the dangers they skirted, decided to remain in Egypt during the war years despite pressure from my Smouha grandparents to join them in South Africa. They themselves had reluctantly repaired there at the urging of the British government as the Nazi threat defined itself more clearly. My father determined that he could not honorably leave because he had an obligation to his clients who wanted immediate release of their funds. My mother had no intention of leaving without him.

They made provision for my safety and arranged with an elderly Swiss couple living in Cairo to take me in should anything happen to them.

✢ ✤ ✢

We found ourselves once again in Alexandria when I was four years and eleven months old, although for this visit the summer with its beach life was long past. It was November of 1942, and the boom of desert battle could be heard over the boom of the waves. Chill winds ruffled the Mediterranean in the distance, and we were housed in the apartment building across my grandparents' garden from the big house. I did not know it, but my mother was pregnant, after having suffered several miscarriages in the intervening years, and the birth of a new baby was imminent. Night after night, the wail of the air-raid siren woke Vera and me, and she pulled me hastily from the warm comfort of my sheets and hurried me down into the bowels of the building. Cousins and older relatives trailed across the garden from the big house and joined us. Rommel and his Desert Rats were coming closer and closer.

Holding Vera's hand as tightly as I could, I stumbled as I tried to match my step to hers, sensing the electricity of her fear. We hurried in the dark and the cold, the illumination of a feeble flashlight wavering ahead of us. When I put my hand out to steady myself, the walls beside me were rough and scraped my fingers. I looked up with apprehension at tall metal grates looming in the wall above my eye-level. Convinced that lions and tigers prowled behind them, and that the roar of artillery that came faintly to our ears was the roar of an assembly of terrifying feral creatures struggling to break free, I couldn't walk past this area fast enough.

Eventually, we reached a round basement room where some benches and old chairs were placed. Sensing the fear that spilled from us all, although for different reasons, my mother's brother, Uncle Teddy, gathered us all into a circle and led us in one rousing song after another. We sang "Little Brown Jug," and "It's a Long Long Way to Tipperary," and "I've Got a Luverly Bunch of Coconuts," and other cheery ballads as loudly and as boldly as we could to drown out the ominous whine and crash of the bombs outside. Sometimes I fell asleep, and Vera had to carry me back to my room when the all-clear pierced the air; sometimes, my eyes heavy with exhaustion, I dragged after her and fell into my bed to sleep soundly until the morning. The day after, my cousin Brian and I would search the garden and find shrapnel from the anti-aircraft shells.

I was beginning to feel the burden of my status as an only child, and I longed for a sibling. I devised a ritual for making a private prayerful request to heavenly powers to provide me with this passionately desired playmate. Perhaps sensing that change was imminent, I had no doubt that my prayer would be answered satisfactorily in due course.

One sunny morning as Brian and I were playing in a wooden pavilion that sat among tall trees and scrubby grass on a slight rise in the center of my grandparents' garden, my father came hurrying to join me.

"Come quickly," he said, his face shining with excitement, "You have a new little brother. You can come and meet him."

My skirt flapped against my legs as I ran beside him and climbed the stairs to my mother's room. I felt no surprise, only delight. With a big smile, my mother gestured toward a white organdy bassinet beside her bed and I hurried to look inside. There, wrapped in a blue, delicately lacy hand-knitted shawl, lay a tiny creature, sound asleep, his skin touched with the orange tint of jaundice. I was silent with wonder. Here was the sibling I had prayed for with such fervor and faith as I stood weaving my secret spells, tucked into a corner by the head of my bed every morning. I had no doubt that here lay the direct result of my prayers.

My brother, Jeff, was born on November 9, 1942, a date that has a place of its own in the history books of World War II, for he arrived in the world with the guns of the battle and allied victory of El Alamein ringing in his ears. According to tradition in my father's family, he should have been named Joseph Nessim after my Mosseri grandfather, but in my mother's Smouha family there was a superstition against giving a child the name of a living relative lest it shorten that person's life, and my living Smouha grandfather's name was Joseph. So my brother was named Jeffrey Nessim (which means "miracles" in Hebrew), and the name Victor was added to mark his arrival on the day of the allied victory at El Alamein.

Very soon, it seemed, he grew into a lively little boy with a wide smile, silky dark hair, and a talent for getting into trouble. My mother longed to have a big family, but it was to be five years and many miscarriages later before she gave birth to a third child, my sister, Susan. Determined to have another child, she had accepted to stay in bed for most of the nine months preceding my sister's birth, so the summer of 1947 we did not go to Alexandria.

In our house in Cairo, and throughout that long hot summer, Jeff and I played around my mother's bed, sweating and sweltering in the unrelieved ferocity of the Egyptian summer, allowed sometimes to run around in our underwear in the privacy of her rooms, creating our own breezes in the room with our activity to give ourselves an illusion of cooling down. If we were able to play outside, we ran upstairs to show her some treasure we had found in the garden. We picked flowers to take up to her room to bring a smile to her face. We did not quite understand the reasons for her interminable stay in bed, but we knew she was hot and uncomfortable and we tried to divert her in small ways.

Effervescent and charismatic with an endless capacity for mischief, Jeff was beloved by all. Bored with charging around the garden at top speed in the hot sun followed by an exhausted Vera, he spotted an abandoned garden hose lying in the grass spurting its muddy water onto the lawn near the open kitchen window. Quick as a wink, the hose was in his small hands and turned in to the large kitchen, spraying Granny Mosseri, Osta Mohammed, and the kitchen through the open window with cold, dirty water, while he laughed aloud with delight. The delight was quickly followed by consternation as he observed the chaos he had caused and saw that a tearful Vera had hurried off to inform our mother. Drawing on all his four-year-old charm, he persuaded my grandmother and the cook to hide him from her wrath, and to Vera's dismay, it was some time before she could convince them to release him to the inevitable.

My father's beloved dog, Rex, died that summer. Some time later, Jeff, Vera, and I were drooping around the nursery table one hot afternoon when my father walked in with a tiny squirming bundle of brown and white fur in his coat pocket. Jeff and I were enchanted. However, Blimpie, the pedigreed pointer puppy he had brought us, was never very healthy. His back legs were weak, and he did not live to a ripe old age. He slept downstairs in a corner under the staircase, and he ran and played with us in the garden whenever we were allowed out of the relative cool of the house. He was never supposed to follow us upstairs, but one memorable day, having observed us taking flowers to my mother day after day, he limped his way up the endless marble stairs, a flower from the garden in his mouth, and deposited it on the floor beside her bed. She had never much liked animals, but this determined puppy won her heart that day.

*Teaching Jeff to ride a bicycle*

As the time for my mother to give birth approached, Granny and Grandpa Smouha arrived from Alexandria and brought a flurry of excitement in their wake. My sister was in no hurry to make her appearance in the world. Days passed and Grandpa Smouha grew impatient. Still the baby did not arrive. Then one morning as I lay reading on my bed, I could hear the sound of Marietta shuffling slowly across the vast upstairs hall to the door of our nursery. The door burst open, and she stood there, her face wreathed in smiles, her bright blue eyes almost disappearing in the intricate network of her wrinkles. As I listened to her tell me I had a little sister, my book fell to the floor, I felt dizzy, and such a rush of emotion welled up in me that tears spilled over. My aunt Helen walked in at that moment.

"Aren't you pleased?" she asked, surprised.

"I'm *sooooo* happy!" I sobbed.

It was October 14, 1947. I was almost ten years old and although I didn't realize it, the magical world I had so far inhabited was on the cusp of change.

✦ ✦ ✦

Our visits to my grandparents' house in Alexandria also meant visits to my father's sister Mary and her husband, Victor Adda. They lived in a big, dark villa in the center of Alexandria, opulently furnished with velvet and damask and dark paneled wood. We went to lunch there whenever we were staying with my mother's family in Alexandria. Their dining room was impressive, with massive furniture and equally majestic silver tureens and candelabras. If weather permitted, we children were sent out into a walled garden in the back that provided protection from the hustle and bustle, the dust and blaring car horns that dominated the busy center of town. We played there, somewhat self-consciously, not quite certain of our boundaries, until we were ushered indoors for lunch.

Auntie Mary, born January 8, 1896, was a large, energetic woman with a hearty laugh and a stellar reputation as a superb cook and hostess. Her husband, Victor Adda, was her second cousin, one of three sons of Sarina (sister of my great-grandfather Nessim Mosseri) and Abramino Adda, the latter having built an immense fortune in Egypt, largely in the cotton trade. Following her marriage, Auntie Mary left the family house in Cairo to set up home in Alexandria, where she was soon surrounded by four daughters, a house staff, and two governesses for the girls. She must have missed her family, but the rigors of a demanding husband and social life and the needs of her four girls soon filled every waking moment.

*Auntie Mary*

My Adda cousins were all older than I was, and our lives did not often intersect as children. Suzanne and Jackie, the two eldest, were under the stern tutelage of Miss Turner, and Helene and Colette were charges of Miss Berkshire (Buckbuck). The two governesses disliked each other and were always at loggerheads. The undeniable tension that flowed from their interaction spilled into my tentative ventures into their domain and made me uncomfortable.

Auntie Mary's jolly disposition was in deliberate counterpoint to Uncle Victor's gruff interpolations and long silences. She bustled in and out of the kitchen, making sure that her unrivaled reputation as cook and hostess remained untarnished, while her husband observed her movements with a penetrating stare on his whiskery face. I was afraid of him and only discovered later that his alarming exterior masked a gentle nature and kind disposition. He had a passion for collecting and had many ancient Egyptian artifacts of museum quality. He had also amassed a valuable stamp collection and a rare and prestigious collection of ancient Roman gold coins, one of the finest in the world.

In the muted splendor of the dining room, steaming dishes appeared through the door that led from the kitchen, ornate silver platters borne aloft by a procession of *suffragies* in navy *galabyas* brocaded with gold, wide sashes round their waists and red *tarbushes* on their heads. The dining room chairs towered above me and I had to be helped up, waiting for the chair to be pushed in so that I might reach the table. The soft pile of the antique carpet underfoot was resplendent in jewel shades of red and blue. The chandelier cast a golden glow that echoed the hushed dignity of the meal, broken only by Uncle Victor's gruff clearing of his throat as he savored a special wine and shared it with my father, or Auntie Mary's infectious laughter as she bubbled over with delight at having her little brother and his family in her home. Used to the freedom of nursery meals or the smiles of indulgent adults in the dining room in Cairo, I hardly spoke, recognizing that the chatter of small voices was not part of the symphony of sounds that accompanied this meal.

Auntie Mary and Uncle Victor counted many dignitaries from the Egyptian aristocracy and from foreign diplomatic circles among their guests and friends. Known throughout the cosmopolitan Alexandrian communities for her warm and generous nature, her infectious laugh, and her talent as a hostess, Auntie Mary's generosity nonetheless did not extend to the sharing of her recipes. Her daughters were eventually inducted into the mysteries of her legendary food secrets, but those secrets were jealously guarded from the rest of the world. In a social environment where a woman's assets were measured by her skills as a homemaker, family recipes had the value of industrial secrets and were protected as such. Women smiled politely and gave their recipes to the intrepid visitor who dared to ask, but they usually left out the crucial ingredient that had made their signature dish so special.

Auntie Mary made a particularly succulent salted-and-pickled tongue that was sliced paper thin. It tasted more like *pate* than tongue. Under dire oath of secrecy, she passed that recipe to my mother, her sister-in-law, who treasured it and guarded it carefully. It involved leaving the raw tongue in the refrigerator for several days in a bowl of kitchen salt and salt peter, with chopped-up carrots, celery, and onions. The tongue was slashed all over, small slashes with a sharp knife to allow the juices from the vegetables and the salt mixture to penetrate effectively. It had to be turned over every night. Once the salting process was complete, the tongue was washed and placed in a large pan with peeled onions, carrots, celery, and some garlic, and allowed to simmer for a minimum of four hours. The process of then peeling off the skin and removing nerves and small bones was a slithery mess and had to be done while the meat was still hot, so it was hard on the hands. The tongue was then coiled into a small bowl and returned to the refrigerator with a weight on top. The resulting slices produced a mellow taste and color unequaled anywhere.

Once, visiting Auntie Mary I found myself pushed gently into a small back room where a very elderly lady sat on a couch, her skin like crushed parchment. She sat ramrod straight, her head ornamented with a formidable black hat. "Say hello to Aunt Ida," whispered Auntie Mary, as the elderly lady leaned forward and uncovered a tray holding *sherek*, tiny delicious egg breads still warm from the oven, sprinkled generously with sesame seeds, the specialty that she herself had baked that day. "Help yourself," said

*The magical Khashabanarti in Aswan*

Auntie Mary, beaming. "They're very good." I had never imagined anyone so old and stared at the lady in awe as she pulled me gently toward her, patted my head and pinched my cheek.

"Jeanne's granddaughter?" she inquired of my aunt in a quavery voice.

"Who *was* that?" I asked my father as we got into the car to drive back to the Smouha household. He explained that it was one of Granny Mosseri's older sisters who had married a handsome gambler, Alfred Nahman. He lost her fortune as well as his own and ruined them both. She had spent most of her married life in respectable poverty, and often came to meals at her niece's house.

"She is almost one hundred years old," he added, smiling.

In the winters, my aunt and uncle repaired to their island in Upper Egypt, Khashabanarti, a beautiful retreat in the waters of the Nile above Aswan. The Agha Khan, who lived across the river, had developed a fondness for Auntie Mary's legendary chocolate cake and frequently came over in his boat to have tea with the family. He and Uncle Victor maintained a friendly rivalry over their agricultural ventures. In question were the watermelons that each of them grew on their lands. The Agha Khan came to dinner one night and was mightily impressed with the Adda watermelons, conceding that they were the best he had ever tasted and had an exceptional flavor. Little did he know that Uncle Victor, whose gruff exterior hid humor as well as kindness, had injected the watermelon served at dinner with *maraschino*.

Granny Mosseri and Auntie Helen traveled together to Khashabanarti every winter for a month, where they could sit and gossip with Auntie Mary to their hearts' content and enjoy the gentle breeze on the palatial outdoor terrace. Meanwhile, Uncle Victor roamed the island, tending to his agriculture and the delicate gazelles that leapt gracefully behind a netting he had erected in one area of the island. Bridge games were organized for the evenings, and friends from the mainland arrived on graceful *faloukas* to socialize and play cards with the inhabitants of Khashabanarti.

My mother loved these times when the older ladies of the household were away and she could actually run the house in Cairo, indulging her otherwise cramped creativity and personal taste and receiving her own guests as she pleased. It was a great hardship to her that she and my father were unable, for twenty years, to move out of the big house into a home of their own. One evening, having organized every detail of an imminent dinner party with great care, she walked into the dining room to discover that the beautiful flower arrangement she had created had been replaced by a disorderly mass of green leaves sitting in the center of the table. Angry and mortified, she called the head servant, Ali, to task, asking him why on earth he had thought it necessary to change her arrangement. He insisted indignantly that he had done nothing to it, and upon closer inspection she discovered that the unusual, brilliant flowers she had chosen from the garden had bowed their heads and closed their petals for the night.

*Faloukas on the Nile*

*Joyce Esther Mosseri*

# My Mother

*My mother*, Joyce Esther Smouha, was born in St. Anne's-on-Sea near Manchester, England, on March 13, 1914, just as the world was plunging into the First World War. She was the sixth child in a family of nine children born to Joseph and Rosa Smouha. Photos of her as a small girl show a delicate heart-shaped face, her large, innocent eyes shadowed by a worried expression, an endearing vulnerability—the sort of child one wants to pick up and hug into smiles and laughter. Later, she had long, straight red hair braided neatly and hanging down her back, warm rust-colored eyes, and freckles standing out on very fair skin. My father used to say that her eyes were the color of burned sugar.

Like my father, my mother had grown up in a multilingual environment. A world traveler from a young age, she was four when her family first moved from Manchester to Alexandria. Although based in Alexandria, in the period between the world wars my Smouha grandparents and their children spent half of every year traveling in Europe, where my mother and her younger sisters went to a Parisian nursery school, the Cours Fenelon, and learned French and the delights of the French *gouter* every afternoon, thick rich slabs of chocolate buried in a roll of fresh bread.

When my mother was eleven, she joined her older sisters at the Roedean School, a girls' "public school," a boarding school high on a cliff above the Sussex Downs with the cachet for girls that Eton or Harrow had for boys. She started at the Junior House, which she hated. She and her younger sister, Peggy, couldn't manage their thick hair, and they crept out and met their older sister, Hilda, by the bushes that led to Number Three House, where she lived. There, crouching so as not to be seen, dark curls bobbing as she ran, Hilda listened to her little sisters' troubles and dispensed advice while disentangling, brushing, and braiding their long red hair before sending them back.

My mother had an intense love and admiration for her sister Hilda, and as my father came to know Hilda after he and my mother married, he too enjoyed her quick intellect, her charm, and sense of fun. When I was a baby, as ominous rumblings of yet another world war echoed in the pristine beauty of the French Alps where my parents were vacationing, my aunt Hilda, her husband, Felix, and their two small daughters traveled to Courmayeur from their home in Paris to join us.

My mother never saw Hilda again.

Sometime after that vacation, Hilda and Felix left Paris with their children for the south of France, planning to escape to Switzerland. They left their tiny daughters with a French family, giving them false names, and hid nearby, making repeated unsuccessful efforts to escape the growing Nazi peril that was spreading into every corner of France.

Miraculously spared the concentration camps, they all made it safely through the war. "*We are safe,*" Hilda wrote to her parents in Alexandria, "*I am so happy. I can't wait to see you again and for you to see how Mary and Jackie have grown.*"

The letter arrived after her parents had received word of her death following a minor surgical intervention, resulting from a nurse's carelessness in giving her Epsom Salts that produced a toxic reaction with the other medications she had been given.

*My mother (right) with her sister Hilda (left)*

The laughter, the wit, the warmth of her beloved older sister gone forever from her life, my mother nonetheless worked hard at maintaining a cheerful atmosphere for her young children, but I sensed something was wrong and was caught in a creeping uneasiness.

I was eleven before we were able to travel to Europe again, and there I met Uncle Felix, a slight man, quiet and gentle, seeming always haunted by his loss. He spoke barely above a whisper, and sadness clouded his eyes even when he smiled. My cousins Mary and Jackie clung to each other and to their father and spoke in sweet, high voices, planing above the reality of their loss. It seemed to me that they communicated with each other in an unspoken language incomprehensible to the rest of us. The terrifying world they had inhabited during the war encased them forever in an invisible dimension of their own.

✦ ✦ ✦

After my mother left the Roedean school at the age of seventeen, she returned home to live in the house in Alexandria. Although she had so many brothers and sisters, few of them were in Alexandria with their parents at the time. Her older sisters, Marjorie and Hilda, married by then to two brothers, Bertie and Felix, were already both living in Paris with their families. Her younger sisters Peggy and Edna were still at Roedean. This was my mother's year as the only daughter at home with her parents. Her older brother Ellis, having graduated from Cambridge with the law degree that led to his later years as a renowned international lawyer, was also living in Alexandria with their parents.

Ellis Smouha, strong and big from the start, with red hair and milky white skin, was born in 1906 when his mother was still in her teens. His merry antics and creative mischief were a source of anxiety to his young parents, who were eager to take their place in Manchester society. They were appalled to receive a visit one day from a sharp-eyed neighbor who was all too happy to bring disquieting tidings.

"Mrs. Smouha," said the neighbor, eyeing my grandmother's youth and glancing down at the discreet bulge under her dress that announced the future arrival of yet another child, "Was that your son Ellis I saw riding the milk cart and delivering milk with our milkman?"

This was England at the very beginning of the twentieth century, after all, and class distinctions meant everything. And this was only one of the many scrapes Uncle Ellis got into before he went to Manchester Grammar School and later to Cambridge University. He retained the broad vowels of the North of England for the rest of his life.

At the house in Alexandria, my mother helped Ellis as he dismantled a clock and tried to put it together again, finding when it had been triumphantly completed and closed up that there were pieces he had forgotten to put in. It worked, but backwards. He and his little sister got along very well, and he and my father had known each other as young bachelors and enjoyed each other's company when they later became brothers in-law, sharing a lively sense of humor and a healthy respect for each other's intellect and qualities. My father and Uncle Ellis first met on a ship during the course of a voyage from Egypt to England sometime in the early 1930s, before my father and mother were to meet. The sea voyages were long, and there was much social interaction among the young people on board. My father's new camera attracted much admiring attention, and he took photos of the other young people on the ship, including a photo of my Aunt Peggy Smouha (later Setton). My grandfather, locked into a Victorian mentality and ever mindful of any possible smudge on the reputation of his bevy of daughters, was not amused.

"Get it back at once!" he told his son Ellis, who knew that look when he saw it.

My father had a tendency to be all thumbs when it came to any kind of domestic activity and was struggling to pack his suitcase, his cabin door ajar, when Ellis Smouha happened by. With something approaching horror at my father's less-than-organized approach to stuffing his suitcase, Uncle Ellis stepped in and, with characteristic meticulousness, completed my father's packing. Since he was an accomplished photographer himself, he also offered to develop the film he found sitting on the nightstand. My father was delighted to accept. When the developed photos were returned to him, however, the photo of Peggy Smouha had somehow inexplicably disappeared.

*Auntie Peggy in the Smouha cabin at Sidi Bishr*

My mother remembers dancing with her brothers when she was a young girl summering in the grand hotels of Europe. She and her sisters had exquisite evening dresses made in Paris and wore them to these dances, where they sat docilely with their parents, longing to participate, but forbidden to dance with "strangers." The brothers were urged to dance with their sisters at least once on each such occasion, and while she remembers that her brother Teddy's impatience to be off and about his own business caused her to feel like a broom with which he was sweeping the floor, her brother Ellis was quite a different matter. I learned what she meant when I danced with Uncle Ellis once. It was a revelation. We moved slowly to the dance floor, he held out his arms, and within moments, gently propelled in that safe haven, I was led effortlessly by a true master into the most skillful, delightful dance experience I have ever had. I felt like a queen as we floated among the other couples on the floor, my feet seamlessly interpreting the moves that his arms and feet gently suggested, my dress belling out softly around me as we danced. My great, kind bear of an uncle was a superb dancer.

⚜ ⚜ ⚜

Peggy was eighteen months younger than my mother and, in her own way, was as tough as my mother was vulnerable. Auntie Peggy also had a long red braid down her back, but her face was more oval, her mouth more determined. As children the two sisters were often dressed alike, which they hated, and even put in the same bed when the family went on vacation (in a *char-a- banc*, pronounced "shar-a-bank": a kind of small bus!). Each of the little girls wanted a bigger share of the top sheet, and they pulled and tugged back and forth until Auntie Peggy, knowing how easily disgusted her sister Joyce was, sucked her way along the top of the sheet, leaving my poor mother scrunched into a sliver of bed, at the very edge, in order to escape the saliva-drenched sheet that made her shudder.

Their nanny, Nanny Lawley, stern and puritanical, favored Peggy, raving about her big dark eyes, but somehow managed nonetheless to convince both sisters that they were plain. Nanny's bed was next to my mother's, and when the timid little girl coughed in the night, Nanny lashed out with her arm and commanded, "Joyce, stop that barking!" I am sure that this sudden violence in the night when she was a small child instituted in my mother a lifetime fear of the dark and the terrors of the night.

Despite their youthful squabbling, my mother's sister Peggy figured prominently in our lives and in my childhood. She was my mother's closest sister in age. Aside from the sibling wrangling when they were small, and the differences in personality, they were the only two of the Smouha clan to settle in Cairo when they married, and they remained close throughout their lives. By then Peggy had grown from a feisty little girl into a tall woman, her hair a darker red than my mother's, her face less triangular. She was always immaculately dressed in the latest fashions and had beautiful jewelry that she often changed and redesigned to match her whims and the fashion of the moment. Her interest in appearance made her the ideal teacher on how best to apply makeup for most of her nieces when they reached their teens, and we all consulted her on haircuts and clothes, knowing that her interest was real and her taste impeccable.

Her home, the lovely villa situated off a quiet street in Zamalek where she lived with Uncle Cesar and their three children, reflected this emphasis on appearance, novelty, and status. Together my aunt and uncle bought and collected the paintings

and sculptures of many contemporary artists. My uncle, a dignified and sophisticated man, tall and very thin, was a son of Celine
de Picciotto Setton, and he grew up and attended high school and
law school in Paris. (In a charming play of serendipity, the Setton
Paris town house at 38 Avenue Montaigne now houses the fashionable Celine shop, with the name "Celine" displayed in every
window.)

When we were not playing in our own garden, we often set off
with Vera in the car, Osta Hussein driving, to play with our cousins in the Setton garden. It was much smaller but held its share
of attractions. When lemonade arrived midmorning, it came in
Baccarat glasses so heavy that small fingers had a hard time lifting them, but I loved to watch the sunlight glinting and dancing
among the folds of cut crystal. Auntie Peggy and Uncle Cesar's
eldest child, Gilly, was the same age as my brother Jeff, and her
brother Jackie was a year or so younger. Susan and the youngest
Setton, Philippe, were a few months apart in age. Older than all of
them by quite some years, I lingered somewhat uneasily between
worlds, observing both but belonging in neither, as they made up
their own games and Vera and the Setton nanny, Imperia, chatted
and gossiped in low voices under a shade tree.

Uncle Cesar and my father enjoyed each other's company,
and the two couples often socialized together. Once, when the
four of them were spending the evening at a nightclub, King
Farouk and his retinue walked in. King Farouk and his bride,
Queen Farida, had been a charming, handsome young couple
until greedy courtiers preyed on the king's seedier appetites and
he ballooned into an obese, tyrannical monarch with debauched
tastes. His eye for beautiful women was common knowledge. He
had only to make his desire known and denial became dangerous, since he considered himself entitled to the *droit du seigneur*.

Well aware of this, my father became very concerned when the king's eye seemed to settle on his beautiful wife as my parents were dancing, my mother, with her red hair and delicate features, graceful and alluring in her Paris dress.

*My mother in a Nina Ricci evening gown*

The two young couples left the nightclub in a hurry, and Uncle Cesar advised my parents to leave the country for a while, since the king took his royal prerogative very seriously and did not countenance any refusal. It was said that if he admired an object it must immediately be offered to him, and often as not if the object was large, such as a painting or a piece of furniture, a royal van arrived at the house next day to take possession. Understandably, many people were wary about inviting him into their homes.

✤ ✤ ✤

Well before her marriage to my father and her arrival in the Mosseri household, however, my seventeen-year-old mother at her home in Alexandria in 1931 undoubtedly had no thought of tangling with kings and the *droit du seigneur*. Thrilled to have attained the status of young lady and to have her school years behind her, she filled her parents' house with music and laughter. She practiced her singing, piano, and violin. She made silk lingerie by hand, seamed and embroidered with tiny, exquisite stitches. She went to the hairdresser with her mother every Friday and spent time having her dresses fitted to her graceful figure by Madame Perouze, the pear-shaped dressmaker who worked in the house and performed wonders with needle and thread. Dr. Puy-Haubert came to the house whenever anyone had a health problem. He was an immaculately groomed gentleman who slowly dispensed words that drowned into mumbles in his whiskers and provided gruff and caring medical advice. He took good care of anyone in the family with health problems, and then, as he was leaving, the staff lined up by the door to ask him their questions.

Under the acquired layer of British values and sophistication, Grandpa Smouha remained a Middle Easterner at heart. The worlds of business and the business of politics were not for the women and children in his family, so he shielded them from seri-ous involvement in either. However, during summer vacations in the mountains, my mother and her sisters acted each in turn as my grandfather's secretaries, carefully writing out his letters for him, thrilled to be allowed a glimpse into his world. When it was my mother's turn, he was involved in a complex series of land purchases, and my mother wanted so badly to please him that she nervously swallowed great gulps of air and developed a per-sistent cough. Fearing tuberculosis, her parents called the doc-tor, who eventually diagnosed air pockets in her stomach caused by an anxiety syndrome and suggested that my grandfather ease up a little. My grandfather was deeply distressed and took great care to be particularly gentle with her from then on. As well as being the quintessential patriarch and stern moralist, he was very softhearted when it came to his turbulent brood. Once, when his youngest, Desmond, was being particularly difficult and the child continued his mischief even after his nanny threatened to tell his father, the nanny threw her hands up in despair.

"I'll tell your mother, then," she said, beyond exasperation.

"Oh no! Not that!" cried the little boy. "When *she* spanks, it hurts!"

✤ ✤ ✤

There were nine years between my mother and her young-est brother, Desmond. Born in 1923, he was to be the youngest child of my Smouha grandparents. Arriving as he did when they were middle-aged, he was really the child of different parents from those his oldest brothers and sisters had known. He was a handsome little boy, full of charm and mischief, and he reveled in the security of the love and attention of his large, indulgent family. His father had little tolerance for any rebellion against the straitlaced family culture he had instituted for his independent-minded brood, and because he pushed constantly against that culture, much of Uncle Desmond's life was a struggle. He was always in trouble and always caught out. It must have been difficult to express his individuality as the youngest in such a strong-willed artistic family, and as the youngest by far of three brothers, the urge to distinguish himself must have been overwhelming. Consequently he and my grandparents were often locked in conflict.

*My mother with five of her siblings circa 1922:*
*(Left to right) Teddy, Hilda, Marjorie, Joyce, Ellis,*
*and Peggy in the front*

✦ ✦ ✦

The year that my mother left Roedean and returned to Alexandria, her brother, Desmond, was eight years old. She was very fond of her little brother and kept an eye on his antics, having fun playing with him when she had the time. She and her brothers and sisters were all musical. The girls were gifted at the piano and the violin and had exceptional singing voices, Uncle Ellis played the cello, and Uncle Teddy played the accordion. My mother played both piano and violin, and she had a silvery *coloratura* voice that planed among high notes with delicacy and ease. In Paris, my mother and two of her sisters took lessons with Madame Marchesi, celebrated founder of the Marchesi Method for singers. Madame Marchesi foresaw a noteworthy operatic career for my mother, whose musicianship was distinguished by her verve and passion, but my grandfather would not countenance such a possibility and forbade her ever to sing in public. While she expressed some regret that she had not been allowed to explore this talent more publicly, she also harbored no bitterness. A nodule on her vocal cord in the early years of her marriage damaged the range of her voice, and loyal to the extreme, she often pointed out how far-sighted her father had been in refusing to allow her to make a singing career the focal point of her life.

There was a tennis court in the garden. As fiery and energetic at tennis as she was at her music, she was out on the court as often as she could persuade someone to play with her. She became an excellent player with a killer serve, but her hours in the sun had accentuated the mass of freckles that obscured her fair complexion. Fair skin was still considered a mark of great beauty and women shielded themselves from tanning with pretty parasols and large-brimmed hats, staying indoors as much as possible.

"No self-respecting Syrian beauty would accept to keep those freckles," said my grandmother, practical and uncompromising.

"I know a Syrian woman who knows the old folk remedies. She's a sheik's daughter in Damascus, and she has a secret recipe passed down the generations from mother to daughter that will get rid of those."

By that time, my mother had tried everything to rid herself of her freckles, including a recipe given to her by a friend that involved tiny seashells soaked in lemon juice in a Turkish coffee cup until they foamed and fermented.

Nothing worked.

So my grandparents decided to take my mother and her little brother, Desmond, to visit Damascus and travel in the Middle East.

The age of bikinis and suntanned faces had not yet set in. Interestingly, the tide has turned once more as people are urged to seek protection from the sun and its cancer-causing rays.

When my mother arrived in Damascus with her parents and little brother, my grandmother sought out the woman she knew who had the secret treatment for freckles. Since only women and girls were allowed to meet with the Arab woman, a female relative led my mother and her mother deep into the Arab quarter of Damascus, down narrow, twisting passageways, dim, despite the bright sunlight, until they came to the woman's house. The room was small and dark. There were pillows on the floor for seating. Outside was a courtyard with a fountain, and there a chair had been prepared for my mother to sit on. Her terror and her pride fought for dominance and her pride won. She showed no hint of fear or pain. She sat in the chair with upturned face, as instructed, and the woman returned with a liquid in a bowl. She dipped her finger in the bowl and wiped it across my mother's forehead. Then she dipped it again and wiped the left cheek, going from the top of the cheekbone on down. That was when the forehead began to burn. By the time the woman had started on the second cheek, the left cheek was burning too, and the woman stopped in some concern and turned to my grandmother as my mother continued to sit stoically in the chair.

"Is she all right?" she asked Granny in Arabic. "Has she fainted? She hasn't screamed or made a sound."

My grandmother turned to my mother and then assured the woman that her daughter was indeed all right, and the woman continued with the treatment, carefully avoiding the sensitive skin around the eyes and on the neck. Shaking her head as she worked, she muttered, "One young woman actually threw herself into the fountain to stop the burning."

They went back to the hotel, my mother wearing a thick veil to shield her face, as her skin had turned brown. They continued to travel and stopped in various places to see the sights, including at an inn on the top of a mountain. As my mother sat quietly behind her veil, the innkeeper's wife crept up behind her and swept up the veil to see what it hid. My mother shrieked, her mother shrieked, the innkeeper's wife shrieked, and there was quite a commotion. For a couple of weeks she lived under the veil, putting a special cream on to protect the delicate newborn skin as the burned skin peeled off. The freckles were gone, but my mother had to be careful not to go in the sun for quite some time, and she learned to wear some protection when she did.

Lest anyone reading this should think her experience barbaric, the practice was no more so than the use of lead-based face-powder to whiten women's faces at different times in history, or the prevalence of Botox, electrolysis, chemical peels, and other forms of cosmetic surgery common in the Western world today. Women have always been ready to suffer in the name of beauty, and the way they perceive beauty depends on the ways that society decrees the standards by which they measure themselves and their looks.

When I was twelve years old, I had my own initiation into the grooming rituals of womanhood. I had sometimes noticed a large, gentle Arab woman gliding about upstairs in the house in Cairo. At first I thought it was the washerwoman, whose domain was usually the roof of our house where she ruled over huge vats of boiling water and white forests of billowing sheets hung up to dry in the hot sun. Granny Mosseri, dreamy-eyed, had told tales of splendid parties on the roof in her youth, dancing and colored lights, exquisite jeweled dresses glinting in the light from the setting sun, the pyramids visible in the far distance. But by the time I arrived in the household, sadness had moved in, and only the black-swathed washerwoman anonymous in her veils ever spent time there.

This woman, too, was robed in black, veiled except for her eyes, a beaded thread descending her nose to attach her head-veil to her face-veil, leaving her eyes free to see and be seen. She seemed to come to the house every now and then and disappear with my mother into one of the bathrooms. Now it was my turn. She had come for me. Fatma prepared to remove the hairs from my legs with a sticky mixture of lemon and sugar that she heated carefully until it was exactly the right temperature to become a soft, malleable ball that could be spread out and rolled back rapidly, taking the hairs with it. Muttering soft and soothing incantations in Arabic under her breath and swaying hypnotically back and forth as I watched with interest, she patted my legs and squeezed and pulled the *halawa*, as it was called, until she achieved just the right consistency. Too hard, and it would refuse to stick. Too soft, and it could not be removed. Granny Smouha used to make her own. She gave me her recipe and I tried it once or twice, but I could never get it right. The *halawa* experience was a little painful, but the resulting smooth legs lasted a good long time with no prickly shaving stubble as aftermath. Whatever discomfort this rite of passage to womanhood may have caused pales beside the fear and pain my mother endured to rid herself of the freckles she had come to detest.

✢ ✤ ✢

*Joseph Smouha and Rosa Ades on their wedding day*

# VILLA SMOUHA

*The house* in Alexandria where my mother spent so much of her youth and where I was born was a cream-colored stucco villa, expansive and comfortable, large enough to accommodate the different generations and the comings and goings of an expanding family. A generous garden lay in front of the house with a rectangular building of two apartments at the other end. To the right of the house were tennis courts with some wooden spectator benches and an open pavilion. The back of the house faced the sea and had a large swimming pool that was never filled or used during my childhood but had seen use in my mother's young days.

For me, entering my Smouha grandparents' house seemed a very different experience from entering our house in Cairo, where everything was on a larger scale: marble floors clattered under small feet, enormous cathedral ceilings rose above the halls, formal sitting rooms and a majestic staircase linked the world I passed through as I came in from the garden with the rooms upstairs where I lived.

In Alexandria, the immediate foyer was dark but opened into a sitting area with a high red velvet window-seat under a large window facing the Mediterranean, so that golden sunlight poured in and lost itself in the gleaming dark wood paneling of the walls. Rich carpeting muffled the sound of my feet and swallowed the high pitch of children's voices. Some dark, carved pseudo-medieval armchairs and a narrow matching settee were placed against the wall to the right, while to the left were floor-to-ceiling doors leading into the huge dining room.

My cousin Brian and I took our meals in a cheerful blue-and-white nursery at the foot of the back stairs, when we were still too small to be allowed into the dignity of the big dining room where the children ate with the adults and were expected to behave with a semblance of manners and decorum. Brian was the youngest child of my mother's brother Teddy and his wife, Yvonne. He was my close friend and confidant throughout the growing-up years. Nine months younger than me, and as daredevil as I was cautious, he laughed at my fears and led me into adventures. His strength at school was math. He was a math wizard, while I was a real trial to my math teachers. I, on the other hand, was a champion speller, an area that always gave him trouble.

During the early war years, Uncle Teddy's family lived in Cairo and their children attended the Gezira Preparatory School in Zamalek, as did I. Brian and I were in the same grade in school, and we played together often at the Gezira Sporting Club after school, in the care of our nannies. I still remember the horrible sound of the thud that accompanied his fall out of the magnificent sprawling banyan tree at the far end of the large lawn stretching from the clubhouse to the outer borders of the club. Despite wails of remonstrance from his nanny, Nanny West, who stood wringing her hands in despair at the foot of the tree, he had scaled it to the top with simian speed. He broke his nose that day, but that never stopped him later from scampering up every climbable tree at Rickmansworth when his family moved to England after the war. I always watched admiringly from some safe spot where I was anchored to Mother Earth.

He somehow survived his youthful escapades, which included the feat of circling his parents' bedroom in the house in

Alexandria by leaping from the top of the wardrobe to the bed and so on round the spacious room without once touching the floor.

Echoing my mother's pleasure at being in her parents' home, I felt immediately welcomed and embraced by the house as we walked in, since the entrance usually framed my smiling grandmother, her eyes glowing with delight, her arms open wide for hugs. Behind her, radiating from the foyer to the right, a carpeted staircase with a polished mahogany banister curved its way to the upper floors. Alongside it to the right, a short paneled hallway led into the living rooms.

The focal point and heart of the house was a huge rambling room we called "the lounge," comfortably punctuated with several groupings of plump upholstered couches and generous armchairs. The long wall to the left in the lounge was spectacular for its many windows that brought in the clear Mediterranean light and showcased sea, sky, and many a glorious sunset. At the far end of the lounge, around a corner, was a fine grand piano, often used by one and all for music practice, accompaniment for violin and voice, or sending out the sound of piano scales and chords to resound throughout the house. Setting off a corner of the lounge was a dark paneled billiard room, dimly lit. A huge billiard table covered in green baize dominated the space, surrounded by all the accessories needed for an assortment of adults and teenagers to enjoy the game. Next door to the billiard room was a library with a desk, file cabinets, and mahogany bookcases with glass doors, which opened into a small French parlor, the delicate gilt and tapestry period furniture in marked contrast to the chintz and velvet and comfortable coziness of the rest of the house. A small grand piano stood in one corner of the room.

Aside from the wartime summers spent in Alexandria, every winter we also traveled there in the car to spend a couple of weeks with my mother's family. No one knew my grandfather's real birthday or his real age, so at some point, someone designated January 1, New Year's Day, as Grandpa Smouha's birthday. The clans gathered, year after year, and cousins mingled and enjoyed the interaction with peers from other families.

The car trips themselves held their own magic. Osta Mohammed prepared a picnic, which consisted of fruit and mouthwatering chicken sandwiches in white bread. I don't know what he did to make the sandwiches taste so good, or whether the mere excitement of the trip and the fun to come was enough to imbue them with qualities beyond themselves. Since we never ate sandwiches any other time, this was an incredible treat, and the chicken always tasted better between the slices of bread than it did any other way. We knew the picnic sat in its hamper, and our mouths watered from the start of the long drive through the desert.

Granny Mosseri and Auntie Helen waved good-bye and dwindled to two dark specks on the white marble stairs in front of the house as we sailed expectantly round the driveway and out alongside the Nile, and then out of town and off into the desert. Sometimes we coordinated with the Setton family, the other Cairo residents, and the two cars would start off in tandem, but Uncle Cesar liked speed and my father preferred a more austere pace, so we agreed to meet at the Rest House for lunch. The Rest House was about halfway along our route, and inside, warm glass bottles of soda or Coca-Cola could be purchased to round out the picnic meal. Getting out of the car, stretching our legs, and breathing the clean desert air frequently laced with fine particles of sand fed our excitement as the food fed our hunger.

*Car trips*

"Can we have *gazouza*?" we begged, jumping up and down, eager for the tart fizzy lemon drink we knew the Rest House provided.

The Rest House sported toilets and little more. It was a low, open structure surrounded by the dunes, and we were always being told not to stray and not to touch anything on the ground, as there were still hidden bombs and buried mines left over from the war and sharp pieces of shrapnel half-buried in the sand. We resumed the trip, usually singing at the tops of our voices. I remember my father singing "that daring young man on the flying trapeze" with relish and a smile on his face as he drove. We would shift to opera or "How Much Is That Doggie in the Window" at the drop of a hat, and sometimes my parents, glancing at each other with tenderness, would sing "their" songs, "Heaven, I'm in heaven," or "*Je voudrais un joli bateau, Pour promener avec toi sur l'eau*" and we children in the back would fall silent and listen as if there was a code to decipher in the moment, which indeed there was.

All was not always rosy. Sometimes one or other of us was immersed in a sulk which even the excitement of the trip could not dissipate. Sometimes we would find humor in the silliest things. I particularly remember one trip where saying the word "Beethoven" with a pronounced German accent drove the three of us in the back into convulsions of laughter that approached hysteria. We shouted it louder and louder and screamed with laughter until my father became totally exasperated and threatened to turn back unless we quieted down.

As we neared Alexandria, we began to pass some areas with canals. A narrow strip of green bordered them, and women swathed in black walked alongside, pitchers gracefully balanced on a doughnut-shaped object on their heads. Donkeys hurried past, their riders urging them on, feet turned out and flapping as they rode, and a settlement of Bedouin tents appeared to the right of the road. "Look!" my mother would exclaim with unfailing regularity, "There are the Bedouin tents. They are different from other tents because they are flat on top." As the years went by, we would chime in as soon as she began, teasing and affectionate. Let it be noted, however, that while much has been forgotten and discarded along life's path, we all still remember the distinguishing feature of those Bedouin tents. It was part of the mystique of the journey from one place to another, the transition from the quieter, darker culture of the Cairo household to the sunlit chaos that attended the gathering of the clans for celebration of the new year to come, and of Grandpa's birthday.

✤ ✤ ✤

As time passed and World War II slid slowly and ignominiously into the history books, I began to enjoy the yearly celebrations for Grandpa Smouha's birthday more and more. Whereas my brother and sister had peer-cousins in the Setton family who lived in Cairo, my peer-cousins lived in Alexandria, and Uncle Ellis's family, isolated in England during the war, brought two "new" cousins to Alexandria after the war, Judy and Derrick, close to my age and friends for life.

As more and more grandchildren tumbled into my Smouha grandparents' lives, rooms were allocated to babies and their nannies, and to my delight, I found myself sharing a room with two of my cousins in the commodious Smouha house. My roommates for the winter holiday were usually Patricia, Uncle Teddy's daughter, who was three years older than I and already attending boarding school in England; and Gilly, almost five years younger. The shared bond of our sibling parents overcame age differences, and we exchanged whispered confidences after dark, daring, in this safe sanctuary, to talk about our parents, comparing, despairing, and often convulsing into wicked laughter. As we grew older, we speculated about our future and the lives we wanted to lead once we were freed of the parental yoke. We explored the ways our unique family cultures differed from each other, and the way our shared family culture differed from everyone else we knew.

I began to realize that the intersection of multiple worlds made up the mosaic of mine. In my house in Cairo, I grew up with English, French, and Italian interchangeably spoken around me. Down the corridor from the nursery, I sometimes came upon Vera and Marietta frying up eggs, sizzling and spitting in a black iron pan, the smell of melted butter wafting enticingly around them as they laughed and chatted in their native Yugoslav in the small upstairs kitchenette. Osta Hussein, who ruled over the small black Ford and shepherded our comings and goings outside the iron gates, was Egyptian. His father had been my grandfather's chauffeur, and he grew up in our household. Granny Mosseri's chauffeur Santi was Italian. Both the Cairo and Alexandria dressmakers, Madame Marika and Madame Perouze, were Greek. My Smouha grandmother's maid, at the time a forbidding woman called Caliope who rarely spoke to Brian and me in anything softer than a screech, was also Greek. She was sometimes asked to keep an eye on us, and we disliked her immensely. For some obscure reason we nicknamed her "La Chose," kidding ourselves as we referred to her in mocking and mysterious tones that the poor woman had no idea we were talking about her.

Since such a polyglot broth of expression simmered constantly around my childhood, it was easy to adopt a word or a phrase from whichever language best illustrated a thought or a concept. Phrases leapt unbidden to my lips and were often untranslatable into the language being spoken, although my parents strongly discouraged the mixing of languages. Known as "Frarabish," the mixed phrases gathered momentum through the years, as more and more untranslatable expressions took root. My cousins and I giggled about them among ourselves and found in later years that the unique expressions, mixed or not, had come to stay. Phrases like *"trop de zele"* from the French, meaning an excess of well-meaning energy, was once charmingly transmuted into English by Auntie Yvonne as "too many wings." It was metaphorically such a perfect expression of the original that it took up permanent residence in all our vocabularies, although it exists only in our family language. *"Se non e vero, e ben trovato,"* from the Italian, meaning "If it is not true, it has been well devised," or something like that, was a favorite expression of Auntie Helen's in whatever language she was speaking at the time, and she could sometimes be heard to mutter with sarcasm, "*Siamo o non siamo,*" a cryptic statement meaning something like "well, we know who we are," or more literally, "either we are, or we aren't." Her own expression of intense exasperation, "*ammah!*" means nothing at all, as far as I know, but whenever one of us resorts to using it we all smile and know exactly what we mean and who we are thinking about.

✦ ✦ ✦

Since our young aunts and uncles were in the process of getting engaged and married during our childhood, we cousins became fascinated by the dress-up and ritual of weddings, and conducted many an elaborate wedding ceremony for Jeff and Gilly, who were close in age, and once for Brian and myself in the pergola in the garden in Alexandria. These ceremonies became quite elaborate. Once, in a memorable display of his bent for mischief and satire, a mysterious figure in a flamboyantly flowered skirt with what appeared to be bright red hair in a topknot under a bandanna turned up at the pergola as we were "marrying" Jeff and Gilly, my tall cousin Dicky officiating as rabbi. After a moment of stunned amazement, we realized that the apparition was my father dressed as Madame Schubert, my colorful Russian ballet teacher, a mess of red wool on his head and a trail of aunts and uncles following behind, hardly able to walk for laughter. I realize now how young they all were, although at the time we children were stunned to see our venerable parents joining in our game and indulging in such undignified behavior.

Many rituals developed over the years. As we became teenagers and left the family fold to go to boarding school in England, we were no longer within reach of our nearest and dearest on birthdays, so uncles and aunts began to give us our birthday presents on New Year's day.

The first of January must have been a difficult morning for our parents. They had all been out together ringing in the New Year the night before, often at the neighboring Hotel Mediterrannee, which belonged to the Setton family.

Indeed, Uncle Cesar's parents, Celine and Jacques Setton, had first met my grandparents, Joseph and Rosa Smouha, in the early 1920s when both couples happened to be vacationing in Wales. The Settons had told Grandpa Smouha then about the house for sale next door to their own in Alexandria, pointing out that if he bought it, they could possibly cut a door in the connecting garden wall, and the two families of children could play together. Grandpa subsequently did buy the villa in Alexandria in 1926, but the connecting door never materialized, and many years later, the Setton house was transformed into a hotel by one of Uncle Cesar's brothers. The Hotel Mediterranee's nightclub, Le Romance, became the elegant venue for dinner-dancing in Alexandria after the war, and never more elegant than on New Year's eve.

Consequently, our parents were usually still in bed squinting resignedly at the daylight as we swept in mercilessly in droves of four or five, shouting our New Year wishes, wearing the brightly colored paper hats and brandishing the streamers we had received at earlier stops, loot from the adults' revelries the night before. Lists had circulated among the Smouha siblings and the gifts we received were often the very object of our dreams and desires. All of us were clearly being raised in affluent circumstances, but somehow, the conspicuous consumption that surrounds the lives of children today was absent from our world. Our material longings were usually easy to satisfy.

One of the most treasured gifts I received was a red leather writing case with my initials on it in gold. It followed me through my days at boarding school and through the years that followed, growing shabbier and shabbier with use.

Another year made me the proud possessor of a Parker pen. The complete works of Shakespeare bound in burgundy leather, elegant monogrammed letter paper, four books in a series that had absorbed me, a sweater, a scarf, a small blue portable radio: all these had been deeply desired and they all turned up as if by magic on New Year's day in the house in Alexandria.

Knowing that enticing packages awaited us made the scamper from room to room and across the garden to the flats deliciously tantalizing. We waited breathlessly for the moment when we collectively considered that the adults had slept long enough for us to begin our extravaganza of hugs and kisses that led invariably to the crisp rattle of wrapping paper, exclamations of delight, the squeal of paper horns and the laughter of happiness and excitement in equal measure.

This was merely the start of our New Year's ritual. The previous afternoon, parents and aunts had repaired in secrecy into the billiard room and refused entrance to all and sundry. There, they had smuggled in a large tree, and were busy decorating it with tinsel and streamers, and attaching small gifts wrapped in colorful paper for everyone, each gift carefully labeled with the name of its future recipient. The mastermind here was Auntie Yvonne. Since we did not celebrate Christmas, we and our parents were necessarily deprived of the fun, glory, and glamour of an English Yuletide, so she had worked out a way to provide us with some of the magic by producing a beautiful tree at tea time on New Year's day, to *ooohs* and *aaahs* of delight. The kicker was that in order to receive our gift from the tree, we each had to offer a performance in honor of Grandpa, who sat enthroned in his red velvet armchair, beaming benevolently at the noisy bunch of grandchildren milling about the lounge under his gaze.

Grandpa was very concerned about germs and washed his hands often. He tried to drill into us a proper respect for hygiene, and when we were handed a platter of mouthwatering gemlike pastries and small hands wandered dangerously close, he waggled a finger at us, and said sternly from behind his bristly mustache, "Now remember, what you touch, you take."

For years, we all meekly nodded and after wavering over the tantalizing choices, popped one or other of the chocolates or pastries into our mouths as he smiled encouragingly. However, Philippe Setton, Auntie Peggy and Uncle Cesar's youngest— sturdy, endearing, and solemn with a slight lisp, a wide grin, and a spray of freckles across his nose—seeing a large box of chocolates come his way, lunged his small person toward it as Grandpa's admonition rang out:

"Remember, Philippe, what you touch, you take!"

A wicked grin spread from ear to ear, and filling his small hands with chocolates, he shouted gleefully, "I'll touch the whole box, then!" The resulting hilarity engulfed the room and included my amused grandfather, who pronounced that this child would have an interesting future.

Philippe achieved legendary status with another of the comments made when he was very small. He had recently been ill, and in those days there was only one way to take a small child's temperature—and he didn't like that way one bit. Soon after, when his mother got the flu, Philippe walked into her room as she sat in bed taking her temperature, a thermometer in her mouth. He stared in horror and then pronounced in a single word, "Dithguthting!"

*Joseph and Rosa Smouha with (left to right)*
*Hilda, Marjorie, Ellis, Teddy, and Joyce*
*In front: Edna, Desmond, and Peggy*

After lunch on New Year's day, dressed in our best and on our best behavior, we all streamed down the patio's honeysuckle-lined stairs past a brilliance of geraniums, to the garden where some chairs had been set up on the lawn facing the house, ready for the annual family photo. My grandparents sat in the center, with various configurations of daughters, daughters-in-law, and the older granddaughters in chairs on either side. Husbands and tall grandsons stood behind, handsome in dark suits, and the younger fry sat on their parents' laps or on the ground at their feet. There was much merriment and shuffling around as the photographer captured a large part of the Smouha clan on film for one more year.

As the afternoon progressed, Uncle Teddy often played the accordion, usually the theme song from the movie *The Third Man*. One year, Dicky decreed that we should make up a combined theatrical production where each of us would satirize and portray our parents recognizably and the adults would have to guess who we were. This effort went off extremely well to the sound of great hilarity and some dismay from the parents as they saw themselves through the merciless eyes of their offspring.

Often, however, the performances were of a higher order. My grandfather's favorite tune was the barcarole from *The Tales of Hoffman*, and my cousin Judy played it for him one year. Another year, Judy at the piano and my mother and I with our violins launched into Bach's *Double Violin Concerto*, after much practice. Jeff performed Mozart's *Marche Turque* with brio at the age of four, a tower of cushions bringing him to the right height to attack the piano keys and his small nimble fingers dancing out the music. Susan, her dark auburn curls bobbing, performed a solo learned in her ballet class as my mother stumbled over the unfamiliar piano accompaniment. Every effort was greeted with enthusiastic applause and much appreciation, from the youngest to the oldest.

Tea was delicious. Clearly Alexandria had an elegant bakery on par with Groppi's, and the small jeweled pastries and delicate tea sandwiches were a feast for the eye as well as a delight to the taste. Barely able to move after so much food and excitement, I joined in the Ping-Pong tournament taking place between the generations on the terrace, and later was induced to join Patricia, Dicky, Brian, and their parents for a brisk walk along the Corniche. I protested their unrelenting pace all the way and must have been a drag on their outing. I was usually limping when we eventually got home, but the cool sea air on my face, the salt on my lips, and the sight of the Mediterranean far below the stone wall of the Corniche, crashing into clouds of white foam against dark rocks piled along the edge, seduced me year after year. The

reassuring warmth of my aunt and uncle and my cousins surrounded me as we forged ahead, tumbling and laughing or
engaged in serious discussion, without any goal except to breathe
the salt-laced air, to replay the day's events for each other, and to
enjoy each other's company.

*My father, Guido Mosseri*

# My Father

*My father*, Guido Maurice (Moshe) Mosseri was born in 1908. The indulged baby of his family, brimming with the joy of life and a pronounced sense of mischief, he was a complex man when I knew him, intelligent, sociable, interesting, and blessed with a phenomenal memory, a strong sense of family, and an irrepressible sense of humor.

When he was twenty-three years old, an accident of medical management—a misdiagnosed intestinal blockage—simultaneously robbed his older brother, Nessim, of his life and robbed my father of his youth. He had recently earned his law degree and had begun to practice in the Tribunaux Mixtes, the unique judicial system founded by his grandfather, Nessim, a system based on Napoleonic law and presided over by judges imported from the Hague and elsewhere. The only court of private international law ever to exist, it allowed the nationals of different countries to be judged according to the laws of their country. My father, with his strong sense of tradition and family history, loved the practice of law and enjoyed the connection to a grandfather he never knew.

The indulged youngest in his family, he also loved living to the full and got up to all sorts of mischief with his two cousins, Max Harari and Jacques Sasson. Filled with the exuberance of youth, the three sorely tried the patience of their more sober elders. One night, when Jacques and his father were staying at my Mosseri grandparents' house, the young men waited until the household was asleep and then crept outside and drove into town, where they hit the night spots, returning home with the dawn. Jacques' father was a tyrannical despot whose son was desperately afraid of him, and by the time the car had turned into the driveway, Jacques was already wishing he had stayed in his bed, shaking in his shoes, positively moaning with fear, certain he would be caught and find himself once more the butt of his father's dreaded wrath.

Barely past boyhood, the three crept up the long flights of stairs, choking with silent laughter, pushing and scuffling as they went, Jacques arguing with his cousins vehemently in a whisper, refusing to allow them to turn on any lights. When they had almost reached the bedrooms and safety, unable to see in the dark, he stumbled over a metal urn which bounced down the marble stairs with a tremendous clatter, leaving his two cousins weak with laughter, waking the entire household, and drawing upon his quaking self the fiery parental fury he had so feared.

But in 1931 fate dealt my fun-loving father a different hand. Within a few months he lost a father and brother and became the head of a venerable banking institution and of a family of older women. His golden world shattered, and the explosion propelled him off the tracks of the life he knew, head-on into sorrow and adversity.

My father's law practice and aspirations buried in the rubble of these losses, his carefree salad days at an abrupt end, he plunged unprepared and unsupported into the family banking business founded five generations earlier in the mid-nineteenth century by his great-grandfather, Joseph Nessim Mosseri.

Lost in grief and bowed by the burdens he had taken on, my father looked for guidance from his uncles, his father's younger

*Guido Mosseri at his office at Banque JN Mosseri Figli*

brothers who had split off from the two older brothers and created a bank of their own, but he found no help there. Sibling resentment of the older brother who had tried to take their father's place as they were growing up spilled over unchecked after my grandfather's death. The many Mosseri uncles, bankers themselves, put every obstacle in the way of the young nephew who found himself stepping so sadly and reluctantly into his father's shoes.

Throughout my childhood a large photo of my father's older brother, Uncle Nessim, sat in a polished silver frame on the antique desk in the sitting room across from the staircase. No one ever spoke of him, and I regarded his photographic presence and physical absence with that unquestioning acceptance young children display in the face of so much that they do not grasp of the mysterious adult world that surrounds them. In the photos, Uncle Nessim has a firm mouth, a pleasant expression, and the fine, dark Cattaui eyes. He looks like my father and yet different, although his face carries an unmistakable Mosseri stamp.

He had been a son of privilege, and his life was carefree and full of promise. Summer evenings saw him galloping out into the desert on high-spirited horses with other dashing bachelor friends. The future stretched as golden and infinite as the sands under the hooves of their mounts. No hint of the tensions and tragedy to come had yet shadowed their lives. My father, younger by so many years, surely basked in the glow and admiration of his older brother's prowess. He forged his own path in the secure expectation that Nessim would be the one to take his place beside their father as heir apparent to the Mosseri banking enterprise, the Banque JN Mosseri Figli.

His brother's death profoundly changed my father's destiny, and consequently mine. In the midst of his shock and grief at losing a beloved older brother, surrounded by the anguish of his mother, father, and sisters, he abandoned his fledgling law practice, his international travels, and his predilection for practical jokes and turned his attention to learning about the Mosseri bank and adopting the heavy mantle of family heritage it implied. He had barely begun to make this difficult transition when his father, Joseph, died of a heart attack at the age of sixty-three, six months after Nessim's death. It was said that he died of a broken heart at the loss of his firstborn son.

For many years, my father's energies were considerably bound up in self-defense against the very people who should have been his strength and support, and the reverberations of these events in his early adult life prevented him from achieving his full measure of professional achievement. However, his resilience and strength of character forged in those years enabled his ability to shoulder responsibility and to remake his life when destiny again demanded much of him in midlife.

✠ ✠ ✠

I was not privy to my father's sorrows and struggles. For me as a child, visits to my father's bank were special occasions filled with the clamor and mystery of the world outside the garden gates. We went there infrequently.

The Mosseri bank was housed in the Rue Aboul Sabbah, in the noisy dirty center of Cairo. As we drove into town from the leafy streets of Zamalek or the expansive villas of Giza, ragged children with sores and seeping fly-encrusted eyes, gaunt black-robed women wailing and holding up tiny babies, and men missing limbs or an eye crowded about our little black Ford at every traffic light. Traffic police, their white uniforms and peaked hats gleaming in the sunlight, stood on platforms at intersections attempting to direct cars, trams, camels, donkeys, and a seething, disordered humanity with the crisp movements of their white-gloved hands. When our chauffeur, Osta Hussein, parked and got out of the car to open the door, he first had to shoo the encroaching crowd of beggars away furiously as my mother, terrified of disease, chivied us along urging us to hurry, not to touch anything or anyone, pushing us ahead of her into the building.

The polished plate that said "Banque JN Mosseri Figli" shone out from the grime on the walls. Clutching my mother's hand, I navigated worn marble steps winding to a large door to the left of the staircase. Inside, an unaccustomed smell of furniture polish, stale cigarettes, and Turkish coffee immediately invaded my senses. A brass cage fronted the cashier's office, and my father's cousin Richard Mosseri, the cashier, presided behind the polished brass. Later, as we left, he liked to spill glittering, freshly minted coins into our small hands. He used to tousle my brother's hair and call him *le petit prince*.

*Bustling city street in Cairo*

When not working at the bank, Richard held the prestigious position of curator of the famous Cairo Museum. A wiry, nervous man with a shock of white hair, he spoke in speedy spurts, fizzing with suppressed energy as his words tumbled out of him, and he raced about behind the cashier's shiny fortress and hurried beyond to tell my father that we were there. My father's office was dark, quiet, and calm. His imposing desk faced his cousin Albert Mosseri's desk across the room. We often found my father on the phone when we arrived, and he beamed at us and waved us to the commodious worn leather armchairs and couch that slouched about the large room. Albert, a big man with a bald head and several chins, was as phlegmatic as their cousin Richard was effervescent. He was often absent when we visited my father, his desk surface pristine and unsullied by the piles of papers and files we saw on my father's desk. Behind his desk, heavy paneled mahogany doors opened onto a conference room, and we could sometimes glimpse a long table surrounded by neatly aligned chairs. Portraits of my grandfather and other ancestors hung on the walls.

*Mosseri Bank share certificate*

I was awed by all this evidence of my father's other life, the life he led between the times when he kissed me good-bye in the mornings and when I heard the shrill call of the klaxon horn on his battered little gray Ford as he crossed the Pont des Anglais (now called the Al Gala Bridge) and headed home. He always came home for lunch and a siesta before returning to the office in the afternoon. At noon, the sound of the horn and the eager barking of his large golden Alsatian dog, Rex, running in circles of anticipation in the garden heralded his return and sent me hurtling down the interminable staircase to be in time to greet him in the front hall, his big smile proclaiming his happiness to see his family, and a faint smell of cigarette smoke and coffee still clinging to his clothes.

Always profoundly interested in the complicated links between the various individuals and families who made up the interconnected fabric of the large and varied Jewish community in Egypt, my father knew all their histories, and beyond the histories he reveled in the gossip. He could trace the path of abstruse genealogies with a twinkle in his eye, his expressive face mirroring the characters in his stories with sometimes merciless wit. I sat beside him on the blue silk couch in my parents' sitting room, silent, wide-eyed, drinking in the tales of scandal he sometimes brought home and later served up for my mother, grandmother, and aunt at the dinner table. Sometimes the convolutions of plot and character were too complicated for me to grasp, but my memory of those stories is blanketed in the happiness and indescribable warmth of basking in his undivided attention.

We asked over and over again for the story about the ancestress who was a French schoolteacher and came to Egypt as a part of the Napoleonic retinue. Supposedly, she was a beautiful young woman of impeccable family background, so she was invited to dinner parties in her honor all over town, where she was introduced to the most handsome and eligible bachelors. Max Aghion was far from handsome, but he was ferociously intelligent, and he was the one who won her heart and married her. Their blood ran in our veins, for we knew that my father's mother, our grandmother Jeanne Aghion Mosseri, was herself a part of the sprawling, ubiquitous Aghion clan directly descended from those two.

I listened, spellbound, to my father's rich store of anecdotes about people I knew and people long dead. I began to observe all the adults who came and went in my life with an eye to the humor in their reactions, as did he. I began to understand that adults had faults and foibles and were multidimensional, having relationships to each other and to the world that went far beyond their peripheral impact on my own life. I began to sense the existence of a glowing tapestry of humanity stretching out into the far distance behind me, buttressing my short life with the richness and color of the past, leaving me the sum of their life choices and the strength to make my own.

But although I listened through the years, engrossed and enchanted by my father's stories, I thought he would always be there to tell them. I took no care to imprint them on my memory. I only remember shadows and shifting edges of the tales he told, without the detail that anchored them to reality and made them so wonderful.

A particularly memorable moment with my father took place on a summer day many years later. I must have been about fourteen. The war was over, and we were vacationing at the Lido in Venice, Italy. It was a hot golden day with little breeze, and the sea stretched into the distance in a gently rippling blue-grey carpet until it melted into the sky. My father and I were the only two who wanted to go for a swim, and we started boldly into the warm seawater, but the water went on lapping around our ankles and little more as we walked farther and farther from shore. We walked and walked, and at last the water crept up and was deep enough to reach my neck. We had been talking about poetry and literature, the writers I was studying at school, and suddenly, as we faced each other, our limbs half-floating in the soft undulations of the sea, my father began to recite a superb, poignant poem by Victor Hugo, "*Après la Bataille.*" It began:

> "*Mon père, ce heros au sourire si doux*
> *Suivi d'un seul housard qu'il aimait entre tous*
> *Pour sa grande bravoure et pour sa haute taille*"

—and continued with a powerful description of the battle-field, and of a wounded Spaniard begging for a drink. As the hero of the poem in his compassion bends down to offer the wounded man some rum from his saddlebag, the man points his pistol at him and shoots:

> "*Le coup passa si près que le chapeau tomba*
> *Et que le cheval fit un écart en arrière.*
> '*Donne-lui tout de mème a boire,' dit mon près.*"

I was totally mesmerized by the sound of my father's voice, husky with the pathos and power of the poem, and by the time he reached the end I was adding copiously to the salt in the sea with my tears. That single moment of my father's companionship is branded on my memory, the hot sun on my face, the sea isolating us from the beach, and the intense emotion that the poem aroused. My father put his arm around me and gave me a hug, and then he laughed and splashed me. We swam for a while until my mood lightened and then we waded the long way back to shore.

*Getting acquainted*

His memory was extraordinary. He remembered every word of the major passages from Moliere, Racine, and Corneille that he had studied in high school, and every word of the *Fables de la Fontaine*, and he also remembered a poem about the great god Pan that he learned when he was five years old. I can still see the quizzical amused look on his face as he recited to our bemused wonder, in his slightly accented English, "*Sweet, sweet, piercing*

*Guido Mosseri on Mont Blanc Glacier, 1930s*

sweet, *blinding sweet, down by the reeds by the river, spreading ruin and scattering ban, there he went, the great god, Pan."* The incongruity of our father reciting these lines adding greatly to the charm of the moment.

He spoke French, English, and Italian fluently, and also Hebrew and Arabic. It was said of his Italian that he spoke so beautifully that he had *lingua Romana in bocca Toscana*, a Roman speech in a Tuscan mouth. He was an excellent tennis player, won prizes for fencing, and was an intrepid traveler and mountain climber, striking a chill in his mother's heart whenever he went on vacation. She had lost one son and feared losing the other, so she bribed him every summer to stay away from dangerous mountain expeditions long after he was married, the father of three, and had no intention of doing any such thing. To my mother's horror, the mischief of a small boy lit sparks in his dark eyes as he thanked his beloved mother solemnly year after year and took the bribe.

*Joyce and Guido's wedding cake*

# OF LOVE AND MARRIAGE

*Whereas the* Mosseri family traced its roots to Spain, my Smouha grandparents both came from the Middle East. Granny Smouha, my mother's mother, a small, plump lady with laughing brown eyes and sparkling wit, began her life as Rosa Ades, born in Damascus, Syria. One of the younger of eight children born to Sara Jacoby and Eli Ades, she navigated her life with great charm, which effectively disguised a strong intelligence and an equally strong character. I learned from her that the origin of the name Ades was the Arabic word for lentils, *adz.*

"Imagine that you took a big handful of lentils, flung them into the air, and sprinkled them all over the Middle East," she often said with a laugh. "Adeses are not all related, and they are as far-flung throughout the Middle East as the Aghion families in Egypt."

Firmly planted as I was in my own life as a child, I found myself both disturbed and profoundly fascinated by the stories Granny told me about her mother, Sara, who was sent from the jewel of the Ottoman Empire, Constantinople, to Damascus when she was only eleven years old to live with her husband's family. Sara's own mother had come to Constantinople from Russia, probably Uzbekistan: a beautiful woman with gold coins woven into her long, red hair. Travel must surely have been perilous in those days, and I am left to wonder what precipitated her departure from her home in Russia. Was she fleeing from a pogrom which had decimated her entire family? Was she journeying to an arranged marriage? I wonder still why I never asked Granny those questions when she was there to answer.

"Your mother, Sara, was married at eleven?" I asked in disbelief, close to that age myself.

"It was some time before Sara and Eli lived as husband and wife," I was told. This statement, meant undoubtedly to be reassuring, succeeded merely in confusing my thinking even further. The distinction between childhood and adult life seemed so clear to me. My life in my palatial home was so distanced from adult responsibilities and concerns, so firmly cushioned in my own child's world of restrictions and safeguards, so seamlessly bulwarked by the love of an array of protective adults. I had every expectation that the world would lead me gently and comfortably into the intricacies of grownup existence in the fullness of time. I envisioned my own life unrolling evenly like the long jewel-toned carpet down the staircase in my home, leading me without interruption from one stage to the next. But the intimacy of connection to this tantalizing ancestress, Sara, whose life had precipitously wrenched her out of her childhood and plunged her into the complexities of adult life at such a young age, was one with which I wrestled again and again from within my own framework of context and custom so different from hers. It was a startling concept.

Those sudden seismic shifts that had come so early in my great-grandmother's life were totally beyond my comprehension. Instead of blossoming into adulthood within the security of her family's love and protection, she had found herself under the tutelage of her husband's parents who were strangers to her, transported to a different country where different languages were spoken, sent out to play in the yard with brothers-in-law and sisters-in-law—and a husband who was not a husband.

*My great-grandmother, Sara Jacoby Ades*

I puzzled over this from within the safe cocoon of my own limited experience and the stability of my young life. I wondered if Sara ever returned to Constantinople and whether her parents came to visit her in Damascus, but I wondered silently, gravely trying to put the pieces together in a pattern recognizable to my own childhood and the only context I knew, trying to make sense of it all on my own. I wondered if her new family was kind to her. I wondered if she liked being a wife. I wondered if she knew how to do all the things about the house that grownups did. I tried to imagine what it might have been like to be Sara. I listened and puzzled and wondered. And I never asked.

When I was much older, I learned that playing in the yard had caused several miscarriages before she gave birth to her eight healthy children, and I realized that her full married life must have begun well before she was emotionally ready to be a mother.

Sara died of a gall-bladder infection at the age of sixty, and the single photo that survives her shows a delicate-featured woman with a heart-shaped face and melancholy eyes, who seems to gaze out at the thriving diverse multitude of her descendants with a quizzical expression from under a large-brimmed black hat with a flower. But the photo has never told me who lived behind those eyes, and whether the hand she was dealt made her happy.

✤ ✤ ✤

Far from the cold, gray winters that awaited her in Manchester in the years to come, the little girl Rosa Ades grew up in a group of buildings in Damascus surrounding the square for which the synagogue was the focal point. She could hear men's voices raised in prayer as she and her cousins played together in the fierce Syrian sunshine and watched the young men treading grapes in the communal courtyard. She loved school. Arabic was spoken in her home, and she was learning French at school and was very proud of the embroidery she had started. When her father asked her to tell him what she had learned at school that day, she began proudly to recite a Hail Mary.

"What?" he cried, certain that the very foundation of his life was being threatened. "That's it! You can't go back!"

Little Rosa sobbed and sobbed, begging to be allowed at least to go back to say good-bye to her teacher and friends, and to retrieve the embroidery she so badly wanted to finish, but he remained unmoved and she never returned.

Throughout her life as wife, mother, grandmother, and great-grandmother, I never remember her without knitting or

*Cairo street scene in the 1930s*

embroidery in her hands as soon as she sat down, or some magnificent cross-stitch project such as a large tapestry or seat covers for a set of antique chairs. She may have lost that first, beloved piece of work, but all of her children and grandchildren are the proud owners of some of her artistry and industry.

Once, when she was a very small girl, she was sitting on the dusty steps of her parents' house in Damascus in the hot gold of midday, playing happily with some translucent silky threads, draping them on herself and chuckling with delight. Her mother came by, glanced her way, and came to her at a run, snatching the threads off her and hurling them away. They were baby snakes, newly hatched, and that night and for several nights to follow, my great-grandmother Sara put a saucer of milk out on the front step to placate the mother snake. When she saw a black ring around the saucer, she was comforted that all would be well and that the snake would not go after her baby. I shivered when Granny told the story, remembering the black snake behind the flower pots in my garden in Cairo.

Granny Smouha had a cousin, Rosa, who was about the same age and had the same name. The two little girls were playing together one day when they noticed a crowd gathered about a holy man sitting in a corner of the courtyard. The man was telling fortunes. They crept to where the grownup women were gathered about the man, giggling and chatting, babies crawling at their feet, their daily tasks forgotten. Rosa, the cousin, by far the bolder and more mischievous of the pair, bobbed up in front of the man.

"Tell our fortune! Tell our fortune!" she demanded. Telling the future was frowned upon, but the young women were too intent on their own agenda to shoo the two small girls away. The old man pulled little Rosa, my grandmother, toward him.

"Life will be good to you," he said, smiling at the intent little face upturned to his, "You will travel far, far away across the sea and you will have many fine children." He paused and then nodding to himself, added, "You will be wealthy, and you will be happy."

"And me! And me!" the other Rosa cried, jumping up and down in her excitement.

His smile disappeared. He hesitated, but as she kept jumping in the dust, he said slowly, "You will live in these lands all your life, and you will see your share of sorrow and tragedy."

Chastened by this unexpected vision, the two little cousins held hands and crept away, leaving the women and babies to crowd again around the old man.

Many years passed, and they were separated by geography and the overwhelming demands of their lives and their families. They ceased to communicate.

During World War II, when my Smouha grandparents left Alexandria to take refuge in South Africa, they stopped off in Ramallah, Israel, for a few days on their way, and Granny went with Auntie Yvonne to consult a doctor there about some minor health problem. The waiting room was full, and they sat down and began to talk to each other. Suddenly a woman got up from her seat and came over to them. Looking at my grandmother intently, she said, "Are you Rosa Ades?"

It was the other Rosa Ades, who now lived in Jerusalem with her family and who had miraculously recognized the voice and speech cadences of her childhood friend.

✣ ✤ ✣

When Nebuchadnezzar, King of Babylon, caused the first Diaspora in 600 BC, it is probable that my Smouha grandfather's ancestors found themselves exiled to Iraq, which led directly down the years to Joseph Smouha's birth in Baghdad around 1878. He was the elder of the two sons of Habiba (which means "beloved") Djeddah and Ezekiel Smouha.

Like so many young men of legend, Joseph Smouha left Baghdad at the turn of the century to travel, see the world, and seek his fortune. Because of his family's link to the British government and because 1917 saw a dramatic drop in value of the pound in the Middle East, he was given the assignment to go to Egypt to see if he could help to stabilize the currency situation. Traveling on a Royal Navy battleship, he was housed in the British Embassy in Cairo. For three months he worked with Arab leaderships and with Lawrence of Arabia, and succeeded in reestablishing the value of the pound sterling in the Middle East. He left Cairo for England and a job in Manchester.

Once again, the First World War plucked him out of the comfortable order of his days working in the cotton trade in Manchester, sending him on a government mission to the Middle East to set up a cotton plant for the Bradford Dyers Association. The best long-grained cotton came from Egypt, and his prior experience had given him business connections there. This time he developed more interests and contacts that later led to his decision to move his young family to Alexandria, Egypt, after the war ended.

Grandpa Smouha was a man of strong moral fiber, profoundly religious without ostentation. Although his intelligence and entrepreneurial vigor led to a vast fortune in Egypt, he avoided the intense, flamboyant Alexandrian social life, focusing instead on his business and his family. The Alexandria that Lawrence Durrell discovered and wrote about so compellingly in his novels comprising *The Alexandria Quartet* was as far from my grandfather's world as the moon is from the earth. He merely lived in a town of the same name.

He was a great philanthropist, but following the Jewish tradition in which he had been raised, he believed that true charity should be kept private, known only to the giver and the recipient. He left behind no hospitals or museums with his name on the door, but he left a multitude who blessed his discreet intervention in their lives. His charity was ecumenical, and if he funded the building of a new synagogue, he made sure that he also funded the building of a mosque and a church. A rare visionary who was firmly rooted in values and tradition, he transformed himself from a young man applying a Middle Eastern sensibility to a new life in England, to one who established a new life in the Middle East which he infused with a British sensibility.

✦ ✦ ✦

All of the many disparate and distinct paths across time and space that came together to cause my own existence began to converge when my parents met in London in the fall of 1936. Both the Mosseri and Smouha families, seeking relief from Egyptian summer heat, found themselves in London at the time of the High Holidays that fall.

I never tired of listening to my mother tell the story of how she and my father met. While I never analyzed the fascination this snippet of family history held for me, I suspect that I was somewhere subliminally aware that this was the moment that had predicted my place in the world, standing as I did squarely between the Mosseri and Smouha heritage, linked to both by love and by genetics.

In the fall of 1936, unaware that her presence there was to decide the course of her life and certainly unaware that mine hung in the balance, my mother stood shyly beside her mother and sisters in the Ladies Gallery of the Lauderdale Road synagogue attending Rosh Hashana services, trim in her elegant outfit, a pert Paris hat balanced at a fetching angle on her red hair, prayer book in hand. Almost magnetically, her gaze was drawn to two magnificent dark eyes fixed on her from the men's section downstairs. The eyes belonged to a handsome young man, and the owner of those eyes introduced himself after the service. He was in London with his mother and his sisters. His name was Guido Mosseri.

The families were acquainted with each other. They had met during the lengthy sea crossings by ship that were the only way to travel from North Africa to Europe at that time, and it seemed the most natural thing in the world for my Smouha grandparents to invite the Mosseri family to dine that evening with them and their children at St. James's Court, the grouping of apartment buildings where they usually stayed when they were in London. There was a piano in their rooms and my mother played and sang after dinner, very conscious of the gaze of those dark eyes. My father, who loved music and opera above all things, became more and more enchanted with this delicately lovely young woman with the distinctive red hair and exquisite voice. When the two families left London to cross the Channel to France, the Smouhas exclaimed in surprise to find Guido Mosseri and his family on the same boat. My father had found out the date of their departure and set about changing his own booking to coincide with theirs. It was late October.

My mother returned to Alexandria, and my father to Cairo, but their dreams were of each other. My mother kept hoping he would come to Alexandria, and she stood at her bedroom window gazing across the garden, singing her heart out with the famous aria from the Puccini opera *Madama Butterfly* as Butterfly awaits the return of her love. "Un Bel Di Vedremo" rang out in the Smouha household with fervor, day after day. My father came to Alexandria, ostensibly to visit his sister Mary and her family. They went to the Smouha house for tea, and my mother watched my father as he played with his nieces and her small brother and sister. Handsome, yes, but he also loved children. Her heart was won.

My father formally requested her hand from my Smouha grandfather, who gave his consent. On a small bridge on the golf course at the Smouha Sporting Club in Alexandria on December 25, Christmas Day, 1936, my mother in a dark-green wool dress that set off the beauty of her red hair and fine features, my father asked her to marry him, and she accepted. He had to return to Cairo but an exquisite antique silver Venetian casket arrived for her, filled with white sugared almonds (*dragees*) and accompanied by a small box covered in the blue mirror that was later to accent their bedroom in the house in Cairo, with *dragees* just for the two of them, as was the custom.

In my mother, my father found the fun-loving vitality, the love of music and opera, the positive energy that had dissipated in his own household with the many losses that had shaped his young adult years. Auntie Helen gave her brother and his new wife a satiny baby-grand piano as a wedding gift. It was a light rust color, the color of my mother's eyes, and was placed by a window in one of the smaller sitting rooms leading off from the dining room of the house in Cairo, to welcome her there when she arrived. She loved it and spent many hours there, playing and singing, and later supervising our music practice as we were introduced to piano, violin, and voice.

The big house resonated with the fire of her personality. Her voice was my father's delight until some time after my birth, when the nodule that developed on one of her vocal cords caused her to lose the high notes. Still, she continued to exhibit the vibrancy and richness of a trained and exceptional singer. When I was very small I heard her sing the mad song from *Lucia di Lamermoor* along with the record on the gramophone, the lovely modulations of her voice following the flute into the upper reaches of exquisite sound. It still resonates in my memory.

✤ ✤ ✤

*Guido and Joyce in Aswan on their honeymoon*

On February 21, 1937, my parents were married in Alexandria. White flowers cascaded from baskets, and tall vases filled every room of the house with fragrance and beauty, dozens and dozens of exquisite floral arrangements in delicate shades of cream and white accented with green. As the wedding date approached and the array of magnificent gifts filled table upon table of the house in Alexandria, my mother began to panic that people would not also send flowers, and that there would be no flowers at her wedding. My grandmother became infected by her concern and ordered masses of flowers to fill the house. No sooner were they delivered and tastefully deployed about the house than an avalanche of floral arrangements began to arrive, sent by the relatives and invited guests after all.

My mother was terrified of thunderstorms, and a big storm was brewing as she was being helped into her wedding dress in her parents' room, bridesmaids with crowns of woven orange blossom in their hair, sisters, sisters-in-law, nieces, and cousins milling about the room in a welter of laughter, chatter, yards and yards of delicate white tulle, silks, and satins, a hairdresser and dressmaker standing by, ready to be of help.

A sudden loud clap of thunder echoed through the house and momentarily dimmed the lights.

"Ah, no!" exclaimed my grandmother, looking sternly at her daughter. "Don't you dare say that you are frightened today, with everyone you love surrounding you."

Granny must have been remembering another wedding day, September 20, 1904. She was the center of attention that day, but her own mother and father had not been able to travel from Damascus and were not among the grouping in a photo taken on the roof of the Midland Hotel in Manchester, although her sister Rachel and various cousins were there.

Granny Smouha's wedding photo shows an elegant Edwardian wedding, white dresses drifting in the wind, cascades of white flowers everywhere, mustachioed gentlemen, prosperous and handsome in shiny top hats, ladies in stylish dresses with extravagantly upswept millinery on their heads, the nine bridesmaids resplendent with ruffles seated at her feet, their tiny waists cinched tight, their lovely faces framed in graceful swathes of organdy and lace. And in the center of this romantic grouping, my small, sweet-faced grandmother, her rich dark hair tamed into an elegant roll to give the lie to her extreme youth, her dress stiff with lace and ruffled petticoats, a spray of orange blossom on her head from which the filmy veil floated about her shoulders, a lavish spray of white flowers tumbling down from her demurely clasped hands. Beside her, handsome, dark-haired, dark-eyed, a gleam of triumph lifting the corners of his elegant mustache and a spray of orange blossom in his lapel, stood her husband, my grandfather.

⚜ ⚜ ⚜

Granny Smouha left Damascus when her older sister, Rachel, who was married and living in Manchester, England, sent word to her family in the Middle East that she was very lonely. Great-grandmother Sara, perhaps remembering how lonely it was to be without family in a strange environment, immediately made plans to send little Rosa to England, to live with her sister and cheer her up, and to receive a fine education.

Granny was twelve. She never told me how she felt to be leaving her boisterous fun-loving family and the close community of Syrian Jews to travel alone to the gray skies of a distant country. Knowing her valiant and sunny nature, I imagine her fears were lost in the thrill of the adventure. A gentleman friend of the family was leaving for England, and she was sent along in his care. All at once, there she stood on the deck of a large ship, her small face shadowed by a round felt hat, a suitcase in one hand, and a serious expression on her twelve-year-old face echoing the immensity of the departure she was about to make.

When she arrived in Manchester she brought the voice and lively laughter of home to her homesick sister. Together, they set out to visit the school she would attend, and she grew more and more excited as they scoured the shops for her school uniform and the clothes she would need for the bitter English winter ahead. Rachel kept a hospitable home and welcomed to dinner many of the young students and working men from families she and her husband, Sassoon Shohet, had known in the Middle East. Among their guests was a young man from a prominent Iraqi Jewish family from Baghdad, who had come to Manchester to make his way in the world and to learn the cotton trade. His name was Joseph Smouha. He was working in a bank and living in rooms in the center of town and he had begun to make a name for himself as a hardworking young man with a future.

He was often a guest in the Shohets' house, and one day when he came to tea, he found himself mesmerized by the merry brown eyes and pretty face of Rachel's little sister, newly arrived from Damascus. He came again, and again, discerning the strength and intelligence that had led this young girl of so few years to leave home and fit into the strange new world of Manchester with such poise and equanimity.

He fell deeply in love, and knew that young as she was, he had found his soul mate. It was a love that was to last unwaveringly for close to sixty years.

Laughing to remember how different things were when she was young, and aware of just how very young she was, my grandmother told me how he proposed to her. Chaperoned and shy, she went out with him for a boat ride. She didn't know what to say to this intense young man with the ascetic face and well-trimmed mustache who was paying her such flattering attention. He took her hand and asked her who she liked best in all the world. "My mother," she answered wistfully. Well, he asked, but did she think there was someone else she could like? Perhaps love? Could she perhaps bring herself to love him? Flattered, bemused, and bewildered, she didn't know what to answer. She did like him, she liked him a lot, but what did that mean?

Back home at her sister's house, there was consternation.

She was too young. Her parents had sent her to England to go to boarding school. The legal age for marriage in England was sixteen. She was too young! There could be no question of this marriage for some time ahead, much as they liked Joseph Smouha and respected his family.

Even as a young man, my grandfather was a man used to having his way. He insisted that they get engaged, and agreed that he would wait for her to finish school. She was willing to enter into the engagement, undoubtedly flattered and intrigued to be the focus of such intense attention, but still excited about starting school in the autumn. Both families were pleased by the match and the engagement was announced in the Sephardic communities of Damascus, Baghdad, and Manchester, with the understanding that marriage lay some years ahead.

My grandfather made the trip to the Shohets' house more and more often. The more he learned of her, the more determined he was not to let her slip away. She was a rare jewel, and she was his. He learned that he would hardly be able to visit his lovely Rosa once she started boarding school. There would be a few weekends now and then, half terms, the holidays...Finally, and very firmly, he informed Rachel and her husband that his work was suffering, that he couldn't concentrate anymore, that this could not go on. They must marry now. He needed her presence in his daily life. He would get teachers for her. Forget school.

⚜ ⚜ ⚜

What was young Rosa Ades thinking that windy autumn day at the Midland Hotel under cloudy Manchester skies? Her mother was far away. Instead of school, she had linked her future with this brilliant, driven stranger who looked at her with such love and longing. Was she happy? In her wedding photo, she is not smiling. The enormity of the moment seems to weigh on her, as her dress and coiffure undoubtedly did. Smiles and laughter were for less important moments.

She was soon pregnant, and found herself with an intimidating staff to manage. One night, a fierce storm was raging. Draughts swept through the house and extinguished the lamps. She waited anxiously for my grandfather to come home, but he was late. She felt so alone and afraid in the big dark house so far from the sunshine and loving bustle of her home, accompanied only by the roar of the tempest and the fury of the thunder. She could hear the hum of animated conversation coming from the kitchen downstairs. Holding onto the carved banister, she crept to the bottom stair and sat there until her husband came in, near the closest human contact she could find, but wrapped staunchly in the forlorn dignity of a fourteen-year-old lady of the house.

*Rosa Smouha*

My grandfather's business prospered. He always called her his good luck charm, because as time went on, he doubled his financial assets every year. She told me that he never asked her to account for a penny of the housekeeping money. He emptied his pockets of gold coins when he came home, and left them for her use. There was a toy shop down the road, and its window housed the most beautiful porcelain doll she had ever seen. Her bracing daily walks took her past the shop every day, and she stood with her nose pressed against the shop window, her pockets full of coins, longing to step in and make the beautiful doll her own. But then she looked down at her belly straining at her gown. She was going to be a mother soon. The time for dolls was over.

She never bought the doll. She told me the story with a faint tinge of regret, and for a moment as she spoke, I saw in her eyes an image of the little girl standing on tiptoe in a windy Manchester thoroughfare, skirts blowing around her, nose pressed to the shop window, moving inexorably toward adulthood and motherhood and leaving her childhood behind with a sigh and a wistful glance.

I wondered what it meant that circumstance had lifted my grandmother, too, out of her childhood and her birth country of sun and sand. But I knew that while life had propelled her into the perils and responsibilities of adulthood at a young age, it had also given her the ability to deal with them.

There was no trace of melancholy in my grandmother's eyes. As a young woman with a poise far beyond her years, her teen years punctuated with pregnancies and newborns in the restrained atmosphere of post–Victorian England, Granny Smouha ruled over a household of several nannies, nursemaids, and kitchen staff to help her manage eight volatile and intensely verbal children, jostling with each other's fragile sensibilities, vying for attention as they fought, played, and exhibited all the extravagant love, hugs, and kisses of a rambunctiously affection-ate family. She was profoundly and happily engaged in her life. No regrets.

*Grandpa Smouha*

# GRANDPA SMOUHA

*Grandpa Smouha*, the only grandfather I knew, seemed a somewhat formidable figure towering over a little granddaughter, particularly since I sensed that all the other adults who dominated my young life deferred to him. Although he must only have been in his sixties during my early childhood, I do not remember him as anything other than an old man with an arresting ascetic face, deep-set piercing eyes on either side of a narrow nose, a white mustache that pricked my cheek when he picked me up for a hug, and a head of beautiful white hair. He smelled deliciously of Roger & Gallet Eau de Cologne.

He and Granny Smouha often conversed with each other in Arabic, she in the soft consonants and musical intonations of Damascus, and he in the harsher and more guttural tones of Iraq. I couldn't understand what they said, but it always sounded hurried and urgent, and carried an underpinning of mystery and alarm, although clearly this cannot have been the case. I was uneasy in his presence. Without being able to express it to myself or to others, I felt as if he expected something of me that I could neither identify nor achieve.

The exact date of his birth is a mystery. Since Jewish boys in the Baghdad of his youth were conscripted into the Iraqi army at a very young age, mothers hid the birth of boys from the authorities as long as they could, hoping to send their sons out of the country before the army claimed them. Grandpa's only brother was ten years younger than he, and I have found myself speculating that his parents may well have had an unhappy marriage, since great-grandfather Ezekiel spent so many years separated from his wife, returning to father a second son, and leaving again.

Ezekiel Smouha puts in a cameo appearance in a book written in 1875 by Isabel Burton, wife of Richard Burton, British Consul in Damascus from 1869 to 1871: *The Inner Life of Syria, Palestine and the Holy Land, Vol 1.*

> *...the correspondence for Baghdad is sorted, sealed up in bags and dispatched by our faithful Jewish postmaster Smouha with a camel-courier across the Desert; he reaches his destination in a fortnight, and he brings back the Baghdad mail in time to catch the Beyrout steamer.*

Brief though it is, the mention somewhat clarifies the nature of his travels: his family had served as honorary British consuls and couriers for the British government for some generations, and in return for those services had been awarded British citizenship for themselves and their families. Ezekiel's son, Joseph, my grandfather, was consequently able to leave Iraq to seek a new life in Manchester in 1892.

Ezekiel Smouha was an intriguing man of whom many tales are told. He was, it seems, given to prophetic dreams. In one family legend, he was young and restless and had been traveling through the countryside for some time looking for work or adventure. Night fell, and he stopped at an inn to rest. He was soon fast asleep in his bed, his donkey stabled in the area below the inn. Restless in his sleep, he dreamt that he heard a voice calling him to get up and leave at once, danger was coming. He woke with a start and sat up in the bed, but the voice still rang in his ears. He ran to the window, but he saw nothing. Still, the voice had been so insistent, the dream so vivid. Reluctantly, he crept downstairs hoping no one would hear the creaking, unhitched his donkey, led him out of the stable, and rode him into the forest nearby. He hid in the forest, listening to the night creatures rustling around him, but the donkey, incensed at having been disturbed in the middle of the night, began to bray, and fearing for his life, Ezekiel killed him. In the morning, he walked all the way back to the inn, convinced in the clear light of day that he had done a foolish thing and slaughtered his donkey into the bargain, but when he got to the inn, footsore and hungry, he found it silent. All its occupants had been murdered in the night. He alone had escaped.

I am aware with something approaching awe that had he turned over and gone back to sleep that night at the inn, not only would my own existence have been eradicated from possibility, but because of the achievements of his son, Joseph, Alexandria would have been a far different city from what it is today.

The path that destiny takes is only clear at the end of the ride. Once embarked upon it, we can only follow blindly where we are led under the illusion that we do the leading, failing to see around each bend, failing to realize how the dots we make at random connect the architecture of our lives. We never fully understand what each of our choices and decisions might mean in the overall blueprint of our lives, or in the circumstances we create for children yet unborn. It is all part of the mystery we live, where we are given only clues and the ability to dream.

✢ ✢ ✢

During the First World War, when my mother was tiny, my grandfather tried to enlist in the British army, but rheumatic fever in his youth had left him with a heart murmur and he was refused. Subsequently, when he was asked to go to Egypt and evaluate the cotton trade there for the government, clearly having made a name for himself among the textile moguls of Manchester, he left his wife there with their six small children and took the boat to Egypt, where he made many connections with the teeming, thriving Sephardic Jewish community, affluent and respected. He concluded his work for the British government and returned to Manchester, but only to collect his young family to settle them into the gentler clime of northern Africa and weave them into the venerable fabric of Egyptian Jewry.

Keenly aware of the decadent nature of much of Alexandria society at the time and deeply imbued with a combination of Middle Eastern values and Victorian attitudes toward family morals, he took every care to shield his young family from a sophisticated and less-than-moral social atmosphere in the Egypt of the 1920s and 1930s, sending his children to boarding schools and universities in England and maintaining a firm and loving discipline in the home.

When she was a small girl in Egypt, my mother remembers that the prelude to going on a journey was usually a visit from her tall Smouha grandfather, Ezekiel. He arrived at their house to say good-bye to his grandchildren bringing live chickens with him, which he swung in circles over the children's heads to pray for a safe return. His terrified little granddaughters stood bunched together, their long braids down their backs, their eyes huge with distress, the barnyard smell of the chickens and their agitated squawking adding to the strangeness of the moment. The chickens were then immediately conveyed to the kosher butcher for ritual slaughtering and were given for food to families in need.

My mother, always easily disgusted and fearful of anything out of the ordinary, was greatly distressed by these visits.

✦ ✦ ✦

When she was growing up, my mother shared the family's excitement as her father pursued the development that blossomed into what was to become Smouha City, a highly desirable residential area of Alexandria, and its crown jewel, the Smouha sports club. He held a competition with world-renowned town planners to establish a generous plan that included an eighteen-hole championship golf course, for many years the finest in the Middle East, and a race course where swampy marshland once stagnated.

Many years earlier, Grandpa Smouha had been riding in a train with an Egyptian friend when the friend shouted above the clatter of the wheels to get his attention and pointed out the site of the swamp to him.

"Napoleon's forces cut the side of the canal before the battle of Aboukir Bay and created this swamp," said his friend. "It is infested with mosquitoes now, unhealthy, but underneath the land is good. You could drain it and build houses there."

"Why don't you do it yourself?" asked my grandfather, surprised.

"Because I am an Egyptian," said his friend. "I don't have the contacts to bring in the engineers and technical help that would be needed for such a venture. You, on the other hand, could."

So Grandpa decided to look into it, but when he approached the Egyptian government with an offer for the land, they laughed at him. "You can have it for free," they said. "The land is a lake, a swamp. Worthless!" A reverse negotiation began, with my grandfather insisting on paying a fair price for the land, and the government reluctantly acceding in the end. As he so often did when he had his heart and mind set on something, Grandpa prevailed, and the land, roughly equivalent in size to Central Park in New York or Hyde Park in London, was his. He bought up the swampy land little by little, drained it, and developed it within a few years. It was rumored around Alexandria that Joseph Smouha had lost his mind and was throwing his money into dirty water.

*Smouha City*

He set himself and his sons up as a planning authority, promulgating environmental guidelines for land use far ahead of their time. The engineers he brought in dredged the swamp and eliminated the breeding ground for mosquitoes and the miasma of malaria that hung over the area. Any antiquities that were turned up during the process were turned over immediately to the Cairo Museum. There were rules as to how high and how close houses could be built in the residential areas. He built the superb sports club with its fine golf course and racetrack, and he oversaw an industrial development situated in the lower basin of the erstwhile swamp where the land was not as good for building or for agriculture, and where only environmentally clean industry was permitted.

With hard work and a vision far ahead of his time, Grandpa created a city within a city, the wide avenues divided by central gardens. Large squares and roundabouts alternated with private gardens and villas. He returned all the communal land of roads and squares to the municipality of Alexandria. He was close to King Fouad who frequently turned to him for advice, and wishing to honor the king my grandfather proposed to call the area Fouad City. But the king refused, insisting that because Joseph Smouha had done so much good for Egypt and taken nothing away, it must be named Smouha City. The king prevailed, and the area, which has unfortunately fallen into disrepair since the Suez exodus, is still known as Smouha today. At the time of its development, the exiled king of Italy bought a villa in Smouha City, as did many others from the elite of the international and Egyptian communities in Alexandria.

Grandpa Smouha was honest to a fault. When his sons, who saw and feared the writing on the wall, tried to persuade him to diversify the location of some of his great fortune, he refused on the grounds that it could only be done with subterfuge and might even threaten the stability of the Egyptian economy. Consequently the bulk of the fortune he amassed through his vision and hard work remains embattled in the Egyptian courts to this day, with numerous people claiming ownership, and with no further restitution to his dispossessed and numerous descendants.

*Wedding of Rosa Ades to Joseph Smouha, 1904*

✦ ✦ ✦

Despite having fathered a large family, Grandpa Smouha never played favorites and used to tell a tale about a Bedouin *sheik* with many wives and a multitude of children that illustrated his own feelings about his family. The *sheik* was asked by a visitor which of his children was his favorite child. He thought for a while before responding, and then with a smile on his face he pointed at his eldest son. "That is my favorite," he said firmly. "He is the first." Then he turned toward one of his wives who was nursing a baby. "And that is my favorite," he added. "She is the youngest." Just then a frail little girl ran up and hugged him. Turning to the visitor the *sheik* pointed down to her and said, "And this is my favorite. She has always been sickly." Gradually, he looked around him and pointed out every one of his many children as his favorite, for each one held that special place in his heart.

My Smouha grandparents' first child was born in the summer of 1905 in Manchester when my grandmother was fourteen years old. A baby girl with blonde hair and blue-green eyes instantly took her place in my grandparents' lives and hearts. Doubtless more demanding than the porcelain doll in the shop window, my aunt Marjorie was to be the eldest of nine children born to my grandmother, the older sister of five girls. Her birth was rapidly followed by the birth of a lusty boy, Ellis, then by Teddy, Olga, Hilda, my mother Joyce, Peggy, Edna, and Desmond.

My grandparents lost their daughter Olga to scarlet fever when she was seven years old. It was at the time of the First World War, and it seems that the family next door had a child with scarlet fever and the nurse was in the habit of flapping the sick child's blankets out of the window to air them. The wind carried the illness to my grandparents' house. There was no penicillin then, and there were no antibiotics, so what is now little more than a routine childhood nuisance turned fatal. Luckily, they were able to prevent the disease from spreading throughout the household and infecting the other children. My young grandparents were heartbroken.

When my Aunt Peggy was born, she was named Olga Peggy in memory of the sister who had so recently died, but my grandfather could not bear to say the name Olga, so the names were switched and she was always known as Peggy, with Olga as her middle name. My mother must have been a baby at the time, but since this dark period lay buried in her family's immediate history, she was well aware of the tragedy as she grew older, and with the innocent logic of children, she perceived the age at which her sister died to be the danger rather than the illness itself and always worried when a sibling, or later one of her own children, reached that age.

Auntie Marjorie was a renowned beauty much sought-after by an array of suitors, among them Hore Belisha, the inventor of the Belisha Beacons that mark pedestrian crossings in every town in England. At eighteen, she became seriously involved with a young man from an Iraqi family. It was an exciting time for my grandparents. Unfortunately, the announcement of the pending engagement swiftly brought a concerned response from the Middle East. Far from the delighted congratulations they expected, my grandfather's mother informed her son that both the young man's sisters had gone raving mad at the funeral of their mother and had been confined as insane ever since. "You must break off this ill-fated engagement immediately," she wrote, much to the consternation of my young and conscientious grandparents.

Granny Smouha must have been about thirty-three at the time, an age today when many consider themselves too young even to make the commitment of marriage. Hurrying into town for a routine doctor visit, she kept thinking of the gossip that would undoubtedly attend such a rupture and the shadow it might inflict on her beautiful daughter. She longed for guidance and wished for a sign to help her with this painful decision. Would she indeed have to snuff out the radiance of her eldest daughter's first love? Observing her uncharacteristic listlessness, her English doctor persuaded her to share some of her fears and confusion with him. When her dilemma poured out, he shook his head sadly.

"People will forget about any scandal," he said. "But insanity is not something you forget. It doesn't disappear. My wife went mad and I cannot divorce her. It has ruined my life. Don't let your lovely daughter ruin hers. You must break this off. You must not allow her to marry where there is any risk of insanity."

Guidance had come from a most unexpected source. She went home and told her husband what they must do.

When marriage was again in the air, this time to the wealthy scion of a prominent English Jewish family, Auntie Marjorie returned to Alexandria from London for a round of celebratory parties and to prepare her *trousseau* and clothes for a big wedding. But at one of the parties thrown in her honor, she met Bertie (Albert Naggar), a stockbroker from Alexandria, one of a family of eight children himself. He was totally infatuated with her charm and vivacity, and her playfulness that matched his love of teasing. She, too, fell deeply in love. As willful as she was lovely, Auntie Marjorie carried the day. All other plans were stopped and she and Bertie were married.

My mother's two older sisters, Marjorie and Hilda, were trapped in France throughout World War II, unable to communicate with the rest of their family in Egypt. At the mercy of informers as they tried to escape the spreading scourge of the Nazi war machine and the relentless roundup of Europe's Jews, they left their large, beautifully appointed apartments in fine old buildings in the Avenue Henri Martin and the adjacent Rue de Franqueville and fled across France to the Riviera. There, the two sisters and their families eventually separated and each tried to make their way into Switzerland. Neither family was successful.

In Annecy, an attractive lakeside town close to the border between France and Switzerland, Auntie Marjorie and Uncle Bertie were sitting in a cafe with their two daughters, Rosemary and Viviane, and their small son, Guy, a restless two-year-old with a mop of unruly white-blond curls. By that time they were living under false identities, trying to be as unobtrusive as possible, still hoping to make the contacts that would smuggle them to Switzerland and to safety.

A rowdy bunch of German soldiers burst into the cafe, laughing and kidding with each other as my aunt and her family froze into immobility, hoping somehow to escape notice. However, one of the young soldiers kept staring their way. Their terror kept them glued to their seats. His eyes seemed to be focusing on the little boy, Guy. He got up slowly and made his way to their table. When he reached them, he stopped. He pointed at Guy, and then produced a picture from his wallet of his own small blond son, a sturdy little fellow, also with a mop of white-blond curls. He smiled, and they managed to smile back, realizing that he was drawn to Guy because he was reminded of his own child.

Merely one of the profound ironies of war: the little Jewish boy sitting on the knees of his petrified Jewish parents in a French cafe under an assumed identity closely resembled the little German boy back home, beloved child of a man who, in different circumstances, might well have incinerated Guy without a second thought had he known who the boy really was.

During the war years Auntie Marjorie gave birth to a fourth child, a little girl, Ariel. The dangers of hiding in plain view and the pressures and vulnerability that the pregnancy engendered added to their inability to organize the highly perilous escape into Switzerland and further fueled their fears. The unrelieved state of tension combined with the lack of adequate nutrition prevented Auntie Marjorie from being able to nurse the baby, and she had to be bottle fed. The French doctor who prescribed the condensed milk gave the wrong prescription for the proportion of milk to water, and the result perforated the baby's delicate newborn intestines. She lived three days, crying almost continuously, clearly in a great deal of pain, and then she died.

The doctor, meanwhile, had told a school friend of Rosemary's that he had done it on purpose. One Jew less. My aunt and uncle, lost in their sorrow, glared at him when they passed him in the street, while he averted his eyes and refused to look at them. They tried to bring him to justice, but could find no support among the French medical community. When the Germans took over Cannes, he lifted his head and stared right back at them, and the malevolence they saw in his eyes then caused them to move on yet again.

✦ ✦ ✦

Marked profoundly and permanently by the war years, when the Smouha family was once more reunited after the war, the ones who had lived in peril for so long found themselves unable to reconcile their experiences with the war experience of their parents and brothers and sisters, or to reconnect in the same way as before. An undercurrent of unspoken resentment spread gashes and fissures throughout the family. The ripples created by the very different war experiences reached deep and smoldered for many years.

For while the years of the Second World War left the Jews in Egypt in tormenting fear for loved ones engaged in battle or lost across the seas beyond communication, the full impact of what had transpired in Europe only engulfed them when the war had ended. More and more personal accounts of unimaginable horrors trickled out of Europe as survivors told their tales and soldiers shared stories of the sights they had encountered during the liberation of the concentration camps. Sheltered from Hitler's deranged persecutions by fate and geography, those who had been shielded from the unspeakable could only offer their empathy and could not share the inhumanity of the experience.

Nonetheless, along with the sudden explosive rifts and alliances that formed and faded among the strong personalities and prickly sensitivities of the Smouha clan was an even stronger sense of belonging. Like any diverse group of people closely related by blood and youthful experience but often divided by personality and circumstance, the peer groups in my generation often, but not always, managed to transcend the unresolved conflicts of their sibling elders. Where there are wounds, ties of blood form bridges of scar tissue, leaving later generations the option and delight of clambering over the rough spots to find the welcome of family they recognize in a world teeming with strangers.

Once, leaning over the railing of the pier leading from an astounding aquatic museum, I noticed what seemed to be plaques of algae forming and reforming on the sea surface. On closer inspection, what at first appeared to be a single plant undulating with the swells of the sea was in fact huge drifts of tiny fish moving together with perfect precision, closing in, fanning out, occasionally expelling or absorbing other groups that swam into their orbit. Looking back, I realize that they epitomize the peculiar nature of love and warfare in a large, extroverted family.

As the children of my Smouha grandparents spun off into their separate families, they took with them the extension of childhood battles and rivalries, introducing the perceptions and life-views of the individuals they married into an already volatile family mix. My mother was often the peacemaker in her family, despite her red hair and the quick temper that went with it. She managed to steer with an even keel through the stormy seas of disputes and flare-ups that occasionally peppered the social and familial interactions of her siblings. Time and again, she refused to let herself be drawn into the heat of battle, and watching her grow bold at the challenge, I came to believe that there is always a path to family unity even through the most tangled of battle-grounds.

*First day of school at GPS*

# Gezira Preparatory School

*My mother's* brother Teddy Smouha, a wing commander in the RAF, was a trim, handsome man: tall, dark, and slim with large brown eyes and a bristly mustache. A fine athlete, he won the bronze medal for England in the 100 meter relay in the Olympic Games in Amsterdam in 1928. The movie *Chariots of Fire* was based on the Olympic Games of 1924, so many of the distinctive and flamboyant personalities portrayed in that movie were a part of his experience. His wife, Auntie Yvonne, was also athletic, and with her tranquil and capable personality she was the perfect wife for the social life that developed around his important wartime military career.

When Auntie Yvonne and Uncle Teddy and their three children lived in Cairo during the war years, their children attended the Gezira Preparatory School (GPS) in Zamalek near where they lived. My mother and her sister-in-law Yvonne had been friends when they were little girls, and the friendship remained a strong and nourishing one throughout their lives. Because my cousins Dicky and Patricia were older than I was, and because my mother valued her friend's experience and judgment, it was decided that I would start my school years at the GPS with my cousins. So when I was five, that is where I first went to school.

Fall of 1942 saw me standing in our garden dressed in a white shirt and grey tunic, a neat brown satchel in my hand and a grey felt hat on my head with the blue school logo on the front, a quizzical look on my face as I squinted against the sunlight, while my mother took a photo for posterity. Apprehensive about my first real foray into a world outside of my family, I was happy to find myself in the same class as my playmate and cousin, Brian.

Mrs. Whitfield was our kindergarten teacher. She spoke loudly and slowly to us, and somewhat to their irritation, to our parents as well, enunciating every syllable carefully in a high sing-song, a saccharine smile pasted on her face, her soft cheeks smelling of the floury face powder she used, her salt-and-pepper hair escaping gradually throughout the day from the pins she poked in to tame it. She wore gaily flowered dresses and adored little children, having none of her own. Every morning after roll call she showered her small charges with extravagant hugs and kisses before leading us proudly to our place in the very front of the main hall, as the whole school gathered behind us for assembly.

I am not sure how we learned the essentials of reading and writing that year, but kindergarten at the GPS was a happy introduction to schooldays, and one day, turning the pages and looking at the pictures in a book about two little penguins living in the Arctic, I realized that **FLIP** and **FLOP** were their names and that I could read the words. I grew dizzy with the excitement of this revelation and turned the page with eagerness to find that I could read the entire book. Reading is power, and this was the first time I tasted that power and recognized it for what it was. The thrill of opening a book and exploring its treasures only increased with the passing years.

During assembly, Mrs. Bullen, the headmistress, made announcements in her clear British voice and then led the school in hymns, such as "All Things Bright and Beautiful" or "Oh God Our Help in Ages Past," while one of the teachers thundered

*Alexandria: Grandpa's birthday, January 1956*

away on the piano with much enthusiastic pumping of the ped-
als. We were a motley assortment of children from many different backgrounds, speaking many different languages, and as the
years wore on, neat and homogeneous in our gray tunics, gray
felt hats, and white blouses, we became thoroughly inoculated
with the various elements of British culture. We took part in sing-
alongs, belting out "My Grandfather's Clock Stood So Long on
the Shelf," "I Went to the Animal Fair," and many other typically
British songs whose words escape me. We were also introduced
to other thoroughly English pursuits interspersed with the traditional classes in arithmetic, reading, and writing that took up
most of our time.

When we went into the equivalent of first grade, our teacher,
Mrs. Swinburne, was of a much sterner ilk. She had shiny black
hair stylishly arranged into a fashionable roll at the back of her
head, her thin mouth and long nails a vibrant red, and her button
black eyes entirely without humor. Small boys were a trial to her,
and small boys with a more-than-average mischief component

were anathema. She favored long-legged girls with blue eyes, long blonde braids, and pink-and-white Anglo Saxon complexions. She was much harder on the Egyptian girls in the class or those of Italian or other "foreign" extraction, and hardest of all on the boys, although Brian's large green eyes, blond hair, and status as son of an RAF Wing Commander exempted him from much of her ire.

There was another little boy in the class upon whom the wrath of the teachers descended with some regularity. He was a dark-haired, dark-eyed little fellow with a wide, infectious grin. His name was Bobby Naggar. In the spring, led by Mrs. Swinburne's pale stockinged legs in their high heels, her skirts swinging ahead of us, we repaired docilely, two by two, hand in hand to the gym, to learn the mysteries of Maypole dancing. A large pole was erected in the center of the polished gym floor, different colored ribbons descending from it. We were positioned around it, alternating boys and girls, and instructed how to weave in and out to create a braided pattern as the piano thumped along in cheerful rhythm.

Bobby Naggar invariably tangled the ribbons, his merry dark eyes sparkling with mischief, causing irrepressible giggles in his classmates as he clowned about and teased the girls, pulling on their pigtails and stepping on their heels. He usually ended up in a corner of the gym, sent to observe the proceedings as we stumbled and giggled our way through different folk dances and prepared for the end-of-term show for the parents. Bobby's name was really Yves, but he came in for a huge amount of teasing when he first arrived at an English school, where his classmates thought that his name was Eve. So he became known to all of us as Bobby, a mispronunciation of *Bube*, a German term of endearment given to him by a governess when he was very small. To add to the confusion, his middle name, Albert, was used at school for roll call.

*Bobby Naggar and his big brother*

Although I was older, I was still shy, and still uneasy outside my comforting home environment. I watched the others with interest, observing the antics of my bolder contemporaries, never quite daring to join the troublemakers in their fun but wishing I could.

A small, dusty playground surrounded by trees and a tall fence spread itself to the back and side of the school building. We spilled out into its meager attractions every day at eleven for "break." There were no colorful slides or climbing gyms, no swings, sandbox, or other equipment such as we see in the tiniest nursery school playground today. We stood about and gossiped. We played marbles with acquisitive intensity. Some of the older boys played games of catch, or cops and robbers and cowboys and Indians as well as various ball games, as they caromed in herds around the playground. Their playtimes and ours were usually timed not to coincide.

One day, however, I had just emerged blinking into the sunlight in the playground, when a group of older boys playing some game that involved a lot of running and yelling swept past and knocked me over. A tall skinny boy with a shock of black hair turned back, picked me up, and planted me firmly on my feet before continuing on his way. I knew who he was. He was Bobby Naggar's big brother. He swept off to follow his peers and left a small girl dazzled by the encounter. I filed it away as a special memory, little knowing that it would resurface many years later.

Mrs. Bullen retired while I was still at the GPS, and she was succeeded by Mrs. Wilson, whom I liked very much. She had been my form mistress for a year and had introduced me to wonderful stories in the reading hour she instituted. She seemed more accessible than her predecessor, her greying hair puffing out around a broad, smiling face.

Sometime during this period, when I was eight or nine, we had a teacher who taught a poetry class. The homework one night was to write a poem about spring. Long after I was supposed to be in bed, I was eagerly wrestling with words, with rhyme and meter. Finally my mother came into the room and decreed that enough was enough and I must go to sleep. I took the poem to school the next day and handed it in, secretly confident that I would receive an excellent mark for my homework. My parents, usually stern critics, had seemed favorably impressed with my literary effort. A few days later our poems were returned to us. Mine was unmarked. I asked the teacher why, and she launched into an angry speech about cheating and copying instead of writing my own poem as she had required.

"But I didn't copy," I insisted, near tears, and angry enough to forget my timidity and speak out, "This is my own poem in my own words."

"Nonsense," said the teacher. "You couldn't have done this without help," and no disclaimer on my part swayed her in the least. I sobbed, devastated to be so disbelieved, and it took many years before I perceived how she had complimented me.

Meanwhile, I had tasted the magic of words. I knew all about the magic of reading other peoples' words by then, but fashioning words to bring about a faithful image of my own personal perception of the world—that was new. That was wonderful. That was totally seductive. I had been given a gift subscription to *Sunny Stories*, a small magazine run by the well-known children's book author, Enid Blyton, whose dozens of books I devoured with faithful regularity. I learned how to make invisible ink from one of Enid Blyton's mystery novels and I taught my younger cousin Gilly to write in lemon juice, so that the words only showed up when held over a lit match. *Sunny Stories* magazine solicited contributions from its young readers, and without more ado I resolved to have my poem published in its pages in time to present to my parents for their wedding anniversary. I have no idea how or where I acquired a stamp, for such things were not a part of my daily life as a child, but off my poem went to England, into the much-admired hands of Enid Blyton. With the utter innocence of childhood I never doubted for a moment that she would read it and that I would receive a response.

And surprisingly, in due course a handwritten postcard arrived and sat on the mottled marble top of the table in the center of the downstairs hall. It ended with the distinctive signature to be found imprinted on all her book covers. The great Enid Blyton herself had taken the trouble to write to me. Sadly, *Sunny Stories* had ceased to be and was no longer publishing, but her words in the postcard encouraged me to continue writing and seeking publication. There could be no greater honor. Somewhere, she lit a fire that continued to send a glow through all the years and all the difficulties to follow.

⚜ ⚜ ⚜

I stayed at the Gezira Preparatory School until the year before I was due to go to Roedean School in England. I was twelve, almost thirteen by the time I started there. The foreign schools in Egypt at that time were not up to par with the good schools in Europe. Wherever possible, parents who could, made the difficult decision to send their children away to boarding schools to enlarge their horizons and provide them with a broader education. Added to that, my mother and her sisters had all spent their high school years at Roedean School; it was a part of family lore; and my admired older cousins, Patricia and Judy, already away at boarding school, were imbued in my eyes with an aura of independence and sophistication that seemed infinitely attractive to an overprotected little cousin. My parents asked me whether or not I wished to go away to boarding school in England, and fortified with the weight of family tradition, titillated by my voluminous reading of book after book about British schoolchildren and their adventures, I had no hesitation. I wanted to take the exam, and if I got in, I wanted to go to Roedean.

However, it turned out that I needed a further year in Egypt to strengthen my math. I graduated from the GPS and spent that year at the English School in Heliopolis, a distant suburb of Cairo. I had to get up very early in the morning, before my parents were awake. Shivering slightly with cold and interrupted sleep, Vera and I stood every morning, waiting outside the garden gates at the corner of our road, across from the Nile banks. Clutching my lunch and my schoolbag, I could hardly wait to clamber onto the rickety bus and leave my baby life behind me for the day. My brother, by then, had started school at the GPS, and it was my sister's turn to spend time with the daisies and the arbor in the garden.

The school campus was a good hour's ride away, a ride echoing with chatter and shrieks of laughter, through dirty crowded thoroughfares, past Maadi and elegant suburban developments spilling flowers from every wall, along stretches of desert road. I didn't mind it. I didn't mind shivering in the thin winter cold or gasping for air in the turbid heat of spring. I didn't mind any of it, because already vistas of independence opened tantalizingly before my eager eyes.

So far, every school day of my short life, I had been accompanied across the bridge, down shady tree-lined boulevards that led from Giza to Zamalek, Osta Hussein at the wheel of the snub-nosed little black Ford, and my mother or Vera always in attendance. Sometimes blue jacaranda blooms hung heavy among feathery leaves above us, echoing the cloudless sky and suffusing my world in a blue haze, fallen blue petals lining the road. At other times of the year, the predominant color was a brilliant red piercing the green overhead as the poinsettia trees came into flower, leaning over the road in chaotic splendor. Everywhere in Zamalek bougainvillea reigned, red, hot pink, laced with dark green, tumbling in riotous profusion over gates, down walls, cascading from stone urns. We followed the same route returning from school for lunch, and at the close of school in the afternoon, when I knew I could count on seeing my mother straining to catch sight of me as I burst out of class and ran to the school gate. I valued all of this wonderful loving care, but I was eleven and beginning to strain at the leash.

So the fact that I now carried my lunch with me each day in carefully packed thermos flasks, and that a few coins jingled in my pocket and allowed me access to the tiny candy shop on the school premises, seemed a freedom beyond my imaginings. The school was large, and I was in the youngest class. It was coed, and stirrings of interest in the older students added spice to our recreation times. While the school provided a hot lunch for most of the students, I had two close friends, one Jewish and one Moslem, who shared the same food restrictions. We brought our lunches from home and sat together on the same green bench at the front of the lunch room.

Nelly, Summi, and I became a gang of three. We were the three musketeers, we were Sir Percy Blakeney, the beautiful Marguerite and the sinister Chauvelin. Our bible was *The Scarlet Pimpernel*, and basing ourselves on that swashbuckling tale, we stalked the vast perimeters of the playground and playing fields at recreation in search of adventure and romance, developing complicated story lines of our own in tiny notebooks which the talented Summi illustrated. Some of this was written in an elaborate code that we developed, and we plunged happily through the school year, exploring our imaginations and our environment with gusto.

Meanwhile, a cheery round-faced English girl with bright blue eyes named Diana Eady and I vied for the top spot in English, week after week. It was a friendly rivalry, since we knew that both of us were going to attend different boarding schools in England the following year, and we enjoyed the challenge. My math improved, although my father made the grave mistake of offering to tutor me during the winter holiday in Alexandria and emerged from the study quasi-apoplectic after our first session. My mother took one look at his red face and my tearful one, and hired a tutor.

Since the English School at Heliopolis went up to the age of seventeen, and since early arranged marriages were still very much the norm in Egyptian society at that time, we sometimes watched a tearful round of good-byes as a wistful classmate dropped out of school reluctantly, the world of babies and housekeeping instantly taking the place of homework and sports. Once, at recreation time, a bride in fluttering white appeared, beaming and resplendent, to hug her classmates before taking off for the adult world, her sheepish new husband in tow.

✤ ✤ ✤

Winter vacation came around and school closed. I was in a lather of excitement because for the first time, we were going to visit my aunt and uncle in Upper Egypt at Khashabanarti, the island with the magical name I had often dreamed of seeing. By then, I had heard all about Aswan and the legendary Winter Palace Hotel in Luxor where my parents had gone for their honeymoon. I had seen photos of my newly married parents, my mother shy and happy, slim and sporty in a brown skirt and turtleneck sweater, smiling at the camera cuddled into my handsome father's arm, and as I listened to her stories of the two of them in their evening finery descending the majestic staircase of that grand old hotel arm in arm, seeing their own reflection in the mirror at the bottom of the stairs, my romantic soul soaked up a glowing image of their youth, yearning already for the time when it would be my turn.

Arriving by *falouka*, listening to the swish of the Nile waters against the side of the boat, we watched the low-slung dome of the house come closer, and closer, and we were soon listening to Uncle Victor describing the progress of his runner beans with pride. Uninterested in the chatter of his arriving visitors, he solemnly marched me off to admire his tumbling rows of delicately colored sweet peas, and to introduce me to the gazelles and the many wonders of his island kingdom. My stay was dominated by my obsession with finding exactly the right square of rough rose-colored granite to take home as a hopscotch stone with which to dazzle my school friends. But the memory of the *faloukas*—their masts and sails silhouetted elegantly against the deep-blue sky streaked with the orange and fuchsia of the Egyptian twilight swift in its plunge into night, the intimate sound of the opaque Nile waters thunking gently against the wood, and the image of dark men in dazzling white robes and turbans—still lingers.

Banks of rose granite flecked with black and white crystals glittered in the strong sunlight towering majestically on either side of the river, as we left at the end of our stay, and at the center of the island, the sprawling white-domed palace with its stone columns and arches rose from the mist, magic, mystery, and beauty sparking dreamlike images. And like a dream, it vanished from my life forever. I never went there again, and I have never forgotten it.

✦ ✦ ✦

The summer months that year brought an end to school in Heliopolis and to my daily taste of independence, and the hot days brought handcarts outside the garden gates piled high with the most luscious of watermelons, some split enticingly so that their dark green skins contrasted with the sweet pink flesh and black pits inside.

Many wonderful fruits appeared on our dining-room table as the seasons succeeded each other. Winter brought pale citrus globes the size of a small grapefruit, called sweet lemons, *citrons doux*, which revealed juicy golden sections with a particular mild sweet taste all their own. Blood oranges with their pungent flavor and red-veined interior numbered among my father's favorites. I loved best the faintly spicy taste of the perfumed white flesh of *eshta* (the closest equivalent in the Americas being *chirimoyas* from South America, although they do not come close to the flavor I remember), round green fruit mottled with brown, rising to a point at the top, the outer skin knobbly and rough, scales on a miniature turtle shell. When I pulled it open, the fruit revealed a central stem, on either side of which hid a multitude of black pits that slipped easily out of their succulent white pockets to pile up like a gleaming harvest of tiny fish on the side of the plate. We always greeted the first sight of cape gooseberries (*physalis*) with cries of delight, the flavor and juice of the delicious little orange-colored berries bursting tart in the mouth, their many tiny seeds almost invisible in the flesh, each berry waiting like a surprise package in its own individual veined parchment pocket. Known as *amour en cage* ("love in a cage") in French, the Arabic name, *bint taht el namoussia*, means "maiden under the mosquito net."

Clearly, along with the sensuous delight of its distinctive flavor, this is a fruit that evokes romance and mystery in all languages.

Mangos of many kinds, bananas, tangerines, peaches and plums, greengages, oranges, lemons, and limes each had their moment in the limelight and brought pleasure and variety to the changing seasons. Unlike today, it was virtually impossible to find out-of-season fruits, but the advent of the first of each variety marked the turn of the season as surely as the weather and the calendar.

☩ ☩ ☩

Although as I grew older I ate dinner with my parents, Auntie Helen, and Granny Mosseri in the big dining room every day, my parents often spent their evenings after dinner in privacy in their own sitting room upstairs. The sunlit suite of rooms in the big house in Cairo that my mother occupied with my father after their marriage had been redecorated to their taste and needs. Nonetheless, my mother never lost her longing for privacy and for opportunities to exercise her innate creativity that a home of her own for herself and her young family would have afforded her. Since the mansion by the Nile that Grandpa Mosseri had built had become too large for my widowed grandmother and unmarried aunt to rattle around in on their own, my father knew that he could not make the break to a home of his own until his father's house was sold and his mother and sister were suitably housed elsewhere.

Time and again, he sought out buyers, but time and again, various uncles and cousins of my father's who shared in the ownership of the surrounding lands put obstacles in the way of any prospective sale. Despite the passing of so many years, he found himself unable to extricate himself from the financial and familial entanglements caused by the untimely death of his father and older brother, circumstances which bound him to the house itself and to safeguarding the welfare of his mother and sister.

I was intimately familiar with my parents' suite of rooms in the big house in Cairo, not only because as a small child I clambered up into their bed and played among the down pillows, bouncing on the hard blue bolster, but because once I left to go to boarding school in England at the age of thirteen I no longer slept in the nursery with my little sister. I graduated to the comfortable blue couch that opened into a bed in my parents' sitting room for my month-long visits home at the Christmas and Easter breaks. For the summer holidays they came to Europe and we spent the summer months there, so until I left school and returned to Cairo at the age of seventeen, I spent only a couple of months a year at home.

My parents' rooms were to the left of the elevator, at the top of the majestic staircase that led from the downstairs hall. The elevator made its ponderous deliberate way up into an arched stone recess on the second floor, settling to a stop with a thump. It had an upholstered bench along the back wall, clear glass doors, and an accordion metal gate. Granny Mosseri and Auntie Helen used it all the time. My parents used it infrequently, and for me, a ride in the elevator was a rare treat.

My parents' rooms were decorated in Art Deco style, probably quite modern and daring for them to attempt at that time in that venerable house so classical in its furnishings. Their sitting room was a pleasing mixture of pale pink glass shelves behind glass doors that shielded delicate jade ornaments, ivory carvings, and ashtrays of lapis and carved pink quartz. An armchair and occasional chairs framed in a silky blond wood matched the

*Staircase leading upstairs*

low, blue satin couch that later doubled as my bed. A large window faced the Nile, with brown shutters that opened onto a small stone balcony. My mother's desk, with its many neat compartments, opened out into the room. To the far left was a beautifully appointed large closet, basically a small room, which they used variously as a storage room for some of their wedding presents and as a dressing room for their clothes.

The door to their bedroom was by the desk. It was not a very large bedroom, but pretty and light. The satin chairs were often covered with chintz slipcovers with a tiny charming flower print. The night tables on either side of the large bed were of blond wood in a clean design, the top surface and open shelves lined with the palest ice-blue glass. My mother's dressing table was a marvel of the same glass, recessed into the wall across from the bed, with a blue silver-and-enamel dressing-table set of brushes, combs, bottles, and boxes displayed on the top.

To the left of their bed was the door that led into the corridor, and beside it was the door to their bathroom. A small window looked out over the side of the house into the garden, and a floor-to-ceiling cupboard held toiletries, towels, soap, and medicines. The water in the bathroom was warmed by a gas heater that lit up with a *whoosh*. The gas had to be lit with a match to get it going, and then I could see the small burner flame flickering inside the metal heater on the wall. We called it "the *geeza*."

It was an attractive, comfortable suite of rooms, not very spacious, and most certainly not a home of their own, particularly since their children were housed in a separate suite of rooms way across the huge upstairs hall.

*Joyce and Guido in Aswan after WWII*

# AFTER THE WAR

*Wars break* open the patterns of peoples' lives and change the parameters forever. In September of 2001, terrorists flew planes into the Pentagon and Wall Street's twin towers and changed the heart and soul of America. Thousands of people died, and millions more lost their innocence and learned to live with fear.

Although Grandpa Smouha had tried to enlist at the time of the First World War and had been distressed to learn that the rheumatic fever contracted in childhood made him ineligible for military service, he contributed all he could and threw his every support into the war effort as World War II drew more and more countries into its maw. He financed the purchase of two Spitfires for the British Royal Air Force and for the second time was offered a knighthood by the British government. For the second time he refused, claiming that he was only doing what was right for his country.

His three sons and his youngest daughter, Edna, were all in the armed forces. Uncle Teddy rose to the rank of wing commander in the RAF and was then the officer commanding British Transport Command in the Middle East. This position put him in charge of the famous Churchill's Flight and made him one of three organizers of secret movements for summit meetings between Churchill, Roosevelt, Chiang Kai Chek, and Stalin in the early 1940s.

Uncle Ellis, later based in England, had started out in Transport Command before his brother and flew highly dangerous missions to Iceland and the North Atlantic.

Auntie Edna reached adulthood during the war years having just left Roedean School to return home to Alexandria. She joined the WRAAF (Women's Royal Auxiliary Air Force) based in Heliopolis, which was then the British headquarters in Egypt, but Grandpa, ever concerned about the reputation of his daughters, used his pull to make sure that his daughter slept at home every night. A sweet, gentle, generous young woman with large green eyes and light brown hair, she must have chafed at this obvious difference interfering with the easy camaraderie of the other young people she worked with.

General Montgomery and other British dignitaries were dinner guests in the Smouha villa in Alexandria toward the latter part of the war. By then, German troops under Rommel were within spitting distance of Alexandria, and the German radio announced its intention of hanging a handful of influential Jews in Alexandria's central square, first among them, Joseph Smouha. Posters appeared in Cairo listing the names of the first ten people who would be hanged on Field Marshall Erwin Rommel's entry into Cairo. Joseph Smouha was number one on the list there, too. The British government ordered Granny and Grandpa to leave Egypt immediately. My grandparents tried to persuade my parents to join them, but my mother was heavily pregnant with my brother, Jeff, and my father was determined to stay, so my grandparents, Auntie Peggy, and Uncle Desmond left for Palestine and then South Africa, with Auntie Yvonne and her children.

After the war when they moved from Cairo to England, the athletic Teddy family bought a caravan and spent summers enjoying rugged caravanning vacations in Scotland and Ireland, walking, fishing, and climbing together, and skiing in the winter. They also bought a house outside the village of Rickmansworth near London. Juniper Hill House was where I stayed while I was at boarding school and my parents were in Cairo, at half terms and holidays too brief for a return home. Surrounded by lush blackberry woods, the hedgerows teemed with very vocal bird life. It was an exotic place to visit for someone more used to sand dunes than the green richness of the English countryside, and I envied my cousin Patricia her country bedroom and her real antique desk and chair. Auntie Yvonne and her helpers in the kitchen produced lavish meals from what I now realize were rather limited ingredients, since it took many years for Britain to recover from the aftereffects of the war and of rationing.

Brian and I had carved out a hiding place among the blackberry bushes, and we repaired to our "camp" to share confidences and dreams. There was a large elm tree beside the house that had a big smooth bough just the right height for me to climb onto. I rested my back against the trunk, shaded by whispering leaves, and read for hours, or until someone called me in for a meal or a chore. I remember Jeff's horror one half-term at Rickmansworth. I was hidden in my arboreal refuge and deep in the pages of a new book. He was ten, the age of permanently grazed knees and bottomless appetite. His urgent calls finally pierced through the curtain of foliage and my concentration, and when I climbed down anxious that he might have fallen and hurt himself, he cried "Quick! Quick! Auntie's in the dining room! I think we must have missed a meal!" The theme of missed meals quickly became a standard joke.

Rickmansworth is where I discovered a love of old houses with their mysteries and histories, and it was there that I learned to make delicious blackberry jam, stirring the fruit our scratched hands had harvested into a rich syrupy mass that we later poured into jars and sealed. I watched Queen Elizabeth's coronation on the television in the living room, while Patricia, who was three years older and was then one of the stars at the Cordon Bleu cooking school, was selected to serve a meal to royalty at St. James's Palace that night. Awed by her achievement, I watched the coverage of the coronation and attendant celebrations ceaselessly, in the vain hope that I might catch a glimpse of her moving among the royal throng. Of course I never did, but the delicious possibility added a thrill to the event.

⚜ ⚜ ⚜

After the end of the Second World War, we gathered in London every fall to celebrate the High Holidays with my mother's family, staying at St. James's Court in a service flat. Uncle Ellis and his family had their permanent home there. St. James's Court, in Victoria, was steps from Buckingham Palace and, more importantly, close to Victoria Station where Patricia, Judy, and I boarded our train to Brighton and Roedean year after year. The old-fashioned elevator at St. James's Court was a small, clanging metal cage with glass walls. It was propelled by a uniformed attendant who stood to one side pulling on a rope to move it to its destination. The public hallways had a fusty smell, a mixture of stale cigarette smoke and furniture polish. The furnishings were dark mahogany enlivened with shiny brass fittings. Faded, comfortable, chintz-covered couches sat next to high-backed chairs in the living room, facing a gas fire grate.

I loved the beds in our service flat. They were unusually high with dark mahogany frames and headboards, and I had to climb up and then would bounce onto my bed collapsing happily into silky smooth snowy linens, the damp and cold outside held at bay by several blankets, eiderdowns and soft down pillows. The thought of sinking into the sensuous warmth and splendor of the generous furnishings and welcoming mattress and drifting into sleep sustained me through my mother's frenetic London pace and the seeping chill of London's gloomy weather.

The Spanish and Portuguese synagogue at Lauderdale Road in Maida Vale was where my parents had first met and where we attended services rather than at the oldest Sephardic synagogue, Bevis Marks, which was situated in the City, the teeming financial center of London.

Arriving at St. James's Court signaled the final phase in our long summer absence from home. We had vacationed in the Swiss Alps or in Chamonix; we had stopped off in Paris, with a focus on seeing the Paris family and attending the designer fashion shows. New clothes lay packed in layers of tissue paper in our suitcases, and sturdy hat boxes housed the latest creations from my mother's milliner, Madame Dupuy Brival, whose tiny *atelier* was on the top floor of a small building on the Rue du Faubourg St. Honoré.

My stomach churned with suppressed excitement as we settled into our rooms in London, early fall casting a metallic gray light through the leaded windows, the phones ringing continuously from other hotels where uncles, aunts, and cousins were staying. Judy and Derrick, whose home was across the courtyard, dropped by to see if I could be released from my unpacking to go for a walk. The world hummed happily around me as my mother and Susan's governess unpacked, hung up dresses in the tall dark wardrobes with mirrors on the doors, the air inside heavy with the smell of varnish, wood, and furniture polish.

By early afternoon, we had started preparations for the evening. My mother and my aunts hurried down to the banquet rooms to check that the enormous U-shaped table had been set up as ordered, and that the ritual Rosh Hashana dishes prepared by various family members were ready to be placed on the table. Granny Smouha was everywhere, checking her daughters' and granddaughters' outfits, putting the finishing touches to the jams or the omelets, hurrying back from the hairdresser, her lovely white hair framing her smiling face as she began to dress for the evening. The men and young boys in dark suits and hats left in small groups for evening services and returned, bringing the rumble of deep voices and a hint of cold from the outside into rooms filled with the flutter of dresses, jewelry, and excited children.

At last, everyone was ready, last-minute crises averted, and we gathered in groups in the banquet rooms in our finery, commenting on each other's new dresses, new suits, new ties, new hairstyles, new figures, and new plans. As the room filled, the hugging and kissing, the swirl of silks and satins, the sparkle of jewels and bright eyes, the chatter, the exclamations, the shrieks of delight reached fever pitch until suddenly Grandpa Smouha appeared at the head of the table, and we all filed quietly to our places, the occasional murmur or subdued giggle punctuating the quiet to an accompanying glare from parent or other adult as we raised our glasses for *kiddush*.

The table held the traditional holiday foods, each with its own prayer. There were flat green-and-yellow spinach omelets for prosperity in the coming year, glittering crystal jam-jars containing translucent apple jams for sweetness, and golden filaments of marrow (zucchini) jam, to pray that our virtues might swell like the gourd and that we might discard the lesser elements of our character as we discarded the seeds of the marrow in making the jam. There were golden leek omelets, flat and delicious, that we might crush our enemies as we crushed the leeks between our teeth. Sticky brown dates exhorted us by our virtues to stand as straight and as tall as the palms from which they came. Scarlet pomegranate seeds swam in sugar syrup and rose-water, promising that our virtues should multiply like the seeds of the pomegranate. A delicious stew of black-eyed peas (*loubia*) and neck of lamb tantalized us with its aroma as we added our amen to the prayer that we might multiply like the black-eye peas. A sheep's head had been prepared in the traditional Syrian way, but for those too squeamish to taste it, there were platters of pickled tongue or tiny slivers of fish from the head of a fish, to symbolize the wish that the people of Israel might always stand at the head of the nations.

As he prepared to intone each blessing, my grandfather stood, raised his hand for silence, and then started chanting in Hebrew a long-drawn-out introductory "*Ye hi...*" hoping for silence. After each blessing, we ate the food in question with murmurs of appreciation and congratulation for the aunt or cousin who had been responsible for its appearance. In keeping with the theme of sweetness for the new year, it was our custom to have no salt on the table. Salt cellars on the table contained powdered sugar, and there were always those who forgot and liberally sprinkled their food, resulting in muffled giggles from those who remembered.

As the ceremony wore on, the swells of chatter became more insistent, and Grandpa *harrumphed* and tapped his glass and his *Ye hi* became louder with each blessing in the hope of capturing the attention of his rambunctious roomful of happy descendants and returning the evening to dignity. I reveled in these gatherings and the lavish dinners that followed. Parents usually sat closer to the head of the table, with my grandparents in the center, and we younger fry flowed down the sides, grabbing seats next to favorite cousins and chattering away about the summer gone by and the winter to come.

Next morning we got ready to go to synagogue. My mother, Susan, and I climbed the stairs to the Ladies Gallery of the Lauderdale Road Synagogue, where Mrs. Morpurgo, a small and often agitated woman with a pronounced Cockney twang, greeted us enthusiastically. She bustled around us, exclaiming in a loud whisper how we had grown, patting hair and pinching cheeks, asking after my Mosseri grandmother and aunt whom she remembered from the pre-war years, ushering us to empty seats, making sure we had prayer books and knew the page. Meanwhile, since we invariably arrived late, Granny Smouha and various aunts and cousins were already seated, making subtle motions for us to join them.

Downstairs, the formal dress of the men contrasted against the white *talets* and created a dark mosaic around the *tebbah*, the raised dais where the rabbis sat, some men in fedoras, many in black bowler hats, the dignitaries of the congregation in full morning dress, their top hats gleaming in the light from the chandeliers. The Haham, the Reverend Dr. Solomon Gaon, intoned the prayers, his strong voice rising to fill the temple with soaring sound. Beside him, the Reverend Abinun stood by to add his voice to the distinctive Sephardic melodies. A choir of small boys with angelic voices, polished faces, and slicked hair sat in a row in the front with the choirmaster, pushing and nudging each other when his attention turned elsewhere. The service was filled with procession and dignity, tradition and beauty.

My father and brother had joined my grandfather, my uncles and cousins where they sat in front of the *tebbah*. Every now and then one of them would look up to where we were sitting so that we could smile and communicate with subtle hand-signals while the long service proceeded.

Grandpa Smouha never looked up from his prayer book. Wrapped in his white *talet*, a plain black *kippah* on his white hair, his body swayed gently to the sound of the prayers he knew so well while his devout spirit sank deep into communion with his God. We followed the prayers obediently and tried to keep our eyes from wandering to the younger men seated downstairs and our minds from dwelling on our elegant new outfits and the effect they might have.

There was a sudden flurry of activity as the moment for the sacred blessing of the *Cohanim* approached. I hurried to stand next to my mother, who had moved closer to Granny Smouha, and around the synagogue, people moved quietly to stand beside parent and grandparent and bow their heads while the blessing was intoned, while the elders of each family raised their arms to cover our heads in blessing. At Lauderdale Road, my grandfather raised his arms and covered the heads of his tall sons, sons-in-law, and grandsons with the wings of his *talet*, each generation blessing those below and being blessed by those above. It is a beautiful custom, and although not one that is followed universally, there were many in the London synagogue who did as we did, and family communities gathered as the prayer approached, forming like flowers around a central figure and then separating at the end of the blessing, kissing the hand of parent and grandparent in respect. The moment of blessing always floods me with a profound sense of warmth and protection. The combined strength and comfort of generations of women linked by family and by love flowed through the fingers of my mother and my grandmother and flooded my heart with peace.

In the days between Rosh Hashana and Yom Kippur, my mother, filled with energy and consulting long lists of London duties, rushed us around the city, taking care of many things in preparation for the coming school year. We had visits to the orthodontist, the woman who taught eye-strengthening exercises, and other medical specialists unavailable in Egypt at the time. My father had his own busy round of appointments with bankers and others from the London business community while Jeff, Susan, my mother, and I clambered into high black London cabs and sailed off to Dickens & Jones, Debenham's, Selfridge's, and Harrods in search of good strong English shoes and clothes for school.

Haughty salesmen in the shoe departments sauntered to where we sat and measured our feet on a metal measure, and when the shoes were chosen and on our feet, they walked us to the X-ray machine, and we and they peered into the window and watched the bones of our toes wiggle like little white slugs against the outer boundaries of the shoes to see if the size was right. Little did we know then that this was a truly dangerous exercise and that what we were doing, marveling at the wonders of modern science, was subjecting ourselves to massive doses of harmful rays. Luckily, this experience only happened once a year, and our excitement in the moment was undiluted by any sense of danger.

When it was time to pay for our purchases, the salesmen rolled up the money in the bill and tucked them both into a small brass cylinder. Then they sent the sealed package into the store's vacuum system with a *whoosh*, and some minutes later, a thud announced the arrival of the cylinder containing the change back on our floor. During the boarding school years, our shopping was restricted to the department stores that had the exclusivity of different parts of the required uniform. We shopped even more purposefully, lists in hand, checking off each item as we found and acquired it. More often than not, it was pouring with rain when we left the store burdened with packages, and we arrived back at St. James's Court bedraggled and drenched, and sank into the comfortable furniture, clamoring for my father's attention as each of us gave him our own view of the day's experiences.

Two distinctly different restaurants dominated our London visits. Neither of them exists anymore. One was the elegant Berkley Buttery, a bustling enclave in Piccadilly. It was noisy and brightly lit, with black leather banquettes and mirrors everywhere. For our family, its claim to fame lay in its generous platters of luscious pale-pink, paper-thin slices of smoked salmon, punctuated with slices of lemon and accompanied by small triangles of charred toast. The other favorite London haunt was in the heart of a chaotic area behind Liberty's, on Regent Street. The restaurant was housed in a large, unadorned room where a stringy waitress with dyed-red hair, an exhausted bony face, a belligerent manner, and a heart of gold reigned supreme. The name of this kosher restaurant was Folman's West Central Rooms, but to us it was always "Sissy's," and my father asked for her the moment we walked through the door into its echoing cavernous interior. Sissy brought us exotic exciting foods, radically different from the fare we were used to. At Sissy's, we learned to love chopped liver with a dollop of golden *schmaltz* in the center, and we discovered *tzimmas*, diced carrots in a sweet sauce, big juicy sausages boiled to bursting point on a bed of mashed potatoes, thick plates of eggs and *wurst*, tender pot roast in a fragrant gravy, and a host of other specialties. The food there, the smells, the sounds, and the names of the dishes all were so exciting to us, raised as we were with a medley of Mediterranean and Middle Eastern fare, that the visit to London would not have been the same without the yearly pilgrimage to "Sissy's" and the exotica she offered.

In London, Granny Mosseri and Auntie Helen always stayed at the Cumberland Hotel and did not join us at St. James's Court. They invited us to have lunch with them at the Cumberland at least once while we were all in London. It was a chaotic, brash hotel, filled with jostling crowds, color, and noise. The restaurant was famous for its Indian food, and my father loved the strong curry wheeled to the table in a silver cart and ladled onto rice by an Indian majordomo in full dress regalia. After lunch, we were summoned upstairs to Granny Mosseri's rooms; there, nestled in swathes of white tissue paper, lay exquisitely hand-embroidered silk blouses, nightgowns, and tablecloths from Italy, or soft cashmere sweaters in jewel colors from Scotland, the fruit of my grandmother's energetic shopping sprees destined for her daughters, daughter-in-law, and granddaughters. She urged us to choose, her face alight with pleasure and anticipation of our pleasure in the lovely gifts she had found. A dedicated hunter-gatherer, she has passed on to me the thrill of the hunt and the pleasure of giving.

Our London visits always included visits to my father's only surviving aunt, Aunt Vicky Mosseri Alexander, who lived in Hampstead in a large house called Baron's Court, on Bishop's Avenue. I loved Aunt Vicky. She laughed a lot and exuded warmth and kindness. Stout, with a rather red face and a warm smile, she had an ample figure that was firmly corseted into obedience. Looking back, I can see a resemblance to the portrait of her mother, Elena, although tempered with warmth and gentle humor. Although she was the youngest of the Mosseri daughters of Nessim and Elena, she and her mother had shared a room after her father's death and were very close until her marriage at the age of twenty-five to Alec Alexander, a law student who came from South Africa and was the best friend at Cambridge of one of her younger brothers.

*Aunt Vicky*

I loved our visits to Hampstead, for no sooner had Aunt Vicky enveloped each of us in her generous hugs than she hurried to the kitchen to put finishing touches on an equally generous tea. Her baking talents were legendary in my family, and my father used to prime us before we arrived at her sweeping driveway, along with the usual admonitions for good behavior. "Wait until you taste Aunt Vicky's cooking!" he'd enthuse, a big anticipatory smile on his face.

And sure enough, the Scottish griddle cakes were soon borne in by Aunt Vicky, hot off the iron griddle, limp and delicious, small pats of melting butter in the center of each. I have never succeeded in reproducing them, but not for want of trying. The missing elements, aside from Aunt Vicky and her lovely smile, include sunlight streaming into a large pleasant room through leaded windows, a sweep of lawn and flowers beyond, and in a corner, Aunt Vicky's daughter Eileen's dollhouse, filled with rare and exquisite miniature silver furniture, tiny silver tea sets, silver candlesticks, silver kitchenware, and other fascinating Lilliputian objects. I loved the dollhouse almost as much as the griddle cakes, although we were never allowed to touch any of it, since each tiny object was a valuable antique. My parents, elegant and happy, exclaimed over Aunt Vicky's latest changes to the house, and sent us out to the garden after tea, to play with her granddaughter, Kate.

Aunt Vicky's eldest child, Eileen, whose dollhouse I so admired, was one of my father's many first cousins. She was a brilliant eccentric who cultivated her oddities in a particularly British way. Eileen wore no makeup, had her hair pulled back into an unflattering bun, and tended to wander about in shapeless clothing kind to her losing battle with weight. Like her mother, she had a pronounced sense of humor, and a lively intelligence, but the deep, rich, throaty laugh that burst out often, infectious, drawing everyone into its orbit, was distinctly her own. I was somewhat awed by Eileen, who was considerably older than I but who always assumed that I would meet her somewhere on her high intellectual plane as she wandered into the room for tea accompanied by her rumpled husband, Gershon.

I never saw Aunt Vicky wear anything but black because her beloved Alec died suddenly in 1945, leaving her a distraught widow, mother of three strong-willed teenage children, struggling to maintain her home and her family in a London scarred and disfigured by the ravages of the Second World War. By the time I knew her, she was the benevolent focal figure in her household of jousting intellects. Uncle Alec was reputed to have been a formidable lawyer and their three children went on to have distinguished careers. A graduate of Cambridge, Eileen later translated most of the works of George Simenon into English. Lionel followed in his father's footsteps and went into law, and Dicky married my cousin Helene, Auntie Mary's youngest, and was awarded a CBE (Commander of the British Empire) by Queen Elizabeth in 1986.

Both Lionel and Dicky put in command appearances at tea, and their affectionate teasing as they wolfed down their mother's cooking alternated with polite attempts to make conversation with the young second cousins at their table. Sometimes the teasing was hard to take. Already conscious that I was encased in an unusual degree of protective parenting and struggling to emerge from it, I became confused and defensive, simultaneously loyal and embarrassed when Dicky playfully inquired, as he always did, how the princess in the ivory tower was doing.

✦ ✦ ✦

The ten penitential days between Rosh Hashana and Yom Kippur were soon over. My mother explained to me as she did every year that with true repentance, the promises we had made and failed to keep to ourselves or to God in the past year could be erased, but any wrong we had done to another person had to be put right with that person before Yom Kippur.

A few days later on the eve of Yom Kippur, we gathered once again in the banquet rooms at St. James's Court for the dinner that preceded the long hours of fasting and prayer ahead of us, to eat quantities of rich chicken soup, bread, and fruit. In our individual family groups we arrived at Lauderdale Road, having left night bags at a small hotel, Clarendon Court, that was a brief walk away and where we would spend the night. The mood was serious. Those of us who were new to fasting were terrified of not measuring up, and those younger than twelve vowed to themselves to fast at least until lunchtime, whatever anyone said. The solemn tones of the *Kol Nidrei* service began, the repetitive prayers gaining in intensity as the service progressed and as they would continue to do until the final service some twenty-six hours later.

Normally a demonstrative family of huggers and kissers, we refrained from any physical expression of affection as we walked back to our rooms in the hotel after services. We climbed the stairs instead of using the elevator, undressed in the dark, and lay awake listening to the unfamiliar hiss of the hot water through the pipes and the gentle murmur of our parents' voices in the adjoining rooms. Next morning we refrained from brushing our teeth and wearing makeup. This was the one day in the year when we tried to keep all the laws and to plunge ourselves into a mood of self-examination and resolution.

The following day was long and demanding. The services followed each other, the Morning Service, the Additional Service, the Afternoon Service, and then finally the joyous *Ne'illah*. There was usually a break between the Additional Service and the Afternoon Service, and my cousins and I set off for long walks in the deserted streets around the synagogue, scuffing our feet against the gravel, trying to ignore our grumbling empty stomachs, and taking this last opportunity before the full vigor of a new school year to exchange dreams and fears. There were memorable years where someone felt faint, or fainted, and the resultant drama swept us through the rest of the day in an adrenaline rush of concern, smelling salts, and activity. But wherever our thoughts wandered or however much our aching heads and hollow stomachs demanded attention during the long hours, we were always anchored back to the present by the familiar haunting melodies that surfaced again and again, the words and music beating a path beyond consciousness as we shut out the world as we knew it, searching for something more, something other, prayers of repentance and sorrow rising at last toward the end of the day into a crescendo of praise and forgiveness. The dignity and power of the long hours spent together in prayer reached their climax in the thin wail of the *shofar*, the ram's horn that heralded the end of the holy day.

We streamed out of the synagogue, the men's dark formal wear weaving in and out of the bright clothes of the women and girls as we came together and hurried to rejoin the rest of the family at St. James's Court for the much-desired meal that awaited us there, golden chicken soup, glistening roast chicken with green beans, crisp brown roast potatoes, and fat pink sausages. My Smouha grandmother always broke the fast with *zaater*, a mixture of thyme crushed with other herbs and sesame seeds and mixed with olive oil, which she scooped up daintily on bread.

Auntie Yvonne, Auntie Peggy Ellis, and their third sister Betty always had to contend with miserable migraines that kept them in their darkened rooms, far from the rising exuberance of the rest of us as we ate and drank our fill, our hearts light in the knowledge that we had lifted our eyes from our daily lives and reached for something beyond ourselves, the conviviality of the shared experience and the warmth of the large bright room teeming with family provoking a continuous medley of laughter and chatter.

*Roedean School*

# ROEDEAN SCHOOL

*I started* Roedean School in September of 1949. I was twelve years old with my much-desired thirteenth birthday looming a few weeks away in December. Roedean was a forbidding fortress of a building, set high and imposing on a cliff overlooking the main highway from Brighton to Rottingdean, fronting a sea often whipped to a churning fury by gale-force winds. Tall iron gates opened onto a winding driveway that jackknifed its way up the hill through the grounds, the playing fields spread to the right in the distance. A gravel pathway joined the outside entrances to the four Houses of the main building.

Ruled by a housemistress, a second-housemistress, and a matron, each House was a discrete entity with its own distinctive personality, and it was in the House that all personal matters were attended to. We took our meals there, did our homework in the Junior or the Senior Common Room at the preordained times, participated in team sports against other Houses, and had a staff-appointed hierarchy of House prefects and sub-prefects selected from the higher grades. They were expected to keep the House discipline and along with this honor, acquired privileges, such as weekend forays into Brighton or Rottingdean without a teacher, as well as tiny study rooms of their own aligned along the short corridor that led from each House into school corridor.

Houses Four and Three were to the right of a large U-shaped courtyard. Houses Two and One were on the opposite side, with

Houses Four and One facing the outside, while Three and Two faced each other across the courtyard. The center of the U was the main school house (accordingly called Schoolhouse), its imposing wooden doors open whenever weather permitted, presided over by Grace, a kindly woman with a long memory and a jutting chin. To Grace, all her girls remained her girls forever. She never forgot a name, and she never forgot who was related to whom. She remembered the schooldays of each of my aunts as well as my mother, and she showed me the places in the auditorium where their names were inscribed in gold on the multitude of wooden plaques that lined the walls. She always had a kind word or a wave as we hurried about our business, late for class and power-walking down the interminable length of school corridor where running was forbidden, clutching slipping piles of books and papers.

School corridor stretched all the way from the Number Four house corridor, past Number Three, past Schoolhouse with its auditorium and passage to the music wing, and finally past Number Two and Number One. At one end were doors that crashed open into a stone arch open to all weathers, where fierce winds left us gasping for breath and almost swept us off our feet as they funneled through.

A gravel path led out to the games fields on one side and to the left, another wooden door opened onto worn stone steps on the way to the art studio and the quiet, sunlit library. Honey-colored oak tables stretched down the center of the library, with windows on one side leading the distracted eye down the fields to the edge of the cliff. The back wall was made up of shelves upon shelves of books, old books, new books, books of general interest, arts, science, literature, poetry, biography, history, books for every discipline. Wooden carrels jutted out from the walls of shelves, much prized for their relative privacy and usually commandeered by Sixth Formers "swotting" for university entrance exams. The hush in the library hung heavy, the hopes and dreams of past students mingling with the anxious sighs and frantic turning of pages of those at work.

Way down at the opposite end of school corridor was the gym. Ropes hung from the ceiling with iron rings attached and sets of wooden bars lined the walls. Muffled thumps and thuds emanated from its open doors to the accompaniment of crisp orders barked from a platform where a teacher marched back and forth in navy shorts and white shirt, cropped hair and muscular legs signaling a devotion to the toning of the body and a dedication to battle on the sports fields. Beyond the gym lay the chapel, where services were held every morning before classes and twice a day on Sundays.

Junior House was self-contained in a building some distance off to the side, as was the dreaded San (Sanatorium) where we were incarcerated when sick. Whenever any of us were sick with a fever above a certain point, we were summarily removed from our rooms and sent over to the San in the care of the house matron. There we were left to the less-than-tender ministrations of Sister, a woman of formidable bosom and relentless discipline encased in a crisp blue-and-white uniform with a starched winged contraption covering her hair. Since I was an avid reader, and the San had a glass-fronted cabinet filled with assorted reading material dating from the school's beginnings, I tried to curb my boredom when I was there by devouring the shiny yellowing pages of Victorian novel after Victorian novel. Unrelenting in their dark view of existence, the novels were morose reading for a fevered child. In them, the good child always ended up dead, floating in some cherubic heaven while the parents wept into black-bordered linen handkerchiefs at the funeral below. I whiled away the time writing sprightly letters to my cousins Derrick and Brian, who were at Harrow, or listening to *Mrs. Dale's Diary* every day on my portable radio. Things moved reassuringly slowly in Mrs. Dale's world, and even if three months had passed since my last time in the San, I could be sure that as soon as her comforting voice began, "Jim was too tired to go to work today, so I..." there was no difficulty picking up the story where I had last left the characters.

In the San, the fevered pace of school came to a halt. We were left pretty much to our own devices until mealtimes, when Sister often marched in with a plate of stringy beans, some gray boiled fish, and some wobbling pudding. "Now eat it all up!" she would command, her eagle eye roaming the room for every last crumb when she returned. Once, my stomach in revolt at the sight and smell of the food, I resorted to flinging it out of the window to escape her ire. Having learnt from my parents to see the humor in pathos, I described this incident in a woeful letter to Brian, and letting my imagination soar unfettered into the realms of the absurd, I told him in detail how the fish landed on Sister's head as she walked outside for some fresh air, and how she was never able to determine which of her charges had committed this heinous double crime.

Brian and I corresponded frequently during those boarding school years. When I discovered with revulsion that there was a mouse in my room, Brian sent me a mousetrap with complete instructions on how to bait and use it, and also how to dispose of the corpses, carefully taking into account my female sensibilities. With no e-mail to sustain us, letters were also the only way to maintain connection with that other life at home. I still have rubber-banded packets upon packets of the loving letters my mother sent faithfully, twice a week, on filmy crackly airmail paper. Her characteristic handwriting danced across the page, filling it with the very essence of her joyous personality. Sometimes there was also a postscript in my father's elegant sloping hand. As I read the letters I could hear my mother's voice in my head keeping homesickness at bay as she kept me abreast of the minutest details of the life proceeding without me in Cairo and Alexandria.

✦ ✦ ✦

Arriving at the door of Number Three House for the very first time, I felt itchy and strange in my navy wool suit, navy felt hat with the Roedean logo embroidered on the front in red, my red-and-blue-striped tie neatly knotted against the collar of my new white shirt. Because of Rosh Hashana, we had been allowed to miss the first three days of school to attend services with our family in London. I was in a froth of anticipation, part excitement, part dread. My mother had warned me that I must not cry, no matter how much I wanted to, and I was determined not to let her down, although a strange lump in my throat was making it harder and harder for me to swallow as we got out of the car and were greeted warmly by Number Three's housemistress, Miss Will. "Come in, dear," she said in her comforting Scottish accent, ushering us out of the wind. And turning to me, "Jill will take you up to your room while I have a chat with your parents." My mother and father settled down on a comfortable flowered couch facing the log fire blazing in her cozy sitting room, recessed leaded windows behind them, while I trudged up a flight of stairs behind the silent Jill, her forehead and chin blooming mightily with incipient acne. She led me along a narrow corridor to a room at the end. She knocked on the door and it opened to reveal two girls sitting on narrow beds, a skeptical look on both their faces. Valerie and Linda had arrived on the first day of school and had bonded during the three days of my absence. They pointed to the thin mattress on its iron frame tucked into a corner of the room, away from the window and the other two beds. "That's your bed," they said, staring curiously at me as I made my way toward it.

My trunk had preceded me, and I pulled out my sheets and the beautiful plaid blanket I had been so happy to choose. Questions came raining down as I unpacked the navy everyday tunics called *djibbahs* (I have no idea why), and the crisp pink-and-white, blue-and-white, and yellow-and-white striped cotton dresses that were for summer weekend afternoons and evenings. "Where do you live?" they asked, and, "Why are you starting late?" The responses engendered quick looks that passed between them and spoke more than words. Jill, her silence and her acne, had departed without more ado. The lump in my throat grew larger and larger.

My parents stood at the door. "Time to say good-bye," said my mother, trying to exude cheer as she hugged and kissed me. My father gave me a bear hug and turned away. Suddenly, they were gone. I didn't cry, but the ache in my throat drained all the excitement from the event, leaving me sitting shivering on a narrow bed in an unknown room in a vast building perched on a cliff somewhere near Brighton, with two girls who were giggling and whispering together, already friends with each other. My parents were gone and on their way back to London. That night, I learned about homesickness as I wept into my pillow, trying desperately to hide my sobs from my roommates.

Next day, a sign went up on the house bulletin board: "BACKS AND FEET AT THREE." It was signed by Miss Will. Valerie, Linda, and I pored over this cryptic announcement and finally asked one of the senior girls what it meant. She grimaced and said cryptically, "You'll see! You have to line up outside the Will's study in your dressing gowns and underpants. Nothing else." Even more mystified but too new and too shy to probe further, we got ready apprehensively as directed as the clock advanced toward three o'clock. Our room was on the same floor as Miss Will's bedroom, so we crept along the corridor to join the snaking line of girls outside her room, giggling and gossiping nervously as we waited our turn.

One by one we were called into the room to find Miss Will, Miss Ratcliffe, and the house doctor, Dr.W——, lined up on three upright chairs to one side of the room. We were directed to put our dressing gowns on a chair and walk barefoot from one end of the room to the other in front of the lineup, and then bend and touch our toes. This was for Dr. W—— to establish if we had flat feet or incipient scoliosis and needed remedial treatment, and it took place at the start of every school year. It was something of a shock that first year, because the visible changes that had begun to take place in our bodies were new and private and we hated having to parade our bare selves to the clinical stare of the male doctor and his chaperones. However, our embarrassment was minor compared to that of the seniors who had to perform the same routine. It was truly a barbaric custom, and I cannot help but feel that there might have been a more sensitive way for this routine check to be performed.

As the days wore on, Valerie, Linda, and I became good friends, but their initial bonding made me odd-man-out from the beginning, and when the year was over and students were requesting rooming arrangements for the following year, they asked for a two-room; I, who had fully expected to room with them again and had failed to search out a roommate of my own, found myself placed with a new girl, another unknown.

I was always late for everything but most particularly for breakfast in my first year at Roedean. We were supposed to wash, dress, make our beds, tidy our rooms, and thunder down the stairs of Number Three House in a stampeding herd into the dining room in time for grace, which was intoned solemnly by our housemistress, Miss Will, into the brief moment of silence after the doors to the dining room were closed. No sooner had she uttered in her delightful Scottish burr, "For what we are about to receive, may the Lord make us truly thankful," than we fell on the food like ravenous creatures, with a cacophonous scraping of chairs, clatter of cutlery, and chatter instantly swelling to a roar.

Demerits were meted out for any deviation from this morning schedule that began with the wake-up clanging of the big brass bell and ended with the frantic descent to reach the dining room for breakfast before the doors closed. A certain number of demerits meant that we had to memorize a newspaper article and recite it without a flaw to the Senior Common Room the following Saturday morning. My cousin Patricia, as the eldest of us three cousins, felt it incumbent upon herself to keep her juniors, Judy and myself, toeing the line to make sure that we did not disgrace the family name. She always pronounced the word *family* with a capital *F*. We chafed under the yoke of her expectations. The three years between us was a gap too great to bridge with any understanding of her place in the hierarchy of our lives and the hierarchy of the school. We were navigating the treacherous waters of our teen years far from the comforts of home, and were much too self-absorbed to appreciate her concerns.

Patricia was already a senior my first year at Roedean, and so were all her friends. I will always remember her scandalized face when, along with the other convicted criminals, her cousin Jean was led red-faced and giggling into the common room to intone her word-perfect piece of useless journalism. Rolling her expressive brown eyes, she groaned, winced, and muttered in my ear, "What will the Family say? Oh, what will the Family say?"

My younger cousin Gilly Setton's first year at Roedean coincided with my last, and she, in her turn, was a senior when my younger sister, Susan, started at Roedean. We have since established that although Number Three House was the family House and we all lived there in turn, our friendships and encounters with boarding school life led to surprisingly different experiences. Although the older cousins kept a stern eye on the young fry, closeness of family and shared home experience was tightly woven into the fabric of our interactions with each other. Sometimes we pulled against that fabric or tried to ignore it, but when push came to shove we were cousins, shoulder to shoulder against the world. We were all there for each other. That knowledge was a wonderfully reassuring defense in times of adversity, and was to remain with us for the rest of our lives.

Those boarding school years and the shared plane travel and vacation times in Egypt or in Europe created fast friendships with my cousins Judy and Derrick, children of Uncle Ellis Smouha and Auntie Peggy Ellis. My mother's brother Ellis and his family spent the war years in England, surviving the London blitz and the hardships of displacement, rationing, and separation from the rest of their family; thus my relationship with Judy, who was three years older than I, and Derrick, who had preceded me into this world by eighteen months, took root only when they moved back to Alexandria after the war.

We had a whole month of vacation between terms spent at boarding school, and so were able to take the long plane trip home for a nourishing immersion into our family lives before returning to England. In Alexandria, many were the long walks on the golf course of the Smouha Sports Club, where Judy, Derrick, and I pondered together about life in general and our lives in particular. We confronted the difficulties of navigating the shoals of the world opening out ahead of us and the complexities of shuttling between our pronounced family culture and the equally pronounced rigors of an English boarding school. The years that Judy and I spent together at Roedean forged an unassailable connection, and we continue to bridge the distance that life has carved between us as often as we can with phone calls and occasional visits across the ocean.

While Judy and I were still at Roedean, involved in keeping afloat in a churning sea of teenage emotions, friendships and rivalries, sports and studies, Dicky, the eldest of our close-knit group of cousins, married in Alexandria in his early twenties, while still at Cambridge. He is still the only person I know who has eyes of two different colors, one green and one brown. His new wife's grandmother was yet another of the ubiquitous Aghions. Sylvia (Sinigalia) was nineteen, vivacious, attractive, and to Judy and myself—still awkward in our navy boarding school tunics and white ankle-socks—the notion that such a romance and marriage could actually happen to someone so close to us in age set us dreaming and opened new vistas of possibility.

The plane journeys from Egypt to England at the start of each spring term were fraught with anxiety and exhaustion. Uncle Ellis had a chauffeur in London, Bert, who usually met us at Heathrow Airport as we came off the plane from Egypt, and ferried us across London to Victoria Station, where he waited to see that we were safely ensconced in our compartment on the Brighton train, the seats an imitation velvet that pulled at the wool of our navy skirts as we shifted uncomfortably, our luggage in net hammocks above our heads, and the pervasive smell of cigarette smoke seeping into our clothes and our hair. The presence of Bert, the reassuring familiarity of his wiry frame, his big smile, his bulbous nose, and his indescribable Cockney accent, became a welcome part of our lives throughout my teen years, standing in for a parental presence as we made the transition from the comfort of home to the challenges awaiting us at school.

*Uncle Ellis*

Bert had been a taxi driver during World War II. It was hard to find cruising taxis in London at that time, and having picked up my uncle as a fare one evening, Bert gave him his phone number and suggested that he give him a call if he ever needed transportation. One cold January night, driving home from a dinner party Uncle Ellis was hit by a skidding truck, leaving him with painful broken ribs. In need of something from the pharmacy, he remembered Bert the taxi driver, and phoned to ask him if he could pick up the things he needed while on his rounds with his taxi. Bert had decided he was going to stay at home. He had a bad cold, and the weather was appalling. However, at Uncle Ellis's insistence he changed his mind, left his house, and brought Uncle Ellis the medication he needed.

Sometime later, my uncle received a phone call from Bert, thanking him for persuading him out of the house that evening. Surprised, my uncle pointed out that he should be the one to do the thanking, since Bert had left his house to do him a favor on such a miserable night. But Bert revealed that Uncle Ellis had saved his life. His house had received a direct hit from a German bomb while he was out and he would have been killed had he stayed home. Following this incident, he became totally devoted to my uncle, always referring to him as "Sir" as though it were his name, as in "Sir asked me to tell you to hurry."

Because my own family was based in Cairo for most of the year, I spent a great deal of time in the Roedean years with both my Smouha uncles and their families. Since Judy and I traveled to and from school together, I found myself often in their London home, a rambling apartment in St. James's Court. It was a good thing that the apartment was spacious, because my aunt and uncle had a spiky relationship and very different requirements as to their living quarters. Uncle Ellis's wife, Auntie Peggy Ellis as she was known to her nieces and nephews to differentiate her from our other aunt Peggy (Setton), was thin and energetic. She hid a kind heart under a sharp-tongued and bustling exterior. She was happiest in steamy weather and kept her sitting room stifling at all times. Intelligent and well-read, her interests also ran to golf and the martial arts. Her husband, on the other hand, put on more weight than was good for him, compounded by the effects of twenty-five years of cortisone treatment for the asthma that had plagued him since childhood. His study, crammed with meticulously organized files and boxes of papers, was always freezing, the windows open to the elements. Fine dark English antiques filled the room, but I hated the heads of antlered deer staring out at me from the walls, shot by him when he went deer stalking with friends in the north of Scotland.

I loved lunchtimes there, when I could watch Uncle Ellis carving a roast, a task he undertook with sheer artistry at the sideboard in their dining room. The intricate attention to detail that had gone into the reassembly of a clock in Alexandria many years earlier or the packing of my father's suitcase on the ship when both were young was now applied to the roast meat elegantly carved with ritual precision, artistically arranged slices accompanied on each plate by hard green peas and Yorkshire pudding (resembling popovers), or delicious large crunchy brown roast potatoes. The food was wonderful, and so different from the meals at home in Cairo, or the school food we endured at Roedean. There was always a thick brown gravy to accompany the roast, and a dessert, usually something combining stewed fruit with custard. As soon as lunch was cleared, Auntie Peggy Ellis would march determinedly out to her car and her golf shouting parting salvos to her husband as she left, as Uncle Ellis tried vainly to detain her. It was a volatile household, strong personalities and undercurrents crackling electricity through the air, but the warmth and kindness I found there went a long way to alleviating the transitions from home to school.

✦ ✦ ✦

That first year at Roedean, a few weeks after school began, my parents came down to school on the weekend just before leaving England to return to Egypt. They were to take us out for the day and they were anxious to see for themselves how I was settling in at boarding school. Patricia, Judy, and I in our formal navy suits and hats eagerly said our good-byes to Miss Will and Miss Ratcliffe (the Rat), our housemistress and second-housemistress, and we all drove off to Brighton. In what was to become a tradition, my parents had booked a table for lunch at the Metropole Hotel, an elegant Edwardian hotel with rich red carpeting on the floors, polished brass everywhere, a grand staircase, and a large dining room, where we ate as though food was going out of style.

After lunch we went out on the Brighton Pier, clutching the brims of our hats as we advanced into a wind that gusted so fiercely it almost stole our breath away, eating fluffy cotton candy, putting a large copper penny in a fortune-telling machine that loomed up ahead with the face of a gypsy painted on top, screaming with laughter over the results, running and chasing each other, entering the hall of mirrors and shrieking with delight over the distorted selves we saw, buying hard sticks of Brighton rock, and marveling that magically, the words "Brighton rock," usually purple on a white background, continued to be visible however much of the candy stick we ate. It felt like freedom, but all too soon we were back at the iron gates, and then there were hugs and kisses and then there was the reality of separation.

In the five years I spent at Roedean, I never completely settled into the community of Number Three House, although I did my best to fit in and I made some good friends—Hazel and Venice, Angie and Val, Penny and Tricia. There was a pervasive emphasis on sports: lacrosse and netball in the winter and cricket, rounders, and tennis in the summer. I hated "games" and the freezing torture they represented as we were relentlessly herded out of school corridor into the whistling wind and led at a run down the open fields, buffeted and shivering, to the playing field assigned to us that day. "Cradle, Jean, cradle!" the stocky, bowlegged sports mistress would yell in frustration as I swung my lacrosse stick wildly and failed to catch the ball in its leather net. As for cricket, during the daily practice sessions at the nets, I used to bowl down a net and find my ball five nets down. When it was my turn to bat, I spent the time wincing and dodging, certain that the ball was programmed to make straight for my head and knock me out. I enjoyed netball and I loved tennis in the summer, when the winds were gentler and the grass courts rippled with the sea breeze and glinted in the sunshine, but I was never very good at either.

I excelled in my literature classes, however, and was more than ever convinced that I wanted to be a writer when I left school. Two of my poems appeared in the 1953 Coronation Edition of the school magazine, and one of them, my unorthodox view of "games," drew a slightly acid comment from the head of the sports department when I ran into her in school corridor shortly after the yearly magazine came out. "We really didn't need a poem to know how you feel about sports, Jean," she said, a twinkle in her eye. My distaste for organized physical exertion has not changed, and I can hardly put it better today:

*When it's simply a horrible day outside*
*And I've two maths preps to be done;*
*When I creep outside at a snail's slow pace*
*While most of the others run,*
*When I reach Old Flats and I shake with cold*
*Till I just can't move at all*
*Oh how I hate the ridiculous way*
*In which everyone chases a ball!*

*When the sun is gold and the sea is blue*
*And there isn't a care in sight*

*When I'm almost asleep in a drowsy haze*
*And life is exactly right*
*And I have to change and go down to games*
*And I try to hurry—and fall!*
*Oh how I hate the ridiculous way*
*In which everyone chases a ball!*

*When the captain shouts in a furious voice*
*"Have you lost your legs? Quick, run!"*
*And I stumble along past her waving stick*
*While the others yell "What fun!"*
*And they plunge around and they knock me down*
*And I miss the captain's call*
*Oh how I hate the ridiculous way*
*In which everyone worships a ball!*

This masterpiece was written when I was fifteen years old, and the editor of the magazine entitled it "An Unusual View of Games." In all fairness, the accompanying poem of mine was called "The Singing Bird," and was a lyrical evocation of a bird's song at twilight, in quite a different vein.

Much of my spare time was spent in the music wing, where Miss Lucchesi, the violin teacher, and Miss Monk, the piano teacher, reigned supreme. The Luke, as she was called, was a forceful woman with short gray hair that spiked out around her face and a sinister smile that lifted one side of her narrow mouth. She also spoke out of the side of her mouth, possibly the result of a small stroke. From the beginning, she determined to draw out of me what I did not feel I had it in me to give, and some of my fiercest teenage furies were directed at her, causing me to be sent to "the Will" in disgrace more than once, whereupon Miss Will would be heard to mutter, rolling her *rrrrrrs* richly, "Ach! These temper*rrr*amental musicians!"

Because of pressures from the iron-willed Miss Lucchesi, I found myself compelled to join the orchestra and was immediately placed among the first violins. In my second year, I was leader of the second desk. I was awed, because the leader of the orchestra was a Sixth Former and I, a lowly Fourth, was sitting right behind her and next to another senior. But the Luke, who conducted the orchestra with a heavy hand, much sarcasm, and little patience for diffidence, pushed and jostled me into more active participation. Reluctantly, I played in school concerts. I hated performing and always tried to get out of it, but somehow she always pushed me to performance level in time for the next concert, and despite my panic, my name would appear on the printed program whereupon nothing less than *force majeure* would allow my absence. I felt pangs of loneliness as I saw parents rush to the platform after the concert to collect and congratulate their daughters. My parents were at home, in Egypt, and I had no one there who cared at all whether I played well or not. Once, Uncle Ellis came all the way from London as a surprise to hear me play in a concert. I hugged him so hard that I suspect he realized how much his presence meant to me.

I was picked to represent the school and play a violin solo in an international broadcast with selected students from schools around the country. The BBC took my parents who were in London to a special room to hear me play, and my grandparents in Cairo and Alexandria, duly warned, calculated the time difference and heard my name and my violin reach out to them over the airwaves.

Miss Lucchesi continued to push. When the leader of the orchestra graduated and left school, I arrived back at school the following fall to find that I was to lead the orchestra whether I wanted to or not. I argued, I sulked, I stormed out of the room and slammed the door, causing yet another repentant trip to Miss Will's study and the resultant devastating loss of my hopes of being named a prefect that year, but the Luke held firm, maintaining that I would soon be taking the Royal Academy of Music Exam Grade VIII, that I was the obvious choice for the position, and that I would thank her in later life as it would be excellent training in leadership, something I cared little about at the time.

*At Roedean, Mozart's Clarinet Quintet:*
*(left to right) Jean, Bette, Pru, Dee, Mary*

The clarinet player, a petite blonde with short curly hair and a big smile whose name was Libby, had graduated at the end of my first year and had left school. In her place was a tall girl with very long, thin, red braids that she flipped energetically over her shoulders as she settled herself and her clarinet into position. Pru Carmalt-Jones and I became close friends although we were not in the same House. She had spent some years with her family in Hong Kong and had a broader view of life than many of my classmates, most of whom still believed that since I came from Egypt we probably lived in a tent and rode camels to school. Many years later, I was a bridesmaid with Pru's sister Averil at Pru's wedding to Douglas De Lavison, exactly one month before my own. Whenever we have been able to bridge the geography that separates us, we continue the intense conversation that began in our early teens, effortlessly resuming the intimacy that our school years initiated. She has always been what friendship is about.

As the months wore on, Pru and I started a classical record club. We practiced together one free afternoon a week with Delia, Mary, and Elizabeth, to perfect the slow movement of Mozart's clarinet quintet, which we subsequently played in my last concert at Roedean, where I also played a showy Vieuxtemps violin solo, sang in the choir, and led the orchestra, grumbling all the way. At the last assembly that summer, the various sports cups, engraved with the names of many generations of sports achievers, were publicly awarded to individuals who had led teams to victory for their respective Houses. My surprise and delight knew no bounds when I heard the headmistress announce that a dormant cup had been revived and had been won by me for Number Three House. I walked up to the platform in a daze and received the silver cup, the music cup, heavy with meaning and history, and upon which my name and the date were inscribed for posterity.

In a moment of indescribable triumph, "my" cup was placed on the mantelpiece in the dining room of Number Three House to rousing applause that has continued to resonate down the years. Music had at last been afforded the trophy, the glory, and recognition of sports.

✦ ✦ ✦

All of the teachers had their nicknames, the origins of most springing from their names. While some were obscure and lay buried in the memories of Roedeanians long gone, the nicknames themselves were passed along in whispers from generation to generation of new schoolgirls eager to fit into this alien world and to show their ease with it by using the Roedean jargon with casual flair. It was a way of cutting the teachers down to size, of dissipating the enormity of their power over us within the closed confines of the boarding school culture. Their names were never used to their faces, although they must have been well aware of them. We addressed all teachers as "Madam." That was the rule.

Stooge (Miss Sturgis) was the small concise English teacher with staccato speech and an inability to pronounce the letter *r*, who ruled her classes with an iron hand. We were all terrified of coming unprepared to her classes and receiving the serrated edge of her sarcasm directed at us with a fury not commensurate with her slight build. Consequently, she obtained maximum performance from her students and maintained very high standards. Minnie (Miss Godfrey) also taught English classes and took her meals in Number Three House. She was tall and statuesque with a predilection for rather dramatic, flowing clothing. She had a deep, mellifluous voice and pure-white hair always neatly rolled into a bun at the back of her head. Her benign smile and regal manner led to a more relaxed classroom culture. She challenged less and wheedled more out of her students. Miss Butcher was a skeletal woman with skin of an almost unearthly pallor, prominent teeth, faded blue eyes, and wispy red-blond hair escaping from an untidy chignon. She spoke barely above a whisper but was somehow able to communicate her fervor and passion for history. Her nickname, Dwu, was not complimentary, its origin being the words "Death Warmed Up." The headmistress, Miss Horobin, was naturally called the Horror with daring irreverence, and Miss McCullogh, the thin-lipped uncompromising matron of Number Three House, was known as Muck.

Profoundly influential in my school life was a powerful French woman who had known my youngest aunt, Edna Smouha Adda, when she was at Roedean. Therese Lavauden, a brilliant pianist, occasionally gave concerts in Brighton, but her role at Roedean was as head of the French Department. She lived in a small flat in Brighton with the school librarian, Thyra Creyke Clark (known as TCC), who was also head of the Spanish Department. Since I was much more fluent in French than most of my contemporaries, the Lav, as she was called, designed a program for me that involved more literature than grammar. I attended a classical French Sixth Form literature class and we studied the works of Moliere, Racine, and Corneille in depth. I can still see her piercing blue eyes and her leonine mane of pure-white hair which her ringed fingers periodically raked through in exasperation, as she challenged the class, "*Andromaque etait plus épouse que mère. N'est-ce pas? Qu'en pensez-vous, Mesdemoiselles? Allez! Allez!*"

She used these classes as an introduction to philosophical argument, deliberately provoking the more timid among us to heated participation. Life, love, lust, power, revenge, and relationships all came under the microscope of intense discussion in her classes as we explored the literature, and through the literature, ourselves. No subject was taboo. It went way beyond French and most of us lingered reluctantly when class was over, wishing we could continue to talk, to explore, to learn. Mademoiselle Lavauden and I grew to like each other very much, and when I was leaving school and went to say good-bye to her, she shook her head sadly and muttered, "A good mind. A good mind. Such a waste. Knowing your family, you will marry a nice young man, have his children, and do nothing with it. Such a pity." Since I thought some parts of her statement sounded rather attractive, I focused on the last part and wondered why these two goals should be mutually exclusive? She taught me to think and to question, and while I was always a little afraid of her razor wit and sarcasm, particularly when they were directed at me, I valued her classes more than any other and later missed the intellectual stimulation she provoked and required. She, more than any other, convinced me that I should do my utmost to go to university, where I hoped to find more of this kind of challenge.

✦ ✦ ✦

The return to Roedean after a fleeting few weeks at home in Egypt was always hard. Patricia was no longer a schoolgirl after my first two years at Roedean, so Judy and I traveled together, sometimes with Derrick and Brian who were returning to Harrow, sometimes alone. The journeys were long and included stopovers in Rome, where there were frequently delays, sometimes as long as fourteen hours, while we waited for maintenance on the plane or for another plane to arrive from Ghana. We debated endlessly in the echoing halls of the Rome airport whether we should wait for our designated plane to turn up, or whether we should try to get transferred to an earlier flight out; whether we should try to get a message to our parents, or whether we should prove to them that we were on top of things by going with the flow. We never got it quite right and always seemed to end up in trouble, one way or the other.

My cousins and I were among the first to fly in the revolutionary Comets, the first jet-propelled passenger planes. Our parents were excited to think of how much shorter our travels would be as we all hung around the Cairo airport waiting for BOAC to announce our departure, but there had been several unexplained crashes of Comets over the Mediterranean, which later proved to be the result of metal fatigue, an unknown phenomenon in those days. I grew to dread my departures from home and the plane flights that conveyed me back to Roedean. I invariably developed agonizing colitis attacks just as we were about to leave. Derrick vividly remembers the tears at Cairo airport as "the stalwarts of Roedean prepared to launch themselves into the unknown, paralyzed with fear."

*On the Brighton Pier with Auntie Yvonne and Uncle Teddy*

These fears were not unfounded, and were exacerbated after the very Comet we had been scheduled to take from London crashed into the sea between Rome and Cairo. Jeff, who was then ten and at the Abbey School in East Grinstead, had been scheduled to take the Tuesday flight home, and Judy and I were supposed to take the Thursday Comet, but my parents were worried about Jeff having to fly alone and with some difficulty arranged that he would leave a day later and we would leave a day early, so that we could all travel together on the Wednesday flight with Derrick and Brian. Both the Tuesday and Thursday planes crashed, and I shudder even now to think how close we all came to losing our lives but for the reschedule.

However, my friend and rival from my Heliopolis English School days, bright-eyed curly-haired Diana Eady, was on board the Tuesday flight. No survivors. We learned that she and her little brother had been in Rome the day before us and had engaged in the usual earnest discussions as to what to do. Diana decided to wait for the scheduled Comet while her brother, Robin, having transferred to an earlier flight, arrived safely in Cairo.

At Roedean, they grew accustomed to the fact that I invariably returned from vacation with excruciating stomach pains and had to repair to my room for a couple of hours with a hot water bottle. Then it was the big brass bell summoning us to dinner and the instant unrelenting immersion into the thunderous descent down the steep narrow stairs of Number Three House to the dining room, and the cacophony of seventy girls talking about their vacation at the tops of their voices, while chairs scraped, knives clattered, the girls whose turn it was to be at the serving table scurried about laden with clinking dishes, and the nauseating smell of some indeterminate meat drowning in gluey brown gravy filled the air. A day or two later, the food smelled tempting, the noise was comforting, faces and voices resumed their familiarity, and another term was in full swing.

The handful of Jewish girls who acknowledged their religion were given "specials" when bacon or pork was on the menu, and were not expected to attend daily morning services in the chapel, nor the weekly Sunday morning services. Catholic teachers took the Roman Catholic girls to church in Brighton on Sunday mornings, while we received the weekly visit from London of a compact dark-eyed woman, Dr. Blumenthal. Dr. Blumenthal's overly earnest manner and pronounced stutter incited our bunch of assorted teenage girls of different ages and from different houses to fidgeting and inattention. Her accent in Hebrew was almost incomprehensible to my Sephardic ears. She always led off with us standing in a semicircle and reciting the Shema together. Then she would invite us to talk about an upcoming holiday, or read a portion of the Bible and discuss its contents. She was a kindly and well-meaning woman, but we never connected in any significant way, nor did I feel that her weekly appearances kept me connected to my religion. It was an activity that held us in bored torpor on Sunday mornings while the rest of the school was in chapel. Most of us failed to realize the dedication of this woman, who after a heavy work week took the train to Brighton and back to spend a couple of hours just to link a small group of irrepressible schoolgirls to their heritage.

✦ ✦ ✦

The Roedean years saw me through the rockiest period of my teens. I enjoyed my weekend walks and deep discussions with Pru as we paced down together to watch a cricket match on a sunny summer afternoon wrapped in our cloaks, Pru's braids tucked into her hood. My grandparents had donated gray wooden benches in the names of each of their daughters when they left Roedean. These were scattered about the edges of the playing fields overlooking the angry churning of the Channel. I quickly located the bench with my mother's name on it and often made my way to its weathered slats, finding a strange comfort in the letters that spelled her name, convinced that the arms of the bench recognized the contours of my body and offered mysterious emanations of home to soothe my melancholy.

I loved the book-filled hush of the library, the challenge of the classes, the rare picnics and outings when we visited neighboring stately homes in idyllic settings for the Empire Day Picnic or some other school holiday, wandering among lush gardens filled with roses and rhododendrons, watching water lilies float on serene ponds, or attending a concert in Brighton. Those were the moments of harmony with my environment and my classmates.

I remember a hike over the rolling Sussex downs to the village of Rottingdean when I was a senior. Rottingdean, then, was a small enclave of houses perched on a cliff above the clamoring sea. We found a dark basement tea shop there, warm, stuffy, and smelling faintly of cigarettes, fried foods, and toast. We filed into its depths, pushing and giggling, ravenous from the sea air, filled with high spirits from our vigorous walk. We ordered yeasty fresh crumpets slathered lavishly with butter, and generous platters of fried eggs with triangles of fried bread and a mound of crispy fries on the side. It was heavenly fare, if somewhat heavy on the cholesterol, and the brief respite from school food was more than welcome. The food disappeared in short order, and we climbed our way back over the downs and hurried to the school buildings where the everyday awaited us.

There were many good times and many aspects of Roedean that I appreciated, but looking back, I can see that I did not enjoy my time at boarding school. I was often homesick and frequently pushed beyond myself, often lonely and miserable. Nevertheless, it was a deeply formative experience, and with hindsight I have come to value the opportunities it gave me to explore the world beyond the boundaries of my own experience. Fighting my own battles, setting my own goals, and learning to adapt to different rhythms and values gave me invaluable tools for living in the larger world, far from the overprotective shielding of my large and loving family. My parents always made it clear that I could go home at any time if it all became too heavy to carry alone, but my pride never allowed me to confess to them how hard I struggled or how unhappy I often was.

Clearly, much of the misery I remember had to do with the usual teenage angst. But this was compounded with the knowledge that if I wrote a deeply homesick letter home, the two weeks before it reached my concerned parents in Egypt could produce a dramatic turnaround. Experience taught me that by the time I received my mother's anxious response, I would probably have forgotten what my earlier distress had been about. This dislocation in communication compounded my feelings of isolation and vulnerability and made every hardship harder.

✦ ✦ ✦

When I left Roedean, one of my school friends, Linda Croydon, whose father worked in magazine publishing, showed her father some of the poetry I had been writing at school. Impressed, he took it to Jean Leroy, a literary agent with the agency of Pearn Pollinger and Higham. Jean Leroy must have found something there that intrigued her, for she took me on as a client. This small reserved woman with neat gray hair worked in an untidy book-lined office in the heart of London. The agency was well-known and much respected. I could not believe my good fortune.

She sold my poem "The Apple Tree" to *The Listener* and urged me to take my writing seriously, always finding time to sit down with me to explore my goals and my latest writing projects when I was in London, and writing kind, encouraging letters when I was away. Looking back, I am all the more amazed that she took time to guide a seventeen-year-old schoolgirl who wrote poetry and that she actually sent my work out and sold one of the poems. I wish I could have lived up to the promise she saw in me, but instead, my life path set me to trace her steps and become a literary agent myself, so intimately involved in the creative process of others that there was no room for anything else for many years. She died before I had found that path, so she never knew.

Convinced then that mine would be a writing life, I was ready for a deep immersion into the writings of others, anticipating a continuation of those elements of schoolwork that I had most enjoyed, hoping to learn everything that great literature could teach me. I thought I knew much of what lay ahead. I thought the future I anticipated would be mine for the taking.

I little imagined that the Suez Canal, a historical footnote buried somewhere in the shadows of my subconscious, would emerge, sinuous as the black snake of my childhood, and alter the shape of the future for me and for the Jews of Egypt.

*Homeschooling: (left to right) Jackie Fresco,*
*Brian Massey, and my sister Susan*

# Suez

*Leaving Roedean* held sweet promise of my return to my home in Egypt, where I anticipated that the glamour and mysteries of adulthood would gradually be revealed. Jeff, at fourteen, had already gone back to his boarding school in the North of England. I understood little about the movement of politics throughout the larger world. I had been too busy fighting my own battles every day within the closed and protected world of my school. The terrible world war to end all wars was over. Britain was recovering. Nothing but promise lay in the future.

Despite my childhood perception that hidden dangers lurked in the innocent progression of everyday life, I somehow never imagined that the outside world would so suddenly crush my hopes and dreams as I left Roedean to return to Egypt. But in 1956, the Suez crisis swept aside the veils of protection with which my parents had so carefully surrounded me. Home, no longer a bulwark and a haven, had become a precarious island in a heaving ocean of hostility.

We were trapped in a nightmare from which we could see no escape. Auntie Helen and Granny Mosseri were home most of the time, and as evening fell, we all huddled in the dark comfort of the paneled library where the large antiquated radio involved much static and careful tuning of dials as we tried to make sense of the news. Through the whistles and whines, the tension in Auntie Helen's loud commands, and my father's patient twiddling of the knobs, the news came to us in faint bursts. It became increasingly obvious that much more was at stake than a military coup by French and British forces. Ramped-up exhortations from the Muslim Brotherhood echoed from loudspeakers throughout our quiet residential neighborhood, harsh, threatening in tone although I did not fully understand the content, drowning out the distant thunder of artillery. We were of Italian nationality, neither British nor French. We should have been exempt from any repercussions. But we instantly understood that as a result of Israel's involvement, the writing was on the wall for the Jews of Egypt. Passport and nationality mattered not at all. Years of history vanished in a moment. To be Jewish was to be a potential target for whatever forces were unleashed by this war.

My father left the house every day to visit this or that ministry in hopes of obtaining visas and plane tickets to leave. He was gone all day and returned tired, drawn and despondent as night fell. My mother pulled out suitcases, and methodically we packed and made lists. All available suitcases were soon filled. More large brown leather suitcases smelling of the bazaar, the *muski*, magically appeared. We rolled majestic porcelains in blankets and rugs and fitted them carefully away, packing behind closed doors, hoping that the staff of servants were not aware of what we were doing and hoping that they would somehow not notice that this or that valuable or favorite object had disappeared from its accustomed spot. Hoping that somewhere, somehow, a few of these treasured possessions would follow and find us. It was clear we would not be staying for long.

We packed in order of personal significance. Suitcase number one, my mother decreed, was the one we would take if we had to escape suddenly and could only take one piece of luggage with us.

Seeing our sad faces as she packed the most immediate neces-
sities, she said, "Each of us can add something special, one thing
we really care about. It doesn't have to be useful. It could be a doll
or a book. I'll put in photos. Don't worry, I'll make room for the
special things you choose," and she managed to add them to the
warm clothes and small valuables that already filled the space.

Suitcase number two provided for a more expansive departure, and so it continued, as the brown leather cases, packed and
numbered, offered their mute evidence of a family poised for
flight. During the day we gathered objects into the unused room
beyond the library as unobtrusively as possible, and after dinner, when the staff had all gone to their rooms, wooden shutters
locked shut over the large windows, glancing over our shoulders
nervously, we repaired to the dim confines of that room and continued our gradual dismantling of our lives as we knew them.

Then came the startling news that Secretary Dulles in America had pressured the British and the French to pull out before
securing the canal. The threat of Russian involvement had added
a dimension to the situation that had compelled Eisenhower and
Dulles to intervene forcefully to put an immediate end to the
conflict. What had at first seemed to presage a swift victory for
the post-colonial armies and for Israel as we waited for them to
march into Cairo, triumphant, now dissipated into disorganized
diplomatic maneuvering, leaving British and French citizens living in Egypt at the mercy of the Egyptian government's retaliation. Not to mention the Jews.

My father sputtered with fury and anxiety. Although we had
Italian passports, my mother was also registered with the British
Consulate and we were Jewish: a prominent Jewish banking fam-
ily living in a large and somewhat isolated mansion in Giza. We

listened to the muted crash of bombs and the stutter of antiair-
craft fire as we sat shrouded in darkness in the library, blackout
curtains at the windows, and traded our sharp fear of the battle
outside for a stronger and far more pervasive fear of the retaliation
of the Arab masses egged on by the anti-Israeli militant Moslem
Brotherhood and the passionate cries of the *muezzins* from every
minaret of every mosque in Cairo at the hour of prayer. We knew
we were at the mercy of their revenge and outrage. Our hope of
protection had faded with Dulles's intervention and had retreated
with the troops as they were recalled. We were painfully aware of
what could happen to Jews in the wake of Hitler's unchecked bar-
barism, and we knew that Arab fear and resentment at the State of
Israel could turn smoldering ashes into a powerful conflagration
that might well devour us all.

One day my father left the house at the crack of dawn and
returned hours later, and there was much whispering and muttering among the adults. We piled into the car with one small over-
night bag, our chauffeur, Osta Hussein, driving, his face drawn,
his silence as taut as ours. Granny Mosseri and Auntie Helen
were not with us. They had refused to leave the house. My father
hushed our questions. My mother told us not to talk to anyone
about who we were or why we were where we were. Susan and
I looked at each other. We were not sure where we were going
anyway, or what this was all about, but the tense atmosphere and
the utter silence in the car fueled our fears more than words could
have done. The car drew up in front of a plain dark building I
did not recognize. Quickly and silently we were hurried inside
where we saw groups of strangers gathered about, whispering and
circling. It was cold and cheerless, the floors a dirty rough stone,
the yellowing paint on the walls stained and peeling. We were
led to a long hallway where we were given a small area which we

turned into a makeshift bedroom. Women and children milled about. The talk was in Italian, rapid-fire, anxious, spurting and unfolding along the length of the room. My father was to sleep in another room reserved for men. My mother, normally a person beset by every fear under the sun, logical and illogical, became a tower of strength. The Italian Consulate, worried for its European community in the face of unknown political upheaval and the echoes of war, had clustered as many possibly targeted families as they could house in secret in the Italian school building.

We were there for several days. Susan became sick with a raging fever. My parents, frantic with anxiety, considered returning home, but the situation was too unstable. Bellicose crowds were still rampaging through the streets, destroying property and threatening anyone in their path. Hussein brought medicine he had obtained at a pharmacy, but there was no doctor to call. One of the women hiding with us in the school claimed to be able to administer shots, so she was brought around to help. She was unpracticed and the shots were painful, but Susan recovered.

Rumors swirled around us. Jews had been arrested in the dead of night. We heard later that some Egyptian Jewish men were imprisoned and tortured in camps in Abu Zaabal and Tura, beaten, forced to recite insults, and made to walk on broken glass, but all we knew then was that Ralph Green, a neighbor of ours known for his sartorial elegance, his thick white hair and cheerful ruddy face, and the immaculate carnation that was always pinned to his lapel no matter the season or the weather, had been arrested and thrown into jail with common thieves and murderers from the streets. No one had been allowed to visit him. He was accused of spying for Israel. We groaned in horror. Who could imagine the fastidious Ralph Green in such circumstances? For that matter, who could imagine that urbane gentleman spying for Israel?

Other people of our acquaintance were said to have vanished without a trace. The inescapable shadow of Nazi Germany hung over us like a gathering storm, shutting out light and hope. Where would this end? How would we be able to escape?

My father made his way back to Giza to our house every day before dawn, to check on his mother and sister and to appear to be going to his office from there. After a day at work, where he watched helplessly as the inept and greedy custodian frittered away the achievement of generations, he returned to the Italian school by a circuitous route and brought news from the outside world, where the threat was escalating. Together, my parents paced the corridors of the school, casting anxious glances our way as they passed the area where we lay and tried to sleep, worrying, planning, holding onto precious time together since they were separated at night and never knew what the next day would bring. We huddled among a crowd of strangers. Kind as they were, we seemed to be the only Jews there. Would they betray us if it came down to that? At mealtimes, Hussein appeared with a three-tier shiny aluminum thermos, his jaunty side-to-side gait recognizable from far down the corridor, the tassel on his red *tarbush* swinging as he made his way to us. We looked forward to his visits and news from home, and relished the steaming and generous home-cooked meals he brought, enough food for us to invite some of our neighboring refugees to join us as we ate. We shared laundry duties, took turns using the limited toilet facilities, watched as mothers tried vainly to maintain the silence we had been warned to keep, frantically shushing the crying and running of infants and small children in the echoing hallways.

A crowd of Italian sailors joined the crowded refugees, jostling, laughing, shouting, leering at anything in skirts, and causing intense consternation among mothers of teenage daughters as their girls hurried down the dark steps to take laundry to the basement. To the world outside, the schools were supposed to be empty, but at various times we were aware of violence, angry throngs of men gathered in the streets outside throwing stones, shouting, leaving us feeling like trapped creatures as we listened to their muted fury from the safety of the damp walls and stone floors of our refuge.

Eventually, the violence appeared to have somewhat abated, and we left the strange harbor we had inhabited and returned to Giza, to the big house, where Granny Mosseri, now in her eighties, sat in a shadowed corner of the hall. Flanked by potted palms in antique china planters, she muttered sadly to herself, lost in dark musings, unhappy to see her beloved son so beset with worry, unhappy to see such chaos attending her old age, determined not to leave Egypt, no matter what happened. "I want to die here," she said, again and again, to the consternation of my parents and the impatience of Auntie Helen.

A sense of crushing despair had replaced the order and bustle of our lives. My father's bank had first been sealed, then sequestered. Despite my father's unquenchable optimism, it was the loud and obnoxious government official, the custodian sequester, who held sway where for so many years my father had conducted his business in an atmosphere of dignity and respect.

We found ourselves floundering in the alien world around us. My father had become an unwelcome visitor in his own life. Every day he returned to us with tales of misery. He had gone to the *muski* to buy suitcases and had turned his head, to realize with shock that he was being followed. He came home empty-handed and returned many hours later, taking pains to leave from the house and not the office. The government-appointed sequester-custodian had added innumerable relatives to the payroll, including one sleazy character who tailed my father everywhere, and whom he promptly named "*l'espion*," finding small delight in outsmarting him and taking him on every wild goose chase he could think up as he slipped from his grasp to meet with whomever and accomplish whatever he had planned for his day.

Because of my father's irrepressible sense of humor, we were regaled with all the sick jokes and stories that were circulating:

*A man had broken his leg and had gone to the airport to leave Egypt, but the Customs officials had taken him to a small room and broken open his cast, to yells of fury and pain. They found nothing and ushered him back to his doctor's office for a new cast. This time, both the man and his doctor hid a fortune in jewels and cash in the cast. When he arrived at the airport, glowering at everyone, the official who had ordered the breaking of the cast the last time recognized him, and bowing and apologizing, personally ushered him through Customs and onto his plane.*

✦ ✦ ✦

*A woman had hidden diamonds in the heel of her shoe and left with them, flying off to some distant haven, never to be heard from again.*

✦ ✦ ✦

*Gamal Abdel Nasser had been taken on a tour of heaven and hell. In heaven, he had seen angels quietly playing lutes to the whisper of a gentle breeze. In hell, he had seen barebreasted women belly-dancing furiously while all around*

*people laughed and drank, music played, and beautiful*
*girls rushed over and drew him to the center of the party,*
*plying him with fragrant garlands and exquisite dishes.*
*"Where would you like to go when you die?" he was asked.*
*Nasser laughed uproariously. "Who would hesitate?" he*
*answered. "Of course I choose hell." Later, Abdel Nasser*
*died and arrived at the pearly gates. "This is not what I*
*requested," he shouted, "Where is hell?" Immediately a hid-*
*eous devil with a pitchfork arrived and pitched him into*
*a roaring furnace filled with tortured screaming individu-*
*als. "What is this?" cried Nasser, "Where are the beautiful*
*women? Where is the music? Where are the garlands and*
*the food?" The devil laughed. "Ah!" he said, "Last time you*
*came, you were a tourist. Now you are a resident."*

Gaston Naggar, a well-known lawyer, had weathered some
difficult skirmishes with the government through the years and
was fearful of anything that might propel him into an Egyptian
jail. So when he was about to leave Egypt, he exhorted his wife
and mother-in-law that they must not pack anything that might
arouse suspicion. Later, in the plane, he turned to his elderly
travel companion, his mother-in-law, dignified Marguerite
Sapriel—who had faithfully attended Granny Mosseri's Saturday
bridge parties throughout my childhood—and confided proudly
that he had at the last minute included a valuable prayer rug in
his suitcase. She smiled serenely, removed her hat, and showed
him all her jewels hidden inside. She sold those jewels one by one
in her life in Paris, and they enabled her to retain her dignity and
her independence until she died in 1972 at the age of eighty-nine.

*Marguerite Sapriel*

Somehow, we managed to find humor in our days and to laugh through our fears. We mocked the system and managed to simulate a semblance of normal life although we kept ourselves virtually under house arrest.

✦ ✦ ✦

The Gezira Sporting Club, to which we had belonged ever since I could remember, was a holdover of British colonial comfort and ease. Situated in Zamalek, it had always been a social gathering place for my parents and their friends. For the nursery set it provided a vast, exciting playground. Huge expanses of well-tended grass held an open invitation to run and shout. The red-earth tennis courts were among the best anywhere, and members of all facets of Cairo society sat in the bleachers during international tennis tournaments to cheer on the tennis stars of the day. The clubhouse was arranged around a series of descending swimming pools, with the round paddling pool for small children on the lowest level. We were never allowed to use these public swimming pools for fear of polio, and we eyed them longingly as our friends splashed about in them in the heat of the day and called to us to join them. But the specter of Auntie Helen's encounter with the disease held sway and our parents were not to be persuaded. Adults sat on shaded terraces around the pools fanning themselves and sipping Turkish coffee or sodas, chatting and socializing, while German, Swiss, and British nannies, the latter often in full starched regalia, ministered to the needs of the junior crowd. A fine golf course where Uncle Cesar and Auntie Peggy Setton and their golfing friends regularly played golf stretched to the left, velvet green alternating with golden sand bunkers.

As the year of Suez progressed, we gradually ventured back a few times into the Gezira Sporting Club, arranging to meet the friends who had not yet left the country on the terraces near the pools or under the vine-covered pavilion that faced the green expanses of the cricket fields. Sadly, we noticed the absence of many familiar faces. Orderly tables of British and French postcolonial families relaxing in elegance and repose had been replaced by rowdy clumps of Egyptian men in military uniforms, celebrating their entry into a world from which they had been largely excluded. The moneyed, cultured Egyptian aristocracy had always socialized comfortably with their counterparts from other countries, but the brash, newly empowered military had not. Now they were taking possession of that world and claiming it as their own.

Still, we continued to attempt some form of social life outside our home until the day when my parents and I were seated at a table near the pool, and a large officer with greased black hair and a pitted complexion stood up at a table in the vicinity of ours and made his way to our table. My father whispered hurriedly to my mother, "He is from the *Mubahhaz* (the secret police). I met with him to try to get us a visa."

The man sauntered over, grinning broadly, gold glittering around his broad neck, on his sausage-like fingers, and glinting through his smile. He pulled a chair over and sat at our table without asking. We watched him in apprehensive silence. He stared at me arrogantly with what I recognized as a lascivious look, although I could not then have named it. It made me shudder and look down in fear. My father paled.

"Ah, Monsieur Mosseri," said the man. "I see you have a beautiful daughter. Why do you not bring her along next time you come to request your exit visa?"

My father muttered something about my being very young, still in the schoolroom, not allowed to go with him into the world of men and business.

"Bring her," said the officer flatly. He rose and left the table without a backward glance and we hurried home. That was the last time we ventured into the Gezira Sporting Club.

I presume that my father subsequently attempted different routes to obtaining our exit visas, and none of us ever spoke of the incident at the Club, although it was dominantly present in all of our minds and loomed over the many difficult decisions my parents had to make. In their anxiety, they even considered sending my sister and myself with a Bedouin caravan across the Sinai desert to safe haven, but eventually decided that the perils of such a journey far outweighed the possible benefits.

It brought home to all of us, and perhaps more particularly to me, since so much had previously been shielded from me, the extent of our vulnerability and the dangers lurking just outside my field of vision. We stopped going out, and I stopped asking to go out. When we did venture outside the house, I shuddered with fear when I saw a military uniform and tried to disappear into myself. A powerful undertow of menace was tugging at our lives, pulling us deeper and deeper away from the safe, the familiar, the everyday. We didn't know where it would take us. We had no idea where it might wash us ashore, and whether we might be dashed to pieces on the rocks before reaching safe haven.

By 1956, we were all fully aware of the horrors that had attended the Holocaust. As Jews, even Jews with Italian passports and international connections, we knew ourselves to be utterly vulnerable to the whims of a despotic rule and the rage of a vengeful ruler. We eyed the house servants nervously. Would they be loyal? Would they be persuaded or coerced into reporting our clandestine preparations and whispered conversations to the authorities? We developed a language of symbols and inferences. The word "Israel" never passed our lips even in a whisper. It was years and oceans away before I could bring myself to say the word aloud. We spoke in a code that our friends all understood and that we prayed all others did not.

Despite our fears and growing paranoia, Osta Hussein—our chauffeur—and the cook, Osta Mohammed, were above suspicion. They were so tightly woven into our lives that their loyalty was unquestionable and they made it abundantly clear to us that they understood our situation and suffered with us as we prepared to move into uncharted territory. But what about Aboudi, the sneering head gardener who was said to beat his many wives, and whose vicious anger struck terror into the hearts of the little boys who worked with him in the garden? Would he exact revenge for the times that my aunt had argued with him over some small infraction of her rules?

Any unusual expression or request from the other staff seemed suddenly fraught with dangerous possibilities. Often, angry demonstrations brought frenzied shouts and white-robed crowds swirling and wielding sticks and stones outside our gates. The relentless cadences of the *muezzin* from the many minarets around the city calling the faithful to prayer had become a call to arms. The house staff had their rooms in the basement where they slept, leaving families in the upper Nile villages or Sudan to work in the big city. Would they rise in the night and murder us in our beds?

As we sat at our dinner table in the house in Cairo one evening long after my father had come home for the night, the front doorbell rang. An electric flare of fear ran through us all and lodged in each of us, gluing us to our seats. The bell rang again.

"Leave quickly by the back way," said my mother to my father. "We'll say you didn't come home."

"*Qu'est-ce qu'il y a?*" asked Granny Mosseri, looking up from her plate, shocked out of her silent preoccupation by the horrified faces of her family.

"Nothing," said my father, nervously shrugging off his mother's concern and his wife's exhortations as he sent one of the *suffragies* to open the door. The man hesitated, understanding our danger, urging my father first to slip out the back way and take the car. My father shook his head.

The neighbor who had rung the bell to ask for my father's advice on some personal issue must have wondered at the effusive delight with which he was welcomed by the *suffragie* who recognized him and then by the rest of us as he was ushered into the sitting room and accorded every hospitality and attention.

We were Jews. We had become the enemy.

*Villa Mosseri*

Trust became a dangerous commodity. Those considered close and trustworthy were not above the metaphorical knife in the back. Strange tales of deception came to light many months later. Some years earlier, Auntie Edna and Uncle Jacques Adda had engaged a pleasant young Greek nursemaid, Helen, for their two boys. She lived with them and traveled with them as one of the family, and was with them when my uncle and aunt found themselves exiled from Egypt without hope of return. Helen generously offered to help. As a non-Jewish Greek citizen she could return to Egypt and leave again without difficulty. She left for Alexandria with their expressions of deep gratitude ringing in her ears, with many careful instructions and a key to their home, having promised that she would then join her brother in Greece with a suitcase filled with their valuables. She was to contact them as soon as she arrived in Greece. All went according to plan, except that neither she, nor her brother, nor the suitcase ever surfaced again.

My father's uncle Felix, the last of Grandpa Mosseri's siblings still living, was close in age to his nieces, my aunts Helen and Mary, who had been his childhood playmates in the capacious family house in the Rue Fouad. A pleasant portly man, his shiny head ringed by a sparse circle of fading hair, he had a courtly charm and spoke with a marked British accent. Although he is reputed to have had many mistresses, he never married. One of Uncle Felix's mistresses was a certain Belgian woman with whom he lived for many years without ever taking the plunge into marriage. Already an old man in 1957 and trapped in Egypt, he put his considerable wealth into her name so that she might take it out of Egypt for them both to live on. She was able to leave before him. She appropriated all the money and left him as soon as he arrived in Europe. He lived in Brussels after the Suez crisis, quasi-destitute, eking out a living as best he could and traveling to Rome or Geneva to be with his nieces for the religious holidays. He is the only one of Nessim and Elena Mosseri's children who survived into his eighties.

After Suez, many families lost their laughter along with their ease and way of life. From bad investments, some lost the little money they had. It had never mattered before. There had always been enough to cover their losses. Now they plunged from the luxury of roomy apartments and fine houses in a sunny climate into tiny furnished studio flats in strange European neighborhoods. They had made money from money. Now they needed to make money from their wits. Coming from a culture that shielded children from the realities of hardship, the parents of older children continued to shield them from their own failures and stresses. Many were unable to adapt to their straitened circumstances and the other family woes that befell them. Close quarters and lack of money broke marriages apart. A respected insurance executive became an office messenger boy. A lady of leisure turned her skill

*Auntie Edna and Uncle Jacques*

with a needle into a successful business taking in dresses to alter in her home, but the stress and anxiety took its toll. Still in her thirties, she died of cancer. Soon after my father died of cancer, Uncle Jacques fell ill and died, and Auntie Edna battled breast cancer valiantly but succumbed in Paris, in 1973, when she was fifty-four years old.

But along with acts of betrayal and deception, there were also quiet acts of support and kindness. Auntie Helen and my parents had many friends in the Italian diplomatic community. In his youth, Uncle Victor had attended school in Switzerland with a wonderful man who worked for the Red Cross and consequently whose official international position enabled him to gain entry to Egypt soon after the Suez crisis. White-haired, tall, and rangy, his clear blue eyes exuding competence and calm, he turned up at our door in Cairo early one morning, asking for news of Uncle Victor and his family and bearing tidings of our family in Europe.

With him came the hope that he might be able to help effect our departure. Through the kindness of many, we were able to include some furnishings and other objects in crates bearing the household goods of returning diplomats. Storage in Italy held scattered pieces of our former lives for many months. When we found our way out of Egypt, they were there for us.

✦ ✦ ✦

The events precipitated by the nationalization of the Suez Canal in 1956 spun the Egyptian Jews relentlessly out of their comfortable homes and influential positions and scattered them around the globe. To that privileged community, the crisis had exploded with the force of an asteroid colliding with the earth, destroying the work of generations and forcing many lives, including mine, out of what had appeared to be their destined path. Stretching deep into the past, there had always been a significant Jewish community in Egypt, where the great Moses Maimonides settled and taught after leaving Spain during the Middle Ages. Before Gamal Abdel Nasser nationalized the Suez Canal and brought the wrath of nations down upon his head, the Jews in Egypt numbered some 80,000. After the Suez crisis, a continuous heavy exodus of Jews from Egypt, both forced and voluntary, brought the community down to a few hundred.

Much of the written correspondence from past generations sheds light on the day-to-day lives and interactions of this cultured and diverse Jewish community. A substantial collection of writings and fragments of writings, some dating back to the early fifteenth century, was stored in the attic of the Ben Ezra synagogue in the Old City of Cairo and lay there undiscovered for many decades. Now housed in the Geniza collection largely united at Cambridge University in England, scholars are pains-takingly reconstituting and preserving unique archival material that reaches widely throughout the Middle East and vividly docu-ments the day-to-day lives of the Egyptian Jewish community of centuries past. Some fragments were found buried in earth, as is the Jewish custom with sacred documents. Some came to light by chance and were sold to private collectors or sold in the *muski* to tourists.

Housed within this collection lies the smaller Mosseri Geniza collection. Grandpa Mosseri's younger brother, Jacques, my father's favorite uncle, had a strong interest in archeology and Jewish history. A close friend of Chaim Weitzman, he was a dedi-cated Zionist and persuaded two of his older brothers, Joseph and Eli, to put together the financing to build the King David Hotel in Jerusalem. In the course of his years of research, Jacques Mosseri came across and collected many priceless historical documents which now make up the Mosseri Geniza.

Although in my childhood years so much of world conse-quence took place outside my line of vision, looking back I can see that the comfortable tolerance of religion and nationality flow-ing from the dominance of the Ottoman Empire in the Middle East began to falter with the emergence of a series of events that included the weakening of the colonial influence in Egypt. The dissolute reign of King Farouk became imbued with his bitter-ness over British influence in Egyptian affairs that consequently led to his Nazi sympathies. Establishment of the State of Israel in 1948 added to the growing uncertainty of Jews in Arab lands. In 1952, General Gamal Abdel Nasser overthrew King Farouk and sent him and his family into exile. Nasser, too, was a Nazi sympathizer and opened the door to a more overt anti-Semitism. Many Jewish families deeply ensconced in Egypt for generations began to see the writing on the wall. Others did not. Some left the country precipitously, taking vast fortunes with them. Sensing that the stable order that had attended their lives so far was on the brink of major change, many began to seek ways to establish funds in other countries and to educate their children elsewhere.

✦ ✦ ✦

The changes that came about disrupted more than our own lives. We were as much a part of Hussein's family as his own wife and children. Our lives not only intersected for a time, they were permanently interwoven. He was a pious Moslem and kept a small prayer mat in the garage, where he could be seen at all the ritual times, kneeling and touching his head to the ground as the calls of the *muezzin* rang out throughout the metropolis. His understanding and faithful observance of his own religion made him respect the religious observances of others, and he would have been shocked had we failed to observe appropriately the yearly round of feasts and holidays that punctuated our Jewish lives. At Ramadan, he and the house servants continued about their tasks as they endured day after day of fasting in the heat, then spent their night hours in feast and prayer.

Quietly and without asking questions, he had participated in our dismantling of the house in Cairo, the house he had grown up in as surely as had I. He, alone, knew of our days in hiding in the Italian school building and he brought us our meals there. His postcards, sent out into a world he would never visit, asked after each and every one of the family he had lost to the politics of the hour. He wondered about us, worried about us, rejoiced with us. We missed his unfailing protection and gentle participation in our lives. I can still see his neat brown face wreathed in smiles under the red *tarbush* he always wore with a loose-fitting dark European suit, his side-to-side ambling walk as he slid from his seat in the car and came around to open the door for us to jump in or jump out. I can see the quick twist of his head and momentary grin as I sat in the back seat of the car and told my mother some amusing anecdote from school, and the seriousness with which he undertook my mother's request that he teach Jeff everything he knew about electric outlets and electricity. We trusted him, and he trusted us.

After our departure from Egypt, we heard regularly from Osta Hussein. He sent gaudy, sentimental postcards generously illustrated with cherubs, roses, and glitter to Europe and America every year with New Year wishes and wishes for every major occasion of my life, my wedding, the births of each of my children. He made sure that he knew what was happening in our families. He rejoiced in our happiness and shared in each of our losses. Each event saw the arrival of these postcards written for him in a fine slanting script by Madame Marika, whom he visited for this purpose, the misspelled words echoing the halting English he spoke. Beyond the words on the paper, I could feel the silent world of love, loyalty, and loss the postcards symbolized. The heart might be pumping, blood might be flowing as it had always done, his own family might be growing and prospering, but for him, life continued as if a limb had been amputated.

When he drove us to the airport in Cairo for the last time, we all made promises to meet again. We hoped to bring him to visit us, wherever we ended up. He wanted and expected to come to us. There were tears in everyone's eyes. It was many years before we all acknowledged that the visit could never happen. Political, health, and family reasons prevented him again and again from being able to plan to come to Europe. He was the epitome of a good person and none of us who knew him will ever forget his place in our lives.

✦ ✦ ✦

The GPS, where my sister had been attending school, was an English school with students of many different backgrounds, but many of the teachers were British. The school closed. The teachers and the British students and their families were summarily expelled from the country, and when the school reopened it was to teach Arabic only. We knew that sooner or later we would be leaving Egypt for good, and that Susan would have to take her place in an English school in England. Others shared her plight. I set up a schoolroom for three eight-year-olds, complete with roll call, strict hours, and significant homework.

At first, we all considered this a sort of enhanced babysitting that could end any minute as one family or another obtained exit visas and left the country. But the days stretched to weeks, and the weeks to months. Gradually, a curriculum evolved that was a strange medley of traditional spelling and grammar, and eclectic general knowledge. Postcards of Goya paintings, of the *Mona Lisa*, and other famous scenes were tacked up on the wall and discussed. My three small pupils and I all agreed that we hated the *Mona Lisa's* famous enigmatic smile. We built a Norman fort from cardboard and painted it, and read up about the Norman Conquest in the encyclopedia in the library downstairs. The pink night-nursery table was covered with books and papers, and our handiwork covered the walls. No one cared anymore if we damaged the paint.

I managed to keep one small step ahead of my pupils, my sister Susan, a solemn little boy called Brian Massey, and Jackie Fresco, a cheery girl with an engaging smile, freckles, and curly hair. It was homeschooling at its most primitive, but it kept us usefully occupied as the adults tried to figure out what to do to extract themselves and their families from an untenable situation. Susan hated to have her big sister turn into a stern disciplinarian five mornings a week, but we ploughed on regardless. What we had anticipated would last a few weeks eventually encompassed an entire school year. Despite my rudimentary attempts, when they did finally reach real schools in other countries, they were all accepted into the appropriate grades.

As the weeks wore on, it became clear that barring a renewal of hostilities there would probably be no immediate danger. Gradually, as we tried to get a grip on the situation and the new way of life that stretched ahead, we learned of the many summary expulsions of French and British friends and acquaintances, families forced to leave their home in a matter of a few hours with just one small bag, or leaving with only the clothes on their backs. As Italians, we considered ourselves outside the danger net for immediate expulsion now that things seemed to be calming down, and were therefore very surprised one afternoon when an unexpected visitor pushed past the *boab*, the gatekeeper in his red brick guardhouse to the left of the garden gate, and made his way toward where we sat.

Auntie Helen, Granny Mosseri, my parents, Susan, and I were all in the garden on a Sunday afternoon, enjoying near-perfect weather. The *suffragie* had brought out a large silver tray with a plate of *kaak*, the circular crunchy pastries generously sprinkled with sesame seeds that we all loved. Ice cubes clinked delicately in crystal glasses and there was a tall pitcher of fresh lemonade. We were just starting to help ourselves when we turned and saw a short man in an ill-fitting European suit, his hair oiled to his head in dark compact waves, his new brown-and-white Oxfords crunching along the gravel path to where we sat. My father got up and went to meet him. They spoke briefly, turned, and came toward us. After a perfunctory greeting from the intruder my father explained that the man was from the government and was bringing us a message. The man stood impassively by while he spoke. Then in heavily accented English he said:

"You must leave tomorrow. You do not belong here."

"Oh, yes, I do," said my father. "Where were you born, and when did you come to live in Cairo?" The man named a village near Aswan, and conceded that he had only been in Cairo for the past ten years.

"My family has lived here for two hundred," said my father stoutly. "It seems to me that we belong here far more than yourself."

"That makes no difference," said the man. "You must leave tomorrow. You may only take one bag each. You must never come back. Here is the address where you are to go for your exit visa tomorrow morning."

Without another word, he turned and left. We watched him go, stunned into silence. My father glanced down at the paper in his hand. He was to present himself to the government offices on Joseph Mosseri Bey Street to receive his visa to leave his father's homeland forever. As we sat in the lovely flowered garden, the gentle breeze and lemonade forgotten, the irony was not lost on us. I glanced toward the walkways edged with earthenware pots spilling bright flowers, and I shivered, remembering the black snake of my childhood. We trudged back into the house where my father made calls to the Italian ambassador and to various Egyptian officials he thought might be able to help, and we returned to our lists and suitcases, facing the inevitable with silence and little ceremony.

That night, as we worked in the library and prepared our departure, the radio emitted more static than usual. However, through the crackles and spurts of distorted sound we were able to make out that a strong protest had been lodged by the representatives of various governments to the United Nations as to the multitude and manner of the expulsion of French and British citizens from Egypt, and of various Jews of Egyptian and other nationalities.

Next morning, as we were hurriedly continuing our preparations for departure, the doorbell rang. We hurried down the stairs and crowded anxiously within sight of the tall front door as my father moved to open it. A man stood there. He was a stranger. We edged closer together.

"You know that notice of expulsion you received yesterday?" he asked. "You must tear it up. We don't want you to leave. No, we don't want you to leave. You can stay here as long as you want."

⚜ ⚜ ⚜

As the weeks went by, my father set to work to obtain permission for us to enter my Smouha grandparents' house in Alexandria, which had been sealed because it belonged to a British citizen. Claiming our Italian citizenship and the many summer and winter holidays spent in that house, he was able to schedule a visit for my mother, my father, and myself to retrieve "our" possessions. Accompanied by a phalanx of secret servicemen and government officials, we traveled apprehensively to Alexandria and were escorted into the house. No warm and loving presence greeted us. The house was dark and silent, seeming to register an unfamiliar and hostile presence within its walls. We knew of a hidden place that housed my grandmother's silver, but my mother and I had decided that there would be too much risk in trying to claim it. We steadfastly turned our eyes away from it, hoping it would not be found by others, and that with the passing of time, my grandparents might return to their home and claim what was theirs.

This was never to be, and I have often wondered if it remains undiscovered.

I thought of the many happy times I had visited Granny Smouha in her bedroom. It had always seemed so perfect, so special. Her diminutive antique dressing table with its three-sided mirror had an exquisite silver-and-pink enamel set of brushes and glass bottles with matching tops, and elegant crystal flagons of her favorite perfume set out beside them, and was placed across from the bed, under the window. Her blue-and-black-tiled bathroom always smelled of OMY bath oil or some other wonderful fragrance, as did she, and when I was small, I loved to step on and off the medical scale that stood against the wall across from the bath and was exactly like the one in the doctor's office. As the years passed, I felt less of a kinship with the scale, although I continued to find the bathroom glamorous.

Surrounded by the sinister presence of our threatening companions, we climbed slowly and sadly up to my grandparents' bedroom. We did not dare to lay claim to the enamel and silver set of bottles and brushes that lay neatly on the dressing table under the window as if awaiting Granny's return. The room still smelt faintly of her perfume. Opening her drawers hesitantly, we felt like intruders and tried to look purposeful and as if we knew exactly what we were looking for. We had to submit to her delicate lingerie being fingered by those who were the real intruders before they would allow us to check for "our" things. In the end, what we managed to salvage were some photo albums which we exclaimed enthusiastically were our own and which my grandmother was delighted to receive when we were finally reunited, a sweater or two, Uncle Teddy's bronze Olympic medal, and Granny's jade necklace which was in its beige suede pouch in a drawer of her dressing table. Our guards were reluctant to let us take it, but we were able to convince them that it was my mother's and they let it go. It was a strange and painful parting from the house my mother had left as a bride, where laughter and music had rippled through the rooms for so many happy years. It was the last time I ever saw the house where I was born.

✦ ✦ ✦

Weeks of careful diplomacy and patient string-pulling eventually brought their reward, and my father was able to obtain a visa for the four of us, valid for a few days, that would take us out of the country. Triumphant, he rushed to the airline offices, only to find that flights, which had been grounded since the Suez operation, would not resume their travel to Europe until a date beyond the visa's expiration date. He booked us onto the first flight out, and returned to the visa problem. Once again he began the rounds of the government offices, the *Mubbahaz* (Egypt's secret police), and other influential ministries where he sat for hours waiting to make his request. Eventually his persistence paid off and he was able to get the visa renewed. Once again he rushed to the airlines but now they were fully booked until after the renewal expired. For nine increasingly stressful months, he was unable to coordinate visa and airline tickets for us to leave the country. When he was able to get his hands on one of the two elements necessary to our departure, he could not complete it with the other.

While we labored to salvage something of our lives for the future and my father worked ceaselessly to make sure we had a future, we were only able to communicate sporadically with my brother, my Smouha grandparents, and uncles and aunts in Europe through friends in the diplomatic corps who occasionally included our letters in the diplomatic pouch. Meanwhile, fourteen-year-old Jeff, at boarding school north of London, was frantic, hearing all sorts of vastly exaggerated tales from schoolmates, reading about the situation in Egypt in the British press, and unable to assess what dangers his parents and sisters might be facing in the great epistolary silence in which he found himself.

Although we had often been taken to Mena House as children and had ridden donkeys and camels to the base of the Sphinx or the pyramids, we now made a point of visiting palaces and historic sights in old Cairo which we had not yet seen, doubting that once we left, we would ever be able to see these again. We visited the palace of Mohammed Ali and marveled at the intricately inlaid ceilings and floors, the beautiful interior spaces and opulent furnishings. We went to the old city and visited the oldest synagogue in Egypt, reputed to have been built on the very ground where Moses prayed to God to be allowed to leave Egypt. We were told that there was a crypt and an underground river under the foundations of the small synagogue and that it had great spiritual power.

*The Shubrah palace, Cairo*

In despair, after nine months of failed attempts, my father went alone to pray at this synagogue for his own exodus from Egypt with his family. Miraculously, the next day he learned that both the airline tickets and visas were available, and we left precipitously for London. Like the exodus of old, we were allowed to take many suitcases with us, but no currency. The Egyptian government took possession of my father's bank and "paid" him in government bonds due to mature in twenty years, by which time they were worthless. The larger Mosseri family real estate holdings were never sold but were taken over by the government. The house itself and the surrounding land was sold to the Russians as a residence for the ambassador, but due to currency restrictions, the money remained in Egypt and gradually disappeared.

✦ ✦ ✦

About the time when my father was seeing things possibly coming together for our departure, Susan and I were playing in the garden with our Alsatian dog, Lucky, when we noticed him nipping at our heels more than usual. His behavior seemed erratic and we repaired indoors to escape his attentions. Next day, my father took him to the vet, where he became more and more sick, eventually foaming at the mouth. He died of rabies.

The family doctor, Dr. Molco, was sent for. He and his wife, Saretta, and their children were trying to leave for Italy, where they eventually settled. We sat in stunned silence as he explained the tremendous consequences of having been exposed to rabies. He examined fingers and scraped knees, and finally made his pronouncement: unless I could point to a specific incident where Lucky had licked or bitten me, I was exempt from the treatment, but Susan, whose nine-year-old knees were the usual nine-year-old maze of old and new grazes, would have to have the entire round of daily shots in the stomach, starting immediately. Susan had always had a horror of injections, and had once scrambled all the way up my father to claim sanctuary when she was tiny (he only accepted under duress to hand her over to my mother and the doctor). Now she went daily with my mother to a special clinic, where shots from a very large needle were administered. She was very good about it, but the shots were painful. The anxiety and the logistics of the situation contributed mightily to the stress for my parents, too, since it was paramount that the entire regimen of shots proceed uninterrupted and we were about to take a plane for Rome, where we were to stay a couple of days before continuing to London. Matters had reached an unbearable climax. Susan, along with leaving her home and her country, had also to endure the entire series of rabies shots in different clinics, administered by different nurses speaking in different languages and with varying degrees of sensitivity. She was young enough to have to accept the miseries inflicted on her by the adults who controlled her life, but also old enough to understand that she had left her home forever and was being confronted with a hazy future.

I am not sure precisely when I began to yearn for freedoms that seemed destined never to be mine. The close and loving world that followed me everywhere and allowed me only glimpses at the splendid variety of the world outside the walls of my home, had long seemed less real to me than the worlds that emerged from the pages of the books I read with passion and avidity. Reading was both an escape into realms of myself known only to me as well as a release into other worlds whose riches were mine to plunder and to keep.

As a child, even my reading was carefully monitored. I received a gift of a children's encyclopedia that I explored with fascination, since it opened so many doors to places and facts I had never imagined. But before it ever reached my eager hands, my mother had read it and excised the chapter that dealt with various anatomical details, which I can only assume had something to do with reproduction. My mother read every book I received before putting it in my hands. There was no public library available to me, where I might have been able to make my own reading decisions. My world was meticulously monitored and devoid of choice.

She was a loving and careful mother, wary of so much, vulnerable and fearful herself, and determined to keep a close watch on anything that might dismay her or that she feared might alarm or harm me. And her over-care wove me into a translucent chrysalis where I hung in stasis, waiting for life to happen, sensing powerful darknesses around me but never touching them. With time, that tender protection began to seem a profound claustrophobia, a safety that felt far more dangerous than kind. So that the trauma of the moment when the world outside smashed the chrysalis and spilled us all into a harsh, forbidding reality was also the first moment when I sensed that there might be a world in which I could spread my wings, a world where there was promise, choice, the grit of struggle, the magnificence that lies in the possibility of change.

The moment when my parents' world shattered was also the moment that set me free.

Because I slept so close to my parents' bedroom, which was also the only room where they had any privacy, I became an unwilling witness to the volatility that existed at the core of their relationship and sent electricity crackling through the volcanic reaches of their marriage. I could never quite understand how their arguments could reach fever pitch in the evening, raised voices leaving me confused, trembling, certain that they were heading for divorce, and how in the morning, it would all be gone, leaving only the tenderness with which they addressed each other and the new day. The night had worked its alchemy in ways I did not yet understand. What I did understand over time was that their passionate love and commitment to one another always spun bridges over the deep rifts that appeared and disappeared in their relationship as the years went by. Their background overlay appeared so similar, but their differences of family culture and temperament were profound.

*Joyce Mosseri*

I learned a great deal from those solitary moments when I experienced involuntary glimpses into the nature of my parents' marriage. There was no one with whom I could share the terror or the insights. My brother and sister were too young, my aunt and grandmother were tacitly understood to be separate from our family unit, and thus not to be drawn into such intimate matters.

So I wrestled alone with my thoughts as the years led me through adolescence toward the moment when my fears would find a focus and a force outside the walls of my family home.

✢ ✢ ✢

The year of Suez, I spent many melancholy hours in my bedroom, my parents' sitting room, gazing at the muddy Nile waters, watching speedboats circle out, sometimes even with an intrepid water-skier in tow weaving among the houseboats and graceful *faloukas* that carried bales of grasses and lowing cattle from villages of mud huts in upper Egypt to the teeming Cairo markets. Men in white turbans shouted unintelligible orders and grappled with the ropes that controlled the billowing sails, dancing about the decks and ducking as the beams swung around in response to their efforts. I listened again and again to the Grieg and Rachmaninoff piano concertos on my wind-up His Master's Voice gramophone with its signature picture of a dog listening to a megaphone. At night, wary of mosquitoes, I peered beyond the voile curtains through the slats of the brown shutters and watched the moonlight on the water, my heart swelling in melancholy with every ripple of light on the waters of the Nile.

I was eighteen years old, bursting with eagerness for the fullness of life and of experience, and I was housebound.

Most of my friends had either left the country or been forced out, and we lived under constant tension and fear of what the future might bring. Instead of the balls and dances, the stimulating intellectual badinage and the courtship rites of my dreams, I practiced my violin alone in the small room I had claimed on the mezzanine floor; read Dante with my Italian teacher, Mr. Orvieto, who always looked as if he wished he were elsewhere, which he undoubtedly did; and was schoolmistress to three reluctant eight-year-olds in the mornings. Where, I wondered, would I find love, a husband, children, a real life? Where would it find me?

The adults in the household were bowed down and preoccupied with the enormous weight of their responsibilities and their greater understanding of the implications of our plight, but I wandered like a ghost through the days, writing letters to my friends and my cousins that I doubted they would ever receive, scribbling self-pity into my diary, mired in longing for something *other*, something that would offer me open doors instead of locked iron gates with menace circling beyond the railings. I wanted to know what it would be like to interact with others my age. I wanted to have the experiences I read about, experiences that others my age took for granted. I didn't want to be different.

So I spent hours gazing wistfully out of my prison of beautiful clothes and beautifully appointed rooms, waiting to discover myself reflected in the eyes of others. As the months drifted by, my eighteenth year blended into my nineteenth. We began to accumulate clothes for our future lives in colder places. Since we knew that we would not be able to take money with us, we settled for possessions that we would probably not be able to afford in our new lives.

The bizarre paradox of our lives continued. I went to town with my parents to visit the most fashionable dressmakers for fittings of clothes I feared I would never wear, finely crafted copies of the latest Paris designer dresses in silks and soft wools, chiffon, and satin. My mother and the dressmaker circled me, solemn in their dedication to perfection, pulling here, pinching the fabric there, exclaiming to each other, assuring me that I looked lovely.

Lovely. As I watched myself transformed in the mirror, I wondered whose eyes would see me in my finery.

✠ ✠ ✠

My mother was determined to prepare us for whatever future we might be plunged into. She organized cooking lessons with Osta Mohammed, but they did not go down too well because he was locked into a respectful past and was reluctant to let us dirty our hands or get too intimately involved with what we were supposedly making.

Madame Leon, a tall and handsome woman with very black hair that had a dramatic white streak in the front, came to the house and gave me her recipe for a delicious cheese tart as though passing on an heirloom, a rare jewel. She was the wife of our barber/hairdresser, Monsieur Leon, a round-faced man who always had a wide smile on his face and looked immaculate in his white smock as he wielded scissors, dryer bonnets, and rollers in his small, old-fashioned shop, the porcelain fittings and chrome fixtures glittering and bright in the Egyptian sunshine. The Leons had emigrated from Poland early and had escaped the horrors of the Holocaust. While they waited to see if they could leave for Greece and from there move on to find a home in Israel this time around, Madame Leon pored over the nails of the ladies, finishing off her grooming rituals with an array of brilliant Peggy Sage nail colors ranging from a startling crimson to an equally vivid hot pink.

For years, we had all taken music lessons with Monsieur and Madame Menasce, who, together with Monsieur Tiegermann, had also come to Egypt as refugees from Poland and had founded the Tiegermann Conservatoire de Musique. Monsieur Menasce and Monsieur Tiegermann were both so diminutive that I soon grew to tower over them and felt a little like Alice in Wonderland in their presence.

Monsieur Menasce was my violin teacher. He held his violin as if it were an extension of his arm, his long slender fingers dancing delicately on the strings and producing exquisite music seemingly without effort. I used to think that if he had been a performer, he would have been greater than Heifetz, who was Monsieur Menasce's epitome of the greatest violinist of all time. Instead, exchanging the occasional rapid Polish conversation with his wife or Monsieur Tiegermann, he listened to one child after another graduate from squeaks and squeals to something resembling music under his expert tutelage. His wife was rangy and dark-haired, her long thin arms and legs giving an impression of Olive Oyl in the popular *Popeye* cartoons of the time. Although her supple fingers coaxed magical music from the piano, her voice was the least musical voice I have ever heard. Nonetheless, she was a kind woman, a talented teacher, and a star at the Conservatoire.

Every year, the Tiegermann Conservatoire gave a recital in Cairo's concert hall that showcased their most promising pupils. It was taken very seriously, reported in the local newspapers, and attended by *le tout* Cairo as well as the parents and relatives of the performers. The year before Suez, I was to perform the violin solo, a movement from the *Haydn Violin Concerto #2 in G Major*, in a frothy white organdy dress with white organdy wisteria flowers cascading down the back of the skirt from the waist to the floor. I loved the dress but desperately hated the idea of performing. The Menasces and my parents insisted. The dreaded day arrived, and I found myself in the gorgeous dress, clammy and miserable, clutching my violin and towering over my teacher, who was to accompany me on the piano. I peered through the curtains at the audience as the star pianist completed his perfect performance to thunderous applause, and saw my parents' anxious faces as they sat in the front row, holding hands.

"I can't do this," I told my teacher in a panic. "Look at my hand. It has swollen to double its size!"

He glanced at my grossly deformed hand without concern.

"They are waiting," he said, turned on his heel, and walked briskly to the piano. I followed like a lamb to the slaughter and remember nothing of the performance. As I stood outside, radiant with relief, receiving the congratulations of my teacher and parents, someone said, "Look at your hand!" I looked down anxiously and saw that the swelling had completely disappeared.

"You see!" said my teacher, a man of few words.

The year of Suez, with Madame Menasce's help my mother had begun to study for the teaching diplomas given by the Royal Academy of Music in London. She hoped to be able to take the exam and to teach piano if we ran into financial difficulties once we had left Egypt.

As I wallowed in my lonely melancholy, I tried to recognize that my response was a very superficial one. I tried to be grateful that we were all alive, that we were still comfortably living in our own house, that nothing had separated us and we were all still together, and that our lives no longer seemed to be in immediate danger. I knew that my personal preoccupations couldn't possibly matter in the larger scheme of things. But I wanted them to matter. Lost in the narcissism and intense self-involvement of youth, drowning in melancholy and loneliness, buffeted by an intensity of feelings that had no place to go, I wanted, with a passion close to despair, to know that out there beyond the gates, beyond the alien waters of the Nile, beyond the impossibly large moon that mocked my desires, there would be fun and laughter, flirtations and aspirations. I dreamed of a husband and children. I dreamed of engagement with the challenges of adulthood. I dreamed of walking free.

A real life.

❧ ❧ ❧

*With Judy in Piazza San Marco, Venice, Italy, summer of 1960*

# Beyond Suez

*We arrived* in London in September of 1957, early intimations of fall sending a brisk wind to whip color into our exhausted faces. We had barely set down our luggage and were looking around wearily in the service flat at St. James's Court when the doorbell rang. Judy and Derrick burst in. There were tears and laughter and hugs galore, my parents beaming with delight, my head ringing with travel exhaustion and excitement.

"Now," said Judy, "unpack a cocktail dress right away. We have a party invitation for tonight."

"A party?" I said in wonder, as though it were a word in a foreign language. She fanned out a handful of invitations. "These are for you," she said. "I told them you had just arrived from Egypt and everyone said, you must bring your cousin along."

I sat down slowly, looking at the beautifully engraved invitations in my hand. Was this London, or was it heaven? Needless to say, I managed to pull out a dress in record time and I ventured tentatively into the London social whirl with my stalwart cousins at hand to push me through my awkwardness into the fun I had dreamed about: cheese and wine parties, elegant balls, cocktail parties, birthday parties, visits to Glyndebourne with a champagne and smoked salmon picnic. Everywhere they went, I was included and welcomed. I had tumbled out of an empty, forlorn world into a marvelous unreality glittering with possibility, and I was determined to make the most of it.

Meanwhile, my mother set up appointments for us to visit the two women's colleges of London University. Although I longed for Cambridge or Oxford, my parents would not countenance either, having heard abundant tales from brothers and cousins of escapades over the college walls in the dead of night and other extracurricular activities available to the undergraduates of those venerable institutions. London, therefore, was the compromise. They had originally hoped to bypass university completely for me, but the Suez crisis had taken care of that.

We started with Bedford College, an imposing structure that somehow failed to appeal to me. It was the larger and better known of the two. Just as well that my heart was not set on it. A stern-faced individual made it uncompromisingly clear that Suez crisis or not, I would have to take entrance exams for the following year. There would be no possibility of making an exception and taking me right away.

I had already lost a year. I could not accept losing another.

We sighed and repaired to Westfield, where my childhood friend, Vivette Ancona, had already been ensconced for a year, a year painful with the terror of silence from home and the need to stretch her meager finances way beyond what they had been planned to cover, since she had little or no communication from her family in Egypt and no sense of how long that money might have to last.

Miss Chesney, the principal, was gaunt and gray-haired, but her manner was pleasant and she was genuinely interested in hearing about our problems, asking penetrating questions about my qualifications and interests. However, she made it clear that the English department was filled to capacity, and that she had no room in which to lodge me, nor even could another desk and chair be squeezed into the classrooms. Classes had already begun, and I would have to take the entrance exams and start the following year, if I passed. My mother got up dispiritedly as my heart sank slowly into my shoes.

"That's that, then," she said, gathering her coat and her bag. "You'll have to go to a domestic science course for a year." I watched the formidable Miss Chesney blanche and recover.

"Let me have a word with Professor Jenkins," she said. "I'll call you tomorrow."

Surprised, we shook her hand and left.

Next day she called. She had spoken to Miss Horobin, my Roedean headmistress, who had said many good things, so she was proposing a compromise. She truly had no lodging left in the college, but if I could find somewhere to live, she and Professor Jenkins had agreed that these were extraordinary circumstances that required extraordinary solutions. He would find a way to add another chair where necessary, and I could live outside the college, attend my first year, and take my exams at the end of it with the other students. If I passed with honors, I could move into the second year with my peers. If not, I would have to repeat the first year. Either way, I was in.

My relief was so enormous that I could barely croak out my thanks. My mother was still wondering if a domestic science course might not be the answer, but I managed to convince her that enough kind people had put themselves out that it would be incredibly ungracious to refuse. It had already been settled that Susan and Pen (Ivy Davy), a soft-spoken white-haired widow who had been my sister's governess in Cairo for a few years and whom we had all grown to love dearly, would be living in a "maisonette" my parents had rented on Spanish Place, a small street parallel to Marylebone High Street, close to Baker Street and radiating out from Manchester Square. It would be easy for me to travel to and from Hampstead to go to classes.

So we accepted, and then the panic set in. How would I be able to fit in? I had always felt like an outsider at Roedean, and now I would be carrying my strange Suez year on my shoulders like a large and unwieldy burden. I would be "different" again. But I kept my nerves to myself and prepared to register with the bursar at Westfield next day and start my classes right away.

The bursar was a short, compact woman with a brisk manner, wiry hair, and a serious expression. She gave me papers to fill out, handed me my undergraduate gown, and led me down the gardens, her gown belling out behind her in the stiff wind as she hurried from Kidderpore Avenue where the main college building stood, to Finchley Road where a small house was divided into lodgings for the students with a classroom on the ground floor. A class was in progress in Old English. She opened the door, and instantly I felt twenty assorted pairs of eyes fasten on me. I winced and made my way into the room.

The lecturer, a tall pale woman with faded red hair, tired blue eyes, a round face, and a placid expression, motioned to the only unoccupied chair and went on talking to the class. Then she announced that since this was the first Old English class of a new year, we should go around the room, introducing ourselves and telling the class what schools we had attended. One after another, voices spoke out, naming this village school, that grammar school, not one public school in the room. At last it was my turn, and mortified beyond belief, I muttered the name of one of the most famous public schools in England. Perhaps it was my fragile imagination, but I kept my eyes down, convinced that I heard sniggers. The class passed painfully for me. The lecturer left the room, her black gown billowing in her wake, and we made for the door to walk up to the main building for lunch. Miserable, certain I was already a pariah, I was unprepared for the swift enthusiastic invitation from two students who hurried to walk on either side of me. Each was eager to invite me to come to her room for coffee after lunch.

Nan Kerr was the first, and Gill (Wertz) Nolan (who later became the writer Andrea Newman) was the second. Together with their roommates, Lorna and Dorothy, they became the inner nucleus of students whose friendship delighted and educated me. I discovered to my amazement that far from the boarding school desire to reduce everyone to the same common denominator, college students welcomed difference, eager to expand their horizons and learn about the world, and through others, to come to know themselves.

✢ ✤ ✢

Number 4, Spanish Place, to which I returned every night, belonged to Pearl Harper and her elderly mother, whose reedy voice was often to be heard calling for her daughter, but who never emerged from her room. Miss Harper was a worn-looking woman, stringy and gray, her salt-and-pepper hair rolled up into a tight bun at the back of her neck. She wore neat clothing in sober colors and a permanently anxious expression. She and her mother occupied the first floor of their roomy Edwardian house, one of several gracious row houses strung side by side along the short quiet street off Manchester Square, its generous windows looking right into the windows of the Wallace Collection across the narrow street. Miss Harper had rented out the basement apartment of the house to an elderly retired colonel and his wife who had lived there for many years, and she would refer complacently to "the colonel" with a certain pride, although he and his wife eluded our curiosity and remained invisible for the length of our lease. The top three floors of the house she had agreed to rent to my parents, for Jeff, Susan, and myself to occupy with Pen.

The political situation having settled into an uneasy calm, my parents planned to return to Cairo to help relocate Granny Mosseri and Auntie Helen, and to salvage whatever they could of our life and possessions there. Pen and I shared responsibility for the budget, the cooking, and the care of nine-year-old Susan, who was to attend Kensington High School that first year, and of Jeff, then fourteen, when he came home for the holidays from Gresham's, his boarding school in Norfolk. Pen worked part-time as a saleslady at Dickens & Jones and became our "housemother" once she collected Susan from the nearby school every afternoon and walked her home.

The "maisonette" was up two narrow carpeted flights of stairs, past the Harpers' living quarters, and past a half-floor landing that housed a small bathroom that the Harpers used. Our first floor, probably the parlor floor, was dominated by a fairly large living room with floor-to-ceiling windows festooned with heavy, musty-smelling, mustard-colored curtains. My parents bought two single beds and turned this room into Susan's and my bedroom. There was also a small bedroom that was Pen's own private domain. Up another twisty flight of stairs was the bedroom my parents used when they were in London, a small dining room and kitchen, and a big bathroom with a generous bathtub where I spent many blissful hours of privacy, warming up from the pervasive London chill after the trek home from Westfield, soaking in the fragrant water, and peering anxiously into the tiny mirror over the washbasin to achieve the metamorphosis from exhausted and earnest student into the social butterfly that my cousins and our mutual evening social engagements demanded and that my starved soul had so long been denied.

The steep and narrow stairs continued up and led to the highlight of the place, a large mock-Tudor room, a sort of loft with no door, with dark paneling, a sloping beamed ceiling, and coats of arms in polished wood and bright colors accenting the impression of a bizarre Tudor graft onto a dignified Edwardian town house. We all fell in love with that room with its particular atmosphere and blatantly neo décor, and it naturally fell to Jeff, as his bedroom, whenever he was home. When he was away at school, it served as a second living room, and one I often curled up in to read uninterrupted, and where every so often Vivette and I held cheese and wine parties or coffee parties to repay some of the kind hospitality that was being extended to us by our London friends.

Things settled into a comfortable rhythm. We received news that my parents had completed the sale of the big house to the Russians and had moved into a smaller apartment in Cairo having found another apartment for Auntie Helen and Granny to move to when the time came to leave the house. My mother's dream of a home of her own had come about at last, but it came studded with pain and loss, fear and separation, and it held none of the happiness and fulfillment she had hoped for. She and my father perched there uneasily, readying themselves for further flight, anxious to be with their children, reluctant to leave my weary grandmother and valiant aunt, trying to fill their lives with social evenings with the few friends who remained, and trying to persuade Granny Mosseri to leave Egypt with them.

Winter came and went. Spring arrived and filled Manchester Square with golden daffodils, and along with the birds and the buds, the Easter vacation loosened my brother, my sister, and I from our moorings and wafted us to Paris, where so many of my mother's family had assembled. Passover was imminent. We were housed, with Pen, at the Windsor Hotel at the top of the Rue Saint Honoré, near the Arc de Triomphe, and we all trooped off to my grandmother's flat in Neuilly for every meal.

A striped silk sectional couch encircled the walls on two sides of my grandparents' living room in Neuilly, and heavy deep-yellow curtains framed large windows that caught every glimmer of the parsimonious Paris sunlight. Grandpa sat in a moss-green velvet armchair to one side of the couch, gazing silently at the flutter and chatter of the bevy of daughters and grand-daughters milling around my grandmother, laughing and teasing each other, some sitting on the couch, some venturing into the kitchen to see how the meal was coming along—under the expert stewardship of my grandparents' cook and their butler/chauffeur, Minna and Walter—some on the phone, others arriving in a flurry of exclamations, kisses, and conversation. Exiled from his comfortable villa in Alexandria, already in the grip of the arteriosclerosis that was to take his life, he could not remember all our names. "Girl, girl," he would say, "which one is your mother?" And then he would nod approvingly at the answer and resume his musing observation of the traffic around his chair. He seemed in a world apart, lost in thought, but suddenly he called to Granny. She came to his side instantly, impatiently questioning the interruption of so much activity. He smiled at her and said distinctly in English, "Rosa, all your daughters are beautiful. All your granddaughters are beautiful. But you are the most beautiful of them all." This was no magic mirror on the wall speaking. Even the skepticism of youth did not prevent me from recognizing it as the voice of love.

For Passover, the Seder table stretched the length of their dining and living rooms combined, and Jeff, Susan, and I settled ourselves at one end, acutely conscious of our absent parents so far away and in such an uncertain political climate. Our grandparents, uncles, aunts, and cousins tried hard to make us forget our melancholy, but even though so many of the traditional rituals and customs were the same as the ones we had grown up with, many were not. We had always celebrated Passover in Cairo, with my father's family. As we neared the end of the *Birkat Ha Mazon*, the grace after meals, Granny smiled and said, "I know that the Mosseris always sing at the end. Let's sing their songs."

So Jeff, Susan, and I led the gathering in song, but the lovely melodies only stirred our sadness. As we came to the last song, "*Had Gadya*" ("One Only Kid"), a cumulative round with a succession of verses that all end with the same rhythmic chorus, two of our uncles, their eyes on our tearful faces, got up from the table and responding to the rousing nature of the song, pronounced that they would now dance the "*Had Gadya* Rock." Uncle Cesar, tall and angular, and Uncle Jacques, round-faced and stocky, solemnly led a growing crowd of uncles and cousins around the room as we sang out with gusto between bouts of uncontrollable laughter, ending the evening on a cheerful note and consigning the *Had Gadya* Rock to family legend.

✦ ✦ ✦

My first year at Westfield flowed past like a fast-moving river of new experiences and challenges, foaming around any boulders in its headlong rush, burbling and sparkling its way through the days and the nights. Of the tiny coterie of American students spending their junior year at Westfield, Firth Haring was the one most often to be found having coffee with Nan and Lorna, her slow musical speech, gorgeous green eyes, smooth cap of dark hair, and exotic accent charming us all. America was as distant as Mars to us, and it was fun and illuminating to have a Martian in our midst.

As the first year drew to its close, the results of the final examinations entitled me to move ahead into a second college year with my friends, and a room was found for me on campus— a tiny rectangle of a room, with a narrow bed, a window at one end, and a door at the other. There was a small desk and chair, a sliver of closet beside the door, and a strange wooden cupboard with a marble slab inside that served as pantry/refrigerator for food supplies. A gas fire was carved out of the wall, with a meter for shillings and one lone gas ring. We could heat our "milky coffee" or make toast. One or other of us often ran down to Finchley Road in the early morning mist to buy fresh sweet rolls from the local bakery rather than confront the clatter and conversation of the communal breakfast in the dining hall.

After long and arduous effort, my parents had managed to obtain exit visas that allowed for a return to Egypt, and they were able to join us in Europe for the summer months. With Granny Mosseri's situation unresolved, they planned a return to Cairo one more time. As summer sharpened into fall, my mother and I set about equipping my room on campus for my second year. We found a remnant of misty-blue cotton twill in a fabric store and had curtains made for the tall narrow window, together with a divan cover and black and red cushions for the bed. We scoured the local Woolworth store and found a small rug with a bold geometric design in black and red, and a black art deco ceramic vase for one or two flowers. A coffee set, glasses, and stainless-steel cutlery later, I was all furnished and glowed like a queen. My kingdom may have been small, but it was mine, and the dreams it contained were limitless.

My parents returned again to Egypt. The next time they left Cairo, it would be forever. As she had so ardently desired, Granny Mosseri never moved out of the house her husband had built for her. She died in 1958 at the age of eighty-three, before the Russians took possession.

As the second year at Westfield progressed, Nan, Lorna, and I combined culinary forces and became adept at concocting ambitious Sunday dinners, taking turns to prepare a civilized evening for ourselves, sometimes including a few chosen friends: curried chicken spiced with pineapple served with saffron rice; spaghetti in a rich thick Bolognese sauce fragrant with generous dashes of oregano, thyme, marjoram, and basil; beef stew simmered for hours on our gas ring, spiked with a dash of red wine, mustard, and vegetables; and sometimes Lorna's mother's special Parkin cake, lovingly and parsimoniously sliced to last as long as possible. My small room shared a wall with the large room my two friends inhabited, and when my narrow quarters closed in and threatened to crush me I was always able to escape next door for breakfast, coffee, or consultation on a shared study project. I had the best of both worlds: privacy and companionship. Nan and I were both "reading" English, as was Firth; Lorna was "reading" history with an eye to a future in the civil service; and Evelyn was immersed in modern languages and European literature.

My parents had maintained their rental of Number 4, Spanish Place, and I could go there on weekends, although we mainly used the maisonette during vacations, since Susan had started attending Ridgeway, a boarding school close to London. My evening dresses brought from Egypt—an exquisite pale-yellow lace dress, a flowing red silk chiffon, and a Grecian gown of delicate white chiffon with its wide blue satin beaded sash and matching shoes and bag—stayed in the cupboard in the maisonette on Spanish Place, and I ferried them to and from college as the occasion to wear them arose.

We were allowed a limited number of late passes, and at ten o'clock every night, the steps to the main building on Kidderpore Avenue flowered with entwined couples, kissing and sighing, scurrying up the steps with fevered parting glances as the hour implacably arrived, and the porter glared down at his charges from his lodge near the door. Cinderella had to leave the ball or deal with the consequences.

I was going to have friends. I was going to be happy. I was going to study the works of famous writers and write papers about them. There would be the black undergraduate robes and stimulating intellectual fervor of Westfield by day, and the glamour of swirling color and music, admiring swains and idle chatter in the evenings.

I was more than happy. I was ecstatic.

✤ ✤ ✤

It was probably inevitable that I would fall in love. As the second year at Westfield progressed, the energy and persistence of certain young men began to distinguish them for me from the many who attended the same parties as my cousins and I did. There were times when I welcomed having to invoke the strict college curfew. As the year sped along, one man, a law student at Cambridge and an acquaintance of my cousin, Derrick, became a frequent and welcome element in my life.

All around me, my college friends were affirming and forming intense relationships, planning lives that held the promise of marriage, or tasting avidly at various relationships like starving souls at a banquet. I listened and wondered. I shared their hopes, their disappointments, and their plans, and felt the romantic and erotic edge that hung everywhere in the air. Nan's charming tall fiancé, Martin, came down from Cambridge to visit, his hair a wiry halo around a strong, intense face. Nan cooked for him, and after dinner we sat in hers and Lorna's room while he played Elizabethan love songs on his guitar and sang in a rich young voice. I thought they were the most romantic couple I had ever seen. Gill and Terry married in secret and took a room outside college, living on love and very little else, happy as larks. We used to save the tins of pork and beans that graced the Sunday evening dinner trays to help them eke out their budget. Evelyn purred and flashed her distinctive green eyes, playing kitten games with anyone who would play, tossing her blonde mane, her jeans tight as a second skin. She never skimped on details about her latest sexual escapades. Dorothy covered for Gill, who was not allowed to be married and living off campus, pretending she was still single, still living in college, still sharing a room with Dorothy. It was rumored that two of the students who had shared a room their first year and who tended to keep very much to themselves, now actually shared a bed. In 1960 this was still a tale told in whispers.

Friendships formed and feelings were shared that were intense and true. Within the safe boundaries of the college experience, the intimacy of late studies shared in the hush of the library, of elaborate Sunday dinners cooked inventively on one sputtering gas ring, of confidences given and received, of works of philosophy and literature excavated for their secrets, we were able to explore the world beyond our childhoods by peeking into the worlds and values of others around us. We learned much about life and more about ourselves.

And it was within this environment that I sank willingly and wonderingly into love. The young man was intellectual and intelligent, one of the few who loved poetry as I did. He was a law student because he needed to earn a living, but his heart was in literature and he envied me my studies. He wrote long, fascinating letters every day that arrived unfailingly in the afternoon mail, for we were graced with three mail deliveries a day at that time. I could mail a letter to someone in another part of London in the morning and receive a response in the afternoon. At first we concentrated on discussions of philosophy and the literature I was writing papers about, but soon his letters took on another tone, and as we began to go out more and more regularly to dinner, to the theater, meeting at parties and gatherings more and more frequently and usually with intent, I began to wait impatiently for the return of my parents so that I might share this wonderful development with them and move toward the engagement that seemed inevitable.

Unfortunately, all did not go well. When they came, at last, it was to eye with distress and suspicion a relationship that had wandered far afield from the Middle Eastern Jewish background they claimed and understood. Poland and the *shtetl* were not yet in their vocabulary. A long and intensely painful struggle ensued, my father convinced that he was fighting to save my future, and I, deeply committed to a relationship with a person whose qualities seemed self-evident to me and who was clearly doing everything in his power to win my parents' respect. At first disbelieving, I was torn to shreds by my father's reaction.

My family and I were tightly woven together into the rich tapestry of our shared heritage, of love, of memories, of traditions maintained and dangers overcome. I understood enough about myself, and the young man cared enough about me to realize the perilous situation we were in. Clearly, to unravel the ties that bound me to my parents and my family might very well unravel me. The only recourse we felt we had was to agree to separation in the hope that our steadfastness would weaken my parents' resolve. It was inconceivable to me not to have their support in my marriage. It was equally inconceivable to me to give up the love I had found. Our communication went underground. My parents and I became locked into a battle of wills that lasted two years and that almost broke my heart and spirit.

Barely recovered from my week of intensive nine-hour-a-day final examinations at Westfield, worn to a frazzle from the stress of the intense cluster of lengthy examinations and the emotional turmoil of my conflict with my parents—but determined to show my good will and win theirs—I had agreed to join them in Italy for a vacation. My cousin Judy came with us. My parents worked hard at distracting me, alternately gentle and impatient with my indifference. In Forte dei Marmi, I stood in the emerald sea for hours, buffeted by gentle waves and losing myself in sadness. We bought shoes in Rome. We visited Juliet's balcony in Verona. We went to the opera every night. Judy was enjoying herself. We were staying in the same hotel as the opera *diva* Giulietta Simionata, and for Judy, an aspiring operatic singer herself, the flustered state of excitement that flooded her each time the *diva* appeared reached the level of a rock-star sighting. As Simionata prepared to leave the hotel for that night's performance, Judy found the courage to step up, shake her hand, and express her admiration. That moment and the beautiful shoes she bought in Rome invested the vacation with a golden glow that put a spring in her step and a sparkle in her eye all summer.

For me, the summer was different. Nothing seemed to matter. I ate, I slept, I followed where they led. I was buried too deep in my melancholy and nothing came close to reaching my emotional self.

My father had managed to obtain tickets for a performance of *Aida* in the Roman arena at Verona. The extraordinary experience managed to break through the bubble of my indifference to take its place as one of the most memorable theatrical experiences of my life. I will never forget night falling as we sat in the vast arena among multitudes. Above us, stars of a summer sky pierced through the velvet canopy of night, lights flickered in the hands of the audience massed in hushed reverence, and the stately music of the march swelled all around us as villagers and animals wound their way down a series of hairpin turns, seemingly appearing without end at the top of the arena and continuing to fill one third of the arena above the stage, and the entire stage itself. It was stunning.

Eventually, welcome word reached me that I would graduate with a BA Hons. Degree from London University and my certificate would be conferred upon me the following May in a ceremony at the Royal Festival Hall, by Elizabeth, the Queen Mother.

That didn't seem to mean too much, either.

For the next months, I followed my displaced parents from London to Paris to Rome and Geneva, staying in small hotels or tiny service flats as they explored options and weighed possibilities. They needed to settle somewhere, and the decision was difficult, even overwhelming. The driving factors were to reestablish scattered family connections where possible, and to explore my father's ability to start a financial business, and my parents agonized long into the night, night after night, as new possibilities presented themselves. Finally they settled on Geneva, Switzerland, where my father's sister, Auntie Mary, was looking into buying a house, and where Uncle Teddy and Granny Smouha were also planning to live. Business possibilities began to surface, and they found an apartment and made arrangements for some of the furniture they had been able to salvage to make its way to their new home.

My father never allowed his discouragement to surface. It ate at his health but left his spirit undamaged. His family had owned and managed the largest private investment bank in Egypt. In five generations the Mosseri family had built a considerable fortune, had achieved dizzying heights of ease and recognition, and had become woven into the financial, social, and political fabric of the country that now disenfranchised him and claimed all that was his. My father internalized the wrenching dispossession and hid the frayed ends of the rupture from view as he set about reinventing himself and wresting a future for his wife and children. He had done it before as a very young man when fate had claimed the lives of his brother and father, and he would rise to this new challenge even as he faced middle age. My mother, too, plunged into the intricacies of challenge and displacement without dwelling on her losses. She looked to the future with optimism and energy. As long as we were all safe, she could learn what she needed, and she could and did make do with what she had. Tangled and enmeshed in their own challenges and preoccupations, my parents were unwilling to recognize the extent of my distress. They dealt with my pain in the only way they could: by attempting to ignore its existence as they struggled to build a new life for all of us.

*Upper Egypt, 1990: Present, past, and distant past*

# A Silver Dawn

*Many months* later in the fall of 1961, listless and despairing, I found myself once again in Paris. My cousin Rosemary, seeing the overwhelming level of my distress and pain, convinced me to accompany her to visit a clairvoyant in the suburb of Asnieres. This woman, Rosemary told me, had enabled friends of hers to retrieve jewelry they had been convinced was lost or stolen. She actually told them where it had slipped behind drawers or seat cushions of furniture and in apartments she had never seen.

"Ask her your questions," she said. "Perhaps she can relieve your mind and help you to find the answers."

I did not believe for a minute that this was possible. I harbored a healthy skepticism on the subject of fortune tellers and their so-called abilities, but I could feel the direction of my life slipping away from me. Perhaps this woman could offer me some hope. I went along.

Rosemary drove, and I sat beside her in her car, in grim silence. We arrived at a nondescript middle-class apartment building in a gray and dingy neighborhood, and rode up in a creaky old elevator. We were ushered into a room stuffed with Victoriana, a heavy bead curtain separating the waiting room from the room where the clairvoyant presumably plied her trade. My heart sank. It all looked like such a cliché. What was I doing in such a place? A short, rotund woman with bobbing gray sausage-curls and a loose patterned dress pulled aside the curtain and beckoned me inside. I looked beseechingly at my cousin, eager to drop the whole thing, but she urged me on. The woman stepped ahead of me and sat down at a table that held a large crystal ball. In contrast to the waiting room, this room was bare of decoration. As I walked toward the chair, she lifted her hands as if to shield her face, and said, "Ah no! You are deeply troubled. I can feel the pain. You walk on disturbed ground over oars that are crossed on your path and cause you to stumble. You cannot see that right ahead of you, the path clears. You must not be so distressed."

Then she looked at me and asked, "Did you lose a grandmother recently?"

Grandpa Smouha had died recently, so I said tentatively, "My grandfather died in September. But I don't want to hear anything about spirits. I came to ask a question."

She smiled and ignored me.

"I asked about a grandmother," she said gently. "You should know that your grandmother loved you very much. She is close to you and watches over you. She will arrange everything."

I sat down, uncomfortable, and more than ever convinced that I was going to put myself in the hands of a charlatan. She took my hand and studied the palm for a while. I asked impatiently, "I just want to know if I already know the man I will marry, and whether my parents will attend the wedding?"

"Oh, yes!" she said. "You know him. It will be a happy occasion. It will happen within six months. All your family will be there."

I was incredulous.

"He has family in Paris?" she asked.

"No," I said. "As far as I know, no family in Paris."

But she went on firmly, "Maybe he has family you do not know. He will be visiting family in Paris in March."

Then she turned my hand over and asked, "Does he have plans to work overseas?"

"I don't think so," I said, puzzled, "although he does have a brother in America."

"I see him working in a tall building, in an office surrounded entirely by glass, across the ocean. You will cross the ocean," she said.

"We plan to live in London," I muttered.

She went on as if I had not spoken. "I see the letter *a*. Is the letter *a* significant in his name?"

"There is no letter *a* in either his first name or his surname," I said, bewildered by her insistence.

She went on to tell me that I had strong but undeveloped psychic abilities, and that as long as I trusted my intuition I would never go wrong. She insisted that much happiness and fulfillment lay ahead, although she knew I did not yet believe it.

"Is he writing a book?" she asked suddenly, after she had sat in silence for a time studying the lines in my hand. I wondered why she asked, but told her that he was not.

"Well, I think he will," she insisted. "I see a strong image of a book, with great streams of money falling thickly from its pages." She turned my hand over and closed it, looking at the lines below my little finger, and declared that I would have three children. "I hope to have four," I said defiantly. She did not argue.

Drawn into the game in spite of myself, I asked her whether I, myself, would have a career. She paused, twisted my hand this way and that, rubbed it softly, then said, "I see you on a platform giving a lecture to a hall packed with people."

*Not a chance!* I thought. I hated any sort of public appearance, and I knew with certainty that I would never do anything that might involve public speaking.

*Joyce and Guido Mosseri with their children*

I had already told her that I wanted to hear nothing about any deaths or tragedies, so sensing my utter skepticism about the entire session, she smiled pleasantly, shook my hand, and ushered me out of another door across from the bead curtain.

Rosemary was waiting. "What did she tell you?" she asked eagerly.

"The usual rubbish," I said crossly. "She told me I would marry a tall, dark, handsome man within six months and live happily ever after." And I stalked out. We talked of other things on the way home.

I never saw the lady from Asnieres again, and I put her nonsense out of my mind.

⚜ ⚜ ⚜

*Jean's wedding day*

# THE END OF THE BEGINNING

*How can* I possibly capture in words the magic afoot forty years ago, on those crisp spring days, Easter weekend in Geneva, Switzerland, 1962: days that in their clarity and simplicity changed the course of my life and propelled me, ecstatic and disbelieving, into the next chapter of my life?

As the months went by in Geneva, I filled my days with typing lessons, wrote long letters to my absent friends, and taught English to business executives who were about to take a trip to America. I corresponded with Jean Leroy in London, tried my hand at some short stories, wrote mournful poems of love and loss, and worked on the translation of some published French mysteries for a writer friend of Uncle Teddy's. I took afternoon tea in a cafe in the Old Town of Geneva regularly with my friend, Marlene, and we gossiped about everything and nothing. I found a lending library that specialized in English books and I haunted its cramped quarters and crowded shelves, once more finding escape and solace in other lives, fictional and factual, reading my way through every book they had. I attended family dinners in a stupor, rallied to celebrate Brian's engagement and wedding to Hana Btesh. More months drifted by in an emotional wilderness as I tried again and again to convince my parents of the rightness of my life choice, the reality of it fading and blurring at the edges as time marched on.

✣ ✣ ✣

One day, a young man from America came to lunch at my parents' apartment with an elderly relative who was involved in a business deal with my father. Locked uncomfortably into my rebellion, I was convinced that this was yet another attempt to deter me from my chosen path, so I spoke hardly a word and barely raised my eyes from my plate. Nonetheless, more out of politeness than anything else, the young man asked me out. I refused. I knew who he was. He was my elementary school classmate Bobby Naggar's older brother, Serge.

After lunch, I went to the bookshelf in my bedroom and took down one of my favorite books, Rudyard Kipling's *Just So Stories*. Inside was the following inscription in my mother's hand: *Jean Mosseri, from Serge & Albert Naggar. December 5th, 1946.* My ninth birthday party. I looked at the inscription and hesitated. Then I took it into the living room and put it into the young man's hand. Everyone looked surprised.

We did not go out together that day. Jeff is the one who showed Serge around Geneva. Still on my high horse, but slowing from a gallop to a very slow meander, I claimed a pressing engagement. For tea. With Marlene. But through a subsequent series of events we did go out together a couple of times before Serge returned to Paris. A few days later our whole family congregated in Paris for the bar mitzvah on April eleventh of Auntie Edna and Uncle Jacques's younger son, Robin. Jeff called Serge to schedule the squash game they had planned in Geneva.

"Can I talk to your sister?" asked Serge.

They never did play that game of squash.

Serge and I went to the theater. We went out to tea in the *Quartier Latin* with Judy and Derrick, also in Paris for the

*Serge*

family event, and with Serge's high school friend, Michel Mendes France. We went dancing. We went to breakfast at *Le Drugstore*, which had just opened on the Champs Elysees, with Jeff and Susan in attendance. My pearl necklace broke, scattering pearls everywhere and sending us all ignominiously to the floor, weak with laughter, to search them out as they rolled this way and that. I returned to Geneva, my emotions in turmoil, confused, exhilarated, guilty, afraid, disbelieving, but most of all, anxious to hear from him again. Serge had been scheduled to return to America, but miraculously, he was asked by IBM to stay and give some more talks in Europe. It was Easter weekend and in Europe, everything closes down for three days. He decided to accompany his parents, who were stopping over in Geneva on their way to their annual health cure in Abano, Italy, and he called me as soon as he arrived in Geneva. The next three days defined the trajectory of our future.

We wandered the old town and the crowded, traffic-laden banks of the Rhone all day. We stopped at various sunlit cafés bursting with voluble tourists, we balanced on small metal chairs, leaned toward each other across small round tables, ordering two lemonades wherever we stopped. The lemonades stood in the sun, the ice melting, as did the distance between us, which seemed to merge into something fragile, new, yet wrapped in an aura of comfort. It was the week of Passover, and we left our lemonades untouched time and again as we continued our ramblings, leaning companionably side-by-side over the bridge, watching the young green waters of the Rhone churning and swirling below, sitting on a bench and gazing at the distant snow-covered peak of Mont Blanc, threading our way through throngs of vacationing strangers as we saw and heard only each other. We talked and talked. What did we talk about? I don't remember, but I will never forget the growing feeling of familiarity mixed with an edge of anticipation as we wandered without a goal or destination, and yet, without clear knowledge or intent, together discovered a path to the future.

That night we went dancing. We sat holding hands on a moonlit bench in the old city. We kissed in the car, parked outside 47 Route de Florissant, and I froze with fear that neighbors would come by and report my resplendent private moment to the world.

Next day my mother supervised the cooking of a splendid picnic. It was packed into a basket with napkins and fruit, and she waved good-bye from the terrace as the two of us drove out of town to spend the day at the Château de Gruyère. The Swiss countryside, dotted with its impossibly neat villages and steepled churches, unfolded around us as we drove between mountains along stretches of flat fields filled with the early flowers of a beautiful spring day. We stopped in a meadow and had our picnic of delicious meat omelets, fruit, bread, and cheese. A pleasantly cool breeze hovered over us. The sun shone and we could hear cars occasionally swooshing past on the highway, while around us insects buzzed and hummed. We lay on the grass, looking up at the clear blue sky. We kissed, and the warmth and stirring wonder of that sun-drenched moment is with me still. We knew without words that we were deeply, passionately in love, and we knew without words that we would spend the rest of our lives together.

We climbed the worn stone steps in the tower of the Château de Gruyère in a turmoil of senses and delight. The day was idyllic, the sun shone, birds sang, a light breeze hovered, we stopped to kiss and look out of a window, climbed some more steps, held onto each other's hands. We could have been anywhere. We saw no one, heard no one but each other. It was our day, and it took the two distinct strands of our separate lives and wove them tightly into the beginnings of the tapestry of days and years that would follow.

Back in Geneva, we shared our news and our happiness with our parents, who were simultaneously stunned at the speed with which all this was happening and delighted by the engagement. In a daze of happiness, I made plans to leave for New York in ten days with my mother, but something else needed to be done. First, I needed to go to London.

Serge was heading for London anyway for a couple of days of meetings before returning to New York. Much to my parents' distress, I insisted on going with him to tell the young man in London face-to-face that the drift and slide that had recently suffused our relationship had swept it to its end. I phoned him and made an appointment to meet him in a coffee shop we both knew. My parents decided to accompany us to London to drop in on Jeff at Cambridge and to see Serge off to New York a couple of days later.

In a small, dark coffee shop off Baker Street the day I arrived, we sat facing each other in sorrow as an indifferent waitress with tired eyes took our order. The coffees sat untouched on the table between us. I wept bitter tears as I told him that it was over. I wept as much for the pain I feared I was inflicting as for the loss of something I had thought invincible. Guilt also played a part in my distress, for despite my tears I was aware that churning beneath the sadness of this parting lay an enormous tidal wave of joy waiting to be released. I knew that he must have been as conscious as I was that things had been fading between us for some time, but I kept my new love to myself, assuring him nonetheless that my decision was not the result of parental pressure.

"If you ever need a friend," he said as he rose and prepared to leave, "you will always know where to find one."

My parents had arranged a dinner at Prunier, the celebrated London fish restaurant, and I began to allow happiness to engulf me as we sat and made plans for the weeks to come. My father was to wind up some business matters and to follow my mother and myself to New York as soon as possible. We planned to announce our engagement to our families and to the world a few weeks later, on May twentieth, Granny Smouha's birthday.

Serge met us at Idlewild Airport (now Kennedy) in his sleek silvery-blue Corvair, a wide smile never leaving his face, his arms filled with flowers. I would have followed him to the ends of the earth, but New York was all that was required, and New York welcomed me. I, who had never even wanted to visit America, flung myself without reserve into the new world offered to me. Our stay was brief and crammed with new experiences, new people, new places, a new way of life opening out. We set dates and made plans. Every morning before my parents were up, I ran down Central Park South from the Essex House, where we were staying, to meet Serge for breakfast at a coffee shop before he went to work. I discovered waffles, eggs-over-easy, pancakes and maple syrup. To my left, as I ran, Central Park was beginning to awaken from its deep winter sleep, fluttering a profusion of fresh green leaves against a blue Manhattan sky. It was hot and steamy in early May that year. I discovered the magnificent New York City department stores—Bergdorf, Bendel, Bonwit Teller, Ohrbach, Altman, and Macy's, many of them now defunct. I shopped for *trousseau* clothes with my parents. Serge took us to different restaurants every night for dinner. It was a magical time, spilling happiness and excitement like the scent of roses into every hour of every day.

Concerned that I might not be able to obtain a visa to return to the States with him after the wedding, Serge persuaded my parents that it would be expeditious to go ahead with a civil ceremony in New York, so that a claim for a green card for his wife could be set in motion. The day before we were due to return to Switzerland, June 1, 1962, we were married before a Justice of the Peace at City Hall. My mother, intent on adding a little fantasy and celebration to the proceedings, bought me a shocking pink hat at Henri Bendel, which I wore with a simple white linen suit. After the brief ceremony, she triumphantly produced a box of satiny white *dragees*, sugared almonds, traditional wedding fare, and we went to lunch with our two witnesses: Allan Goodridge, Serge's oldest friend from Paris, and Stanley Groggins, a kindly business friend of my father's who had offered to bring my father and our family to the States and stand guarantor for us during the Suez crisis days.

Next day, we left for Europe to prepare for our "real" wedding on July fifteenth.

✤ ✤ ✤

Our engagement progressed in a blur of intensity. I was married, and not married. It was a strange time. Serge remained in New York, working on getting visas for us both to return to the States together after the wedding. He was to arrive in Geneva a couple of days before the great day. In Paris, my Aunt Marjorie gave a glamorous party to celebrate my engagement. My thoughts and longings were elsewhere, winging their way across the Atlantic to my absent fiancé. My future parents-in-law gave a party in their magnificent apartment overlooking the Seine, on Quai de Passy (now Quai Kennedy). Family from both sides attended, the bright eyes, smiling faces, and festive dresses flowing around me in a symphony of sound and color as they admired my dress, my engagement ring, the lovely view from the terrace, exclaimed over the delicious food my mother-in-law had produced, laughing, congratulating, asking about my fiancé and our plans for the future.

✤ ✤ ✤

Finding myself the center of so much attention and activity, I had nonetheless rarely been so lonely. Before, my loneliness had focused on a longing for the unknown or the unattainable. Now I knew where I wanted to be, and with whom, and a feverish impatience built and intensified along with the flurry around me. Love letters arrived from New York and left for New York every day. Throwing thrift to the winds, we spoke on the phone as often as we dared, sharing every moment of this separation that was to bring us together forever.

Despite my impatience, being the focus of so much celebration was heady stuff. I remember arriving at Maison Carven, situated on the Rond Point des Champs Elysees in Paris, the Place de la Concorde visible in one direction and the Arc de Triomphe in the other. This was the headquarters of the Paris designer where my mother routinely bought her best clothes. News there of my pending wedding brought about a flurry of exclamations and excitement.

The clear summer light that poured in from the floor-to-ceiling windows of the salon was amplified in sparkling sconces and crystal chandeliers, delicate gold tracery everywhere, and small gilt chairs scattered on the thick cream carpeting. Sound disappeared into the space, sinking into the deep cushioning of the carpeting. There was a muted sense of excitement as supercilious models, exquisite and fragile, swept through the salon on demand in handsomely designed clothes, showing off the highlights of the Carven collection to clusters of elegant women, each woman's "dresser" (they were never called saleswomen) hovering discreetly in the background with advice and suggestions.

We greeted the receptionist, asked for Madame Nicole, and sat down. Madame Nicole, my mother's "dresser" for many years, appeared, followed by women with armloads of exquisite dresses. More dresses floated by on the models as they walked past, swinging their narrow hips and swiveling in front of us to show off the float of a skirt or a special fold or feature of the outfit they were wearing. We narrowed our choices down to one or two. Madame Nicole rushed off to find Mademoiselle Carven herself to consult with us in this important decision. A small, compact woman with a blunt face and light eyes, her skin a dull tan, doubtless from frequent trips to Cannes or St. Tropez, she wore no makeup and had her dark-blonde hair drawn back into a severe ponytail. She took the deference surrounding her as her due, shaking her head dismissively as the dresses we had selected were held against me, and imperiously waving in another dress we had not yet seen. They brought out a strapless black ball gown, a profusion of gossamer black organdy flowers scattered about a full skirt that billowed from a tiny waist. It took my breath away. My parents nodded, pleased. Mademoiselle Carven pronounced herself satisfied. They would make the dress in pure white, with a simple molded bodice, unadorned neckline, and short sleeves, and would revert it to the more sophisticated strapless style after the wedding. The hairpiece was to echo the dress with two white organdy flowers from which sprang yards and yards of delicate white silk tulle. It was a dream dress.

My first fitting brought the entire staff of Carven into the salon to add their exclamations of admiration to our pleasure as I stood in the center of the tall three-sided mirror, my parents on small gilt chairs to the side. Everyone fell silent as Madame Nicole and Mademoiselle Carven circled me solemnly, concentrated, pointing out the tiniest of details to the fitter, who knelt with pins in her mouth to adjust the tilt of the hem. I stared at myself in the mirror and saw a small girl twirling on a table in the nursery in Cairo, while my mother and Madame Marika patted and pulled at my clothes and circled me with the same intent and solemn expression, the same dedication to perfection.

The fittings proceeded rapidly. I was to leave for London for Pru's wedding and then hurry back to Geneva, where there were many details to attend to before my own wedding day. It was decided that Madame Nicole herself would bring the dress to Geneva, traveling with it on the train from Paris. She would help to dress me in it and would attend the wedding to deal with any last-minute crises or adjustments to it or to the headpiece that might be necessary.

✦ ✦ ✦

By July of 1962, Auntie Helen had moved into an apartment, and alone of all the family had stayed on in Cairo to tie up loose ends and take her departure only when her new living quarters in Rome were ready to receive her.

That summer of 1962, Auntie Helen tried in every way possible to obtain an exit visa to come to Geneva for my wedding. There was nothing doing. The Egyptian authorities were inflexible. She would not be able to leave unless she never came back, and she was not ready to do that. On my wedding morning, we spoke on the phone. In those days long-distance calls were major events, the timing had to be carefully planned, operators were consulted at both ends, static reigned supreme, and through it all, my aunt's emotion-laden voice and my sobs met somewhere in the ether between us. Sad though I was that she could not be with us, I knew she would be following every minute of the day that lay ahead of me. I carried her wishes and her love in my heart as I progressed through the wonderful day that marked my transition into a new life, a new state, and a new world across the ocean.

I often think of the clairvoyant from Asnieres. I thought of her after I had fallen in love with Serge and agreed to marry him and to cross the ocean to live in America. He had come to Paris that March on a mission for IBM World Trade and to visit his family. We were engaged in April and married in July, in Geneva, both families delighting in the marriage. In New York where he lived, he worked in a tall building in an office with glass walls. His grandmother and mine had been friends and distant cousins, and Marguerite Sapriel had often been one of the ladies seated at a bridge table when I entered Granny Mosseri's tea parties on a Saturday afternoon, a shy little girl in a party dress who did not have her mother's red hair. I had known Serge when we were children. His surname, Naggar, which became mine, has the letter *a* in it twice. I had very much wanted four children. We have three.

The book she mentioned puzzled me for a long time. I thought of her when it ceased to puzzle me, and I thought of her when I stood on a platform, knees atremble, facing a hall full of people, preparing to give the closing brunch speech at a writers' conference in Willamette, Oregon, in 1977. Two years later, the manuscript of Jean Auel's *The Clan of the Cave Bear* was in my hands, stirring my heart and my imagination and challenging me to live up to the promise it held.

The woman in Asnieres was no charlatan. She was a true clairvoyant. Without fully understanding all that she was seeing, she foretold the unique and wonderful events that have shaped my life.

# AMERICA

*Strangely enough*, I was not often homesick that first year of my marriage. I had faced the possibility of annihilation and survived. I was deeply in love. I was soon pregnant with my first child, suffused with the joy of carrying new life and the happiness of impending motherhood. Everywhere I went, I carried with me a strange medley of customs and traditions, religious feasts and festivals, superstitions, memories, and dreams invisible even to myself. I only knew that every now and then, I heard myself speaking with the blended voices of all those past generations, all those displaced ancestors who had forged new lives in new countries and who had lived to weave my past and theirs firmly into the challenge of the present and the future.

It was only when I came to America that I became defined by my religion. Here, in the land of "one nation indivisible," I found that the divisions of color, race, and religion were in fact the ones that defined. Even to the majority of Jews I was not quite understandable. I had never thought of myself as Sephardic, but in New York City, I began to grasp that I belonged to a subset of a subset. How was it that I did not "speak Jewish"? If I was Jewish it was inconceivable to those around me that I knew less Yiddish than most non-Jewish New Yorkers. The wry evocative richness of the Yiddish language had embedded itself permanently into the vernacular of America.

Although the Mosseri family claimed Judeo-Spanish origin, none of my family spoke Ladino, the pure Judeo-Spanish language that has survived unchanged from the Middle Ages and is still spoken by many Jews of Spanish or Portuguese descent living in the Middle East or around the Mediterranean.

As I moved deeper into this new world of America, I began to understand that the difference between Sephardic Jews and Ashkenazim is not one of dogma. The two groups are generally of different geographic origin and cultural experience. They differ in their pronunciation of Hebrew, in their rituals, liturgy, and religious customs. When I came to America, I noticed that Ashkenazi Jewish communities had dealt with deep variations in observance by creating specific congregations that adhere either more or less closely to the prescribed rules and are therefore defined by the nature and level of their observance. Sephardic communities, I noticed, generally tended to accept a broader spectrum of religious adherence and to come together in congregations built around place of origin rather than level of observance.

Assaulted every day by the chaos and difference of New York City, I tried to anchor myself to my own reality by reproducing the foods and echoing the rituals of my childhood. Serge's mother and mine had slightly different recipes for *kaak*, but one day soon after our honeymoon, armed with my mother's carefully noted recipe, I decided to surprise him with a taste of the past. I had bought granulated yeast, and I had a large yellow bowl into which I sieved my flour, adding the yeast mixture, measuring each ingredient with the obsessive care of a novice. I lit the oven and waited for my dough to rise. Serge had come home for lunch and, seeing some yeast in an open packet, said, "Why don't you put it all in?" and threw it into the bowl. He had lunch and returned to the office.

A little while later the dough had risen to the top of the big yellow bowl, so I scooped out a large fistful, rolled it into long strips, cut and curved them to make the familiar circular shape, brushed them with egg yoke, sprinkled them liberally with sesame seeds, and proudly popped the tray in the oven. I turned and saw with some surprise that the dough was once more swelling above the rim of the bowl. Hurriedly, I pulled out another baking tray and began the process a second time. By the time Serge had returned home from the office, my baking had turned into a frenzy that resembled nothing so much as a comedy cartoon. Each time I turned to the bowl, the dough had risen above the rim. The faster I worked, pushing and pulling trays of *kaak* in and out of the oven, improvising space as my small kitchen became a chaos of hot baking tins, with tumbled cookies mounding on wax paper on every available counter, the faster the dough returned to the top of the bowl.

Red-faced from the speed and the heat from the oven, flustered, almost in tears as my simple project mushroomed into mania, I was running and rolling, pushing and pulling faster and faster, but like something from a nightmare, the bowl was always full. Taking in the situation at a glance, my husband threw off his tie and suit jacket and joined the fray, and together we eventually vanquished the power of the yeast, convulsing into hysterical laughter as dozens upon dozens of *kaak* filled every receptacle we could lay our hands on. Unfortunately, they were not the best. The excess of yeast had played havoc with texture and taste. But as we crunched our way through weeks and months of *kaak*, laughter lay in every bite.

⚜ ⚜ ⚜

As that first year sped along, I realized that it would soon be fall, and I began to feel the full weight of the responsibility of preparing the traditional foods for Rosh Hashana without the help of a supportive network of aunts and cousins to share some of the burden. I knew it would be a far cry from the family gatherings I was used to, but I wanted to do my best to bring the beauty of family celebration to my new family in this new place. In my family, religious festivals not only marked the turning of the calendar, they were occasions for elaborate ritual and preparation, usually involving foods we loved but never ate at any other time of year.

So I set the table with my best china; I consulted my mother's letters which arrived regularly on flimsy airmail paper, each of them lovingly bringing the gift of a new recipe for me to try; and I produced an acceptable rendering of each of the symbolic dishes I had so enjoyed in the company of the large and turbulent family gatherings in London year after year.

But the greatest challenge surfaced that first April of my marriage, as the leaves on the scrawny Manhattan street trees began to show their strong young green in the weak spring sunlight.

My first married Passover.

My head rang with the memory of Passover preparations in the house in Cairo. I knew that it now fell to me alone to transplant the rituals of my childhood to this new country. By then I was majestically pregnant, as Alan, my eldest child, was born in May of 1963. We were living at 420 East 51st Street, in Manhattan, in a pleasant new two-bedroom apartment, #4C. With the help of a stick-thin, bony, no-nonsense part-time household helper, Mary Cherry, a look of dedicated determination on her pleasant dark face, we scoured every inch of my new home, taking down lighting fixtures, washing walls, moving the refrigerator out from its niche in the kitchen to discover a world of grunge behind it.

*Passover in New York*

My belly leading the way, dressed in a dark-green jumper and white blouse with peter pan collar, I stood in line at Macy's, the only place in town at that time that had a Passover department every year, and I bought dates and nuts, raisins and vinegar, almonds, oil, and sugar. I sorted the rice, although the bags that contained the rice I bought were plastic, and the rice was clean except for a few misshapen grains and the occasional black-tipped one. I peeled onions, saved the rich brown peel, stuffed it into a new Passover pan with a splash of oil, some saffron, and several eggs, and left them to simmer the required nine hours to make the traditional *hamin* eggs. (The word *hamin* meant "oven," and these eggs were traditionally baked in the oven for Sabbath dinner as well as for the holidays, with onion peel saved throughout the week, sometimes with the addition of tea for color instead of saffron.)

With the help of a new Kenwood blender and mixer that stood, majestic and all-powerful, in my small kitchen, armed with the recipe that my mother had sent me, I washed the dates carefully in seven waters, cracked hazelnuts and walnuts until my fingers ached, woke up every hour or so throughout the night to stir the thickening brew, and I achieved the *haroseth*. I wanted to make a beautiful Seder. I wanted to create an exquisite evening in our own home, I wanted to recreate the flavor of my childhood home, and I wanted to seduce my recalcitrant husband into the pleasure I found in the ritual and rigor of this hardest of feasts.

As I stood in my Manhattan living room arranging the fruit and flowers I had just brought home, the phone rang. It was Viviane, one of my cousins from Paris who was in New York for a few days. Could she join us for the Seder? Would we mind if she left immediately after? A young man she was seeing would be picking her up to take her out after the prayers. I didn't mind. I was thrilled. I had a spotless apartment, the *haroseth* was delicious, and I looked forward to having this unexpected family presence in my home for the holiday.

I had not factored in the tremendous pressure of the Passover deadline, and I was hot and flustered when she arrived, way off my schedule and irredeemably late. Together, we finished arranging the flowers, putting out the best china, dealing with the last-minute crises of an ambitious dinner by an inexperienced cook. Exhausted, but triumphant and a couple of hours behind schedule, I lumbered to my bedroom and put on a red velvet maternity jumper. We sat down, Serge put a *kippah* (more commonly called a *yarmulka* in the West) on his head, and we opened our books to start the prayers. I had meticulously checked that everything necessary was on the Seder platter, the *hamin* eggs were a creamy beige with dark brown twirls where the shells had broken as they cooked, the bitter herbs were washed and artfully arranged, the mounded brick red of the *haroseth* was sprinkled with powdered almond, the shoulder of lamb gave forth an enticing aroma, and I chuckled to myself, thinking of Auntie Helen. I had prepared the traditional extra place setting for the Prophet Elijah next to Viviane.

Just as we were about to begin, the doorbell rang, and Viviane jumped to her feet, full of apology, exclaiming over her shoulder that she would have to leave immediately. She opened the door, and a man walked in, beaming with good humor. With an engaging smile he looked around. His eyes fell on the extra place set at the table and he said delightedly, "Oh good! You haven't started yet, and I see you have set a place for me."

He sat down in Elijah's place and never left. He celebrated the entire Seder with us, the first of many. Viviane and Gerry married that summer and there were to be many Seders we celebrated together with our young families, developing rituals of our own until, outnumbered as our children began to spin off into their own families, we could no longer all sit at one table.

⚜ ⚜ ⚜

The months continued to bring new challenges as they accelerated past. By the time December was upon us a second time, a little boy with silky dark hair and laughing eyes had become the center of our lives. I remembered that when I was a little girl in Cairo, every *Hanouka*, Osta Mohammed produced a sticky, sweet fried pastry, twirled and curled and rolled into balls of golden yeasty dough swimming in a thick syrup. I had the recipe and I gave it my valiant best, but the experiment sank into a glutinous mess at the bottom of the pan of hot oil.

Outside our apartment, Manhattan exploded into lights and celebration, Christmas trees glittering in every window. Piped carols sounded in the elevators, the department stores, everywhere I went.

At home, under my husband's somewhat skeptical gaze, the smoke from the ruined *zalabia* lingering in our nostrils, I lit my small menorah and stood it by the window. We sang, the baby in his bouncy seat by our side, and I reflected that in Geneva my parents and Granny Smouha were singing the same songs; in Rome, Auntie Mary and Uncle Victor had lighted their first light; in Cairo, alone but defiant, Auntie Helen must have drawn the drapes and would be standing in front of the menorah of my childhood (and possibly of her own), leaning on her cane with the tortoiseshell handle, poking a disobedient black hairpin back where it belonged.

I had broken out of the chrysalis and flown free, but I suddenly realized how powerfully my freedom floated on the gossamer wings bequeathed me by the past. I felt the silken bonds that linked me to all those I loved in place, lifting me. I felt my melancholy leaving like the unwelcome guest that it was.

I was transported back many years to the small room between the dining room and the kitchen where we gathered every year in December in the house of my childhood and watched as my father took a thin white taper and painstakingly lit a wick in a metal circle, rocking like a tiny boat on top of the oil and water in a small, thick glass. There was a glass holding a wick for each night of the holiday.

As we sang, standing close together in that small room in the house in Cairo that my grandfather built, our eyes were riveted to a beautiful little silver house in the right-hand corner near the window, an intricately wrought metal design, with an etched-glass interior and silver rings jutting from the walls, into which were placed the glasses, the lighted wicks on their tiny oil lakes. As

*Auntie Helen in her 100ᵗʰ year*

the holiday progressed, the windows of the silver house winked and twinkled with more and more light, until on the eighth night, silver and light conspired to fill the night with a mysterious glow. And then, watching the lighted taper bend slightly and tremble in one of my father's hands as he held the prayer book in the other, watching the faces of my mother, Granny Mosseri and Auntie Helen, my little brother and sister, feeling the gentle richness of my father's voice raised in song, the thrilling beauty of my mother's *coloratura* joining with his and rising above us all, I felt indescribably warm and happy, enveloped in love, in safety, in beauty, and in forever.

That beautiful miniature silver house of my memories exists in my heart, although it never left Egypt. Auntie Helen must have given it to a Jewish organization or orphanage before she finally left Cairo for Rome in 1964. She lived in Rome for many years before moving to Geneva to live with her sister, Mary, then a widow. She stayed on in the house with a caretaker after

Auntie Mary's death, and she died in Geneva in her hundredth year, some weeks after her nieces and nephew came together from London, Paris, Rome, and New York with their families, to throw a party in her honor. Family and friends, many of whom had not seen each other for years, gathered from far and wide to participate in this celebration of an exceptional woman and to bathe for a moment in poignant memories of a lost world.

But every year, in December, when I read those first words in Hebrew from my prayer book, I hear my father's voice rising past the years and the distance, past his death at age sixty-three. I smell the oil, I see the flickering wicks and the taper, the intent faces of my family, some long gone, others transformed by the passing years, and I see the exquisite silver house with its door open and waiting.

I am older now than my father ever was. I know there is no forever. But as we sing and watch the *Hanouka* lights flicker night after night for a week, time stands still, and forever is now.

✦ ✦ ✦

Years have passed, and the years have strengthened my belief that food and feasts serve as a path to the nourishment of family ties and of soul. Each holiday brings its religious obligations, and each specific holiday food links the celebration to the past and prepares the ground for the future.

Along with reading the *Book of Esther* every spring, the Purim of my childhood brought with it a cornucopia of melting pastries, *menenas* bursting with the mingled rich flavors of their date-and-nut stuffing, puffs of fine white sugar coating escaping into the air; and *ghorayibbas*, dazzling circles of white crumbly pastry punctuated with green pistachios that dissolved instantly into a lingering sweetness.

*Tisha be Ab*, the Fast of Ab, which commemorates the destruction of the Temple in Jerusalem, brings *mujaddrah* in its wake, a delicious combination of rice and lentils lavishly topped with crisp rings of deep fried onions. I remember as I scoop yogurt onto the rice, that Granny Smouha taught me how good the *mujaddrah* is when eaten with yogurt.

Along with the foods that link me to my childhood, I love to hear the Arabic phrases that have filtered into generations that never knew Egypt or Arabic. The word "*Mabrouk*," for instance, can best be translated by the Hebrew "*Mazaltov*," and is a complimentary exclamation to make if someone exhibits some new event or new item in their lives. Its roots lie in the Hebrew word *baruch*, meaning "blessing." *Mabrouk* is a hard word to abandon, and sometimes pops up unbidden where it will certainly not be understood. Another Arabic word that has tumbled down the generations and into the vocabulary of in-laws from other cultures is "*Yalla!*" an indescribable exclamation that means "let's get going" or "get on with it" or "come along" all in one neat pithy package. *Bukra fil mishmish*, "tomorrow when the apricot blossoms bloom," is an exquisite expression that conveys all the indolence of a vanished world where time waits for all men, where whatever one is awaiting may never come to pass, and if it does not, does that really matter? My mother can never end a meal in my apartment without saying "*suffra daiman*," "may your table always be filled," to which I answer automatically, "*daiman hayatak*," having no idea what it means but knowing she expects the response.

Sometimes Middle Eastern folklore, religious ritual, and superstition have become so closely entwined that the roots of a particular custom or prohibition are hard to define, and ritual, tradition, and superstition have blended into an unidentifiable set of rules by which we try to organize our lives, forming a subculture of mystery in my life as a child. The most powerful of these is the fear of the evil eye, for which the Jews of Egypt rely on turquoise as the antidote.

Babies from families with Egyptian Jewish backgrounds are usually given a turquoise stone at birth along with a *shaddai*, usually a star of David with the acronym of the name of God inscribed on it in Hebrew. Most women born and raised in the Middle East own and wear at least one turquoise ring or pendant. It is also my birthstone, and I love the color and wear it often.

Direct compliments are associated with the evil eye, and are greeted with anxiety and suspicion, often averted by a denial of the admiring comment and the insertion of a negative statement about the object of admiration. The number five is also reputed to work as an antidote to the evil eye and the mother of an admired baby might be observed waving her five fingers in the air as if to ward off flies or mosquitoes, all the while muttering "*hamsa, hamsa,*" under her breath, invoking the number five in Arabic. Understandably, the statement "you are so lucky," uttered in all innocence by someone from another culture, sends shivers down the spine of someone raised with these superstitions since it implies envy, and the power of envy is considered capable of bringing about the influence of the evil eye to set potent negative energies spinning off into a series of concrete negative incidents. If a series of misfortunes befalls an individual who has exposed his or her good fortune too prominently to the public eye, someone is sure to mutter darkly, "It must be the evil eye."

My life was barricaded with many other superstitions. Not only was our view of the world influenced by Jewish ritual and a medley of Mediterranean cultures, but because my Smouha grandparents had lived in Manchester and sent their children to English boarding schools, superstitions imported from England had also become blended indistinguishably into the mix. We were never supposed to eat an egg without adding salt, because an element of the mourning ritual for those in *abel* (or *shiva*, as it is more frequently called in the West) was to eat a hard-boiled egg without salt, while sitting on a low stool or chair, to signify the start of the week of mourning. Another superstition involved the passing of salt from one hand to the other. It had to be put down by one person and picked up by the other, or the two would end in dispute. Grandpa Smouha claimed that dispute would also occur if you dried your hands on the same towel as someone else, but since he was very meticulous about cleanliness and was talking to small children with grubby hands, I have no way of knowing if this was his way of maintaining hygiene or if the custom had a larger context. Hats, we were told, must never be thrown on the bed. If we ran around and around a table or sat on the floor when we were children, we were immediately stopped because of the unspoken association with mourning and death. The gift of a knife, handkerchiefs, or scissors had to be neutralized by the gift of a coin from the recipient of the gift to the donor. Uncle Ellis fell seriously ill, as a child, and his middle name was changed to Hay (meaning *chai*, life). My grandparents believed that this name-change saved his life.

The list of superstitions stretches on and on. Chewing on the Passover knucklebone guaranteed marriage within the year for a young woman, as did drinking the last drop of wine from a bottle for men and women alike. Umbrellas must never be opened indoors; it attracted bad luck. So did breaking a mirror, which could lead to seven years of bad luck, although that could be counteracted by throwing the broken pieces into flowing water.

Following British custom, black cats generally signaled good luck in my family, although the relationship of black cats to bad luck was dominant in the Middle East. A story involving Edmond Safra, founder of the Republic Bank of New York and the Banque Safra, has it that when a black cat crossed his path as he was on his way to close a major business deal, he turned back without a moment's hesitation and abandoned the deal.

Ridiculous as these customs may seem, I see these attempts to avert danger or disaster as a tacit acknowledgment of the dark shadow lurking in all our lives. Clearly, the subconscious knowledge of a precarious relationship with the world despite any evidence to the contrary was ingrained in us from our earliest days.

When I was growing up, before any trip a servant would appear by the front door with a tray of glasses of water. Granny Mosseri became quite agitated if anyone forgot to drink before leaving, since it was believed that if you sipped the waters of the Nile before a trip you would always return. Whether or not any of us actually believed it, we always drank, just in case, and we exported the custom when we left Egypt. In Paris, in London, in Geneva, in Rome, and in New York, glasses of water always appear at the door before a trip and everyone is urged to take at least a sip before departing from the home. We thus ensure that we will return to the banks of the Seine, the Thames, the Rhone, the Tiber, and the Hudson, carefully ignoring the fact that our glasses of Nile water before leaving Egypt did not in fact guarantee us a return home.

⚜ ⚜ ⚜

During the brief period of my engagement, knowing I would be far from all the family, I asked Granny Smouha to give me some of her recipes for my favorite foods. She laughed.

"You know what I suggest, darling," she said. "Why don't you follow me around the kitchen and write it down as we go. I don't know measurements. I cook by feel."

So I learned how to make *pestelis*, *kobebas*, and many different dishes I had loved to eat in her house. The measurements I took as I raced around behind her were far from accurate, and it took much trial and error to produce a semblance of the soul foods of my youth.

Granny Smouha also taught me how to make Turkish coffee. No meal in Egypt was complete without these tiny cups of strong coffee. During our summer holidays in Europe, on a small electric cooking ring in a hotel bedroom, she showed each of her granddaughters in turn how to put the sugar and water into the long-handled *kanaka* to make the traditional Turkish coffee, and how to hold it carefully over the flame until it boiled. It was then taken off the flame, and heaping teaspoons of fragrant powdery Turkish coffee were added. The *kanaka* was carefully returned to the flame, where the contents foamed rapidly and suddenly to the top. The pot then had to be promptly removed from the heat and tapped sharply three times to bring down the contents. This procedure was ritualistically repeated three times before the coffee was poured into small cups, a light brown froth called *wish* on the top. There were three choices: coffee could be made *mazbout* (just right), *succar ziada* (heavy on the sugar), or *sadda* (without sugar).

After drinking the coffee in a social setting, someone often offered to read fortunes. The person who had drunk the coffee placed the saucer on top of the empty cup, turned it upside down, rotated it in a complete circle three times and left it to dry out a little while the rest of us continued chatting. The one who was to read the fortune tapped the top of the cup with a forefinger, muttering an incantation that went something like "*Il ha! Il ha! Ouli il ha!*" (The truth, the truth, tell me the truth!). Then the drinker of the coffee upturned the cup. If it stuck and was difficult to dislodge, it meant that money could be expected in the near future, and smiles wreathed the intent faces watching. The teller of fortunes then perused the inside of the cup with earnest concentration while the recipient observed his or her facial expression with gathering anxiety, all the while laughing dismissively and declaring that this was a pleasant game, not to be taken too seriously.

Images always emerge and offer a tale to tell. My father liked to try his hand at this parlor game in his youth, until the time he saw some ominous signs in a friend's cup that he could only interpret as an imminent tragedy. Uncomfortable with the message that hammered at his consciousness, he kept it to himself but later, with horror, observed the tragedy come about exactly as he had foreseen it. From then on he never read another cup.

# THE LAST TIME

*Sometimes it* is a true blessing not to be able to see around the next bend in the road. Sometimes the future must reveal itself only when it becomes the present. The summer of 1970 was such a time. It was one of the most wonderful summers we had known.

Serge, the children (by now we had three), and I usually braved the summers in Manhattan, a feat made possible by the excellence of the air-conditioning in our apartment. But that year the stars were aligned advantageously for us, and we rented a lovely older house near Mecox Bay in the Hamptons, five minutes from the beach. We bought a rickety old station wagon with torn upholstery and lots of room. My work was freelance and I was able to take a three-month hiatus from my commitments; Serge, a management consultant, was involved in sorting mountains of data and putting together a voluminous report for a major company, so he commandeered one of the downstairs rooms, spread his papers in clumps on the floor, and wrote his report between our forays to the beach, without either of us having to interrupt our idyllic summer by commuting daily to New York. Our children were just the right age for the wide white beaches and thunderous ocean of Long Island, diving in and out of the translucent green waves with their father like fish and shouting in a mixture of terror and joy.

Our first morning in the house, we had awakened to see three small figures outlined in the doorway of our bedroom. Sternly, we inquired why were they not asleep? The three, whose sleep from their earliest days had been accompanied by the roar and clatter of traffic mingling with the intermittent shriek of sirens outside their windows on 72nd Street, a major cross street in Manhattan, replied indignantly: "How could we sleep, with all those birds making all that noise outside?"

With us was Marina, queen of our kitchen, maker of melting *gnocchi, pasta in casa,* sugar-topped *farfalle,* and round rich parmesan breads. With her large heart and sturdy Italian peasant wisdom, she infused the summer with bountiful meals and gave us the ability to enjoy every day to the full.

My parents joined us. The house was large and rambling, and they brought Auntie Helen with them, her first and only visit to America. Jeff drove up from Manhattan in his sleek gray Corvette, the love of his heart. He took my father for a drive to show off his car. It rained heavily and the roof leaked. Then the bottom fell out into the road, to Jeff's acute distress. My father laughed and teased him mercilessly. Susan, too, spent the summer with us. She and Serge discovered a place where used tires in decent condition could be acquired, and they slipped and slid on mountains of used tires in search of four good tires for our ramshackle vehicle. Alan, our eldest, then seven years old, had found and appropriated a tiny crab which he named George, and which he cared for solicitously until it found a way to escape and disappeared.

One day we arrived at the beach lugging our beach towels and thermoses of hot chocolate to find that people were running up and down the sands exclaiming and shouting. Streams of small silver fish were washing onto the sand with every thrust of the ocean, in their death throes as they thrashed about, gasping from their encounter with the air. Close on their tails came the larger fish they were trying to escape, the bluefish, sinewy and voracious, blinded to danger in their greed and desire to gorge themselves on the swarms of small fish, leaping almost into the arms of the ecstatic amateur fishermen who were hauling them in as fast as they could unhook the last one from their lines. A man thrust a rod at my husband, shouting, "Here! Take this! Anything you catch is yours!" We got into the swing of it and returned home with a basket of plump fresh fish, but we were reluctant to gut and clean them. Marina, however, had no such qualms. She exclaimed happily over the catch, gutted and cleaned them without hesitation, and we all sat out on the lawn after sunset, cooking them on our barbecue and enjoying the fresh rich flavor of the bluefish enhanced with herbs, breathing in the cool sea air and sighing with satisfaction. Marina presided over it all, cross-legged in the glow from the barbecue, a bandanna on her head, looking for all the world like an ancient gypsy queen.

My father seemed more tired than usual in the days before their return to Europe, and my mother mentioned that he was going to see the doctor in Paris before returning to Geneva, but he looked fine to me. We laughed a lot together, and he delighted in the spectacular beaches five minutes from the house and the antics of his three young grandchildren. I was profoundly immersed in the demands of my New York life, the balancing act between motherhood and work, managing a young household and forging ahead blithely into a future. This idyllic summer seemed merely a prelude to future vacations, a taste of happiness to come. I never imagined it would be the last time that we would all be together without the shadow of his absence casting its edge of pain into every joy.

The last time wears no warning label. The wise suspect it at every turn and live accordingly. We only know it by the absence of hope that it will ever return. As a child, I had known that darkness could hide under the brightest day, but in Watermill that summer I saw only the sea and the sunshine, the bright faces of the people I loved, and I forgot.

✦ ✦ ✦

For our summer vacation the following year we made plans to take the children with us to Geneva, where my parents were living, but it began to look as if we might not be able to swing it, so I called my mother and told her we might not come.

"You must come," she said, an edge of panic in her voice. "Don't you realize that Daddy is very seriously ill? He has cancer. I've been trying to tell you in letter after letter. I couldn't tell you directly before, because he doesn't know. He *mustn't know*. I don't want him to give up, I want him to fight."

Immersed in the day-to-day of my life in Manhattan and in seeing to the needs of my young family, I had indeed been receiving the usual wonderful chatty letters from my mother and had read the words without reading between the lines. Looking back, I realized that she often made mention of my father's health problems, the fact that he was losing weight, and also that he might have to have an operation.

Once, Serge said uneasily, "Do you suppose he might have cancer?" But I was deep in denial. I turned on him roundly and scotched any such thought.

The news was devastating. I reeled under it and couldn't regain my equilibrium. We began to make preparations to travel to Europe. In an extraordinary stroke of luck, an executive with whom Serge had business dealings asked him to come to Switzerland for three months to undertake a thorough analysis of his company.

My mother called again. "Don't tell *anyone* about the cancer," she begged, so I stumbled about my daily business in a claustrophobic haze of pain and grief. Finally I went to see my kindly doctor.

"I don't know how I can face him, knowing what I know. I don't know what to do," I said, barely holding back tears.

"You must just treat each day as a wonderful gift," he said. "Don't look beyond. Make the most of every day that you have him with you." It was invaluable advice and helped me through those bittersweet days of my father's last summer.

In Geneva, our three children stayed with my parents at their Florissant apartment and my husband and I stayed just outside the main part of town, in Conches, where Granny Smouha had a pleasant house where she lived the last years of her life. Salève Mountain rose beyond her small garden. Granny said little, but her loving attention to our creature comforts and the peace and beauty with which she had surrounded herself were balm to my aching soul. Every morning, as Serge drove to Lausanne to confer with his client, I walked along the road to Florissant after a breakfast of croissants and café au lait, sometimes taken outside on the comfortable swing-seat on Granny's patio to the side of the house, early morning summer sunlight outlining the mountain in radiance. None of it seemed real.

I listened to the songs of Georges Moustaki endlessly, the songs "Le Méteque" and "Grandpère" always made me cry, and it felt good to cry about some French singer's deliberately poignant song rather than about the reality I was so afraid to face. His songs were filled with the melancholy of exile. He, too, had grown up in Egypt, and he, too, had left.

Along the road outside, the horse-chestnut trees were in bloom, their rich brown nuts hidden in spiky green clumps among the leaves. They would fall to the ground in the autumn, revealing their gleaming contents to the light. It was a long walk to my parents' apartment, but the steady exercise in the warm summer breeze, crunchy gravel underfoot, was a good way to dissipate some of my tension before arriving there. My father showed us his new car, a sleek white Lancia that he had permitted himself after years of roomy family cars, now that Jeff was working in Montreal and I was living in New York. Only my sister, Susan, still lived at home, attending Geneva University in the medieval Old Town of Geneva, and driving my father to and from his "treatments," helping him with his work and his papers, steadying my mother in her moments of weakness. In an ironic echo of our father's own experience, she was twenty-three years old, plunged into a maturity that sat ill on her shoulders.

Looking after three small grandchildren pinned everyone's minds to a safe place. We drove my father to the farmer's market in the *Place Neuve*, where he walked from stall to stall with a cane, gaunt and exhausted, looking as he might have looked twenty years later had he lived. We weighed and sniffed the sun-released fragrance of mangoes and melons, peaches and plums, tomatoes and zucchini, and returned home laden with our bounty in dozens of brown paper bags. On weekends, we drove along tree-lined winding country roads to vine-covered *auberges* by the lake, flowers brilliant in the summer light, to eat exquisite meals that went on for hours. My father ate little, and smiled to watch his grandchildren at their play.

My mother planned a tea party at their home for our ninth wedding anniversary and invited all the family, aunts, uncles, cousins, and their children. She looked so beautiful in her pale green dress, her jade pendant swinging as she moved, her smiling face bringing a smile to my father's face as he sat with Granny

Smouha on the couch under the window, watching groups form and disperse around the laden tea table and enjoying the cheerful chatter.

A veil of unreality seemed to have settled in my heart. The evidence was before my eyes, but my heart refused to accept its possibility.

My parents were scheduled to spend a few days at a hotel in the mountains, and we were to join them there with the children for the weekend. They left for the mountains as planned, and we followed at the end of the week, but instead of the relaxation we were all anticipating, we found my father in great pain. We all drove back together to Geneva, where he went immediately into hospital for surgery to alleviate an intestinal blockage. We paced the brick-lined terrace of the hospital with my mother during the surgery, afraid he would die, almost more afraid that he might live and have to endure months of pain. The surgery was successful, but the cancer was too far gone. The doctor told us it was a matter of a few months at most.

Autumn was beginning to spike the evenings with chill. The leaves were turning brown. It was time for us to return to New York for the children to start school. Our departure could no longer be delayed. We made plans to come back to Geneva for the winter vacation. My father was still recovering in the hospital. I said good-bye to him, tortured by the need to leave and take care of my family's needs. I think we both knew we would never meet again. His hand clutched mine and our eyes gleamed with unshed tears, but we kept up the charade. See you again in a few weeks.

I nearly turned back when we stopped off in Paris to see my parents-in-law, but my mother was certain that he would interpret a return as a clear sign that he did not have long to live, and she did not want him to stop fighting. So I returned to my home in New York in a waking nightmare. For two weeks, my body went about the motions of setting my home in order, equipping my children for school, preparing for the imminent Rosh Hashana holiday while my mind and my heart stayed in Geneva, at my father's bedside. I made the traditional jams. I polished the silver. I took each child to the first day of a new school year. I wrote cheerful letters to my parents every day. Philippe Setton was in New York and planned to join us for the second night of the holiday. I had just placed the fragrant round golden omelets on silver platters and was about to find room for them on the festive table when the doorbell rang. I went to the door and let Philippe in. The phone rang. I ran to answer. It was Jeff, who had gone to Geneva to spend Rosh Hashana with our parents, telling me to leave at once, our father had taken a turn for the worse.

Serge got on the phone immediately and set about finding me a place on the next plane bound for Geneva, and I packed with fingers like lead and a heart even heavier as Philippe kept the children entertained. Shuddering, I included dark clothes in my suitcase and traveled in a navy wool dress and coat. On the plane, my habitual travel anxiety lifted and I found myself convinced that I would be there in time. So deep was my certainty and the peace that came with it that I was stunned and disbelieving to see my red-eyed sister, Uncle Teddy, and Auntie Yvonne waiting for me at the airport, their sad faces obviating any need for words. My sister and I hugged, and hugged again, and wept. We drove straight to the clinic where my mother and brother waited. Auntie Helen came in after I had arrived, and taking in her beloved little brother's mourning family at a glance, she uttered the most wrenching wail of pain and sorrow I have ever heard. It shook loose our own pain from its moorings and we wept together.

My father was twenty-nine when I was born, and I was thirty-three when he died.

✝ ✝ ✝

For the eight days of *abel* (shiva), we sat on low chairs, and Auntie Peggy Setton and Granny Smouha brought food from Granny's kitchen to the apartment and tried to coax us to eat. Family and friends came from near and far and sat with us, helping each of us through the first days of shock and grief. My closest cousins, Suzanne, Judy, Gilly, and Patricia, each offered tears and hugs, their loving memories of my father, and their unbounded sympathy. In our close-knit group of cousins, we were the first to lose a parent; it was the first collective loss of an uncle. There was a *minyan* for prayers every night, and my sister, Susan, standing next to Gilly, expressed what we were all feeling: "I can't believe this is happening to me," she whispered as the sound of the *kaddish* filled the room. My brother, Jeff, went unshaven for thirty days and attended early morning services every morning with our cousins. Prayers continued in our home every night.

Upon our return from the funeral, my mother had told us to pin an old handkerchief to our clothes. Even knowing what was to come, the shock and the sudden sharp hiss as the rabbi tore each piece of linen amplified the tearing of our hearts. I still remember how it felt to walk outside with my sister for the first time after the week at home. Susan and I felt as though our skin had been ripped from us, leaving our vulnerability open and aching in the air. His hat still hung on a hook by the door when we came home from the funeral. His coat still held his shape and his scent. It did not seem possible that he was gone from our lives forever. But we knew that he was.

Serge and the children flew in from New York. The children slept in the home of my cousins Dicky and Sylvia Smouha, and it was arranged that they would go to school with their cousin, Caroline. They came to visit my mother each day and brought smiles and comfort with them. In the most somber moments, one or other of us would comment on an incident, pointing out the humor my father would have found in it, and laughter spilled hesitantly, guiltily from us, lightening the dark sorrow that filled us. My family and I were in Geneva for a month.

⚜ ⚜ ⚜

The bright Rosh Hashana memories of my youth carry a dark shadow now. For many years after my father's death, I could hardly bear to cook the leek and spinach omelets, or to set a beautiful table for the second night of the holiday. I hated the first brown leaves of fall. But time dulls that first raw pain. When we returned to New York, I often thought I glimpsed him on a bus or walking down the street ahead of me. Tears rushed to my eyes and my hand reached out, until the person turned and became so clearly not my father. With the passing of the years, the fine memories remain, polished to a high gloss. The laughter, the love, the humor, the ability to take the best of life as it was offered and to make light of the worst—these were a part of him, and they are his legacy to us, his three children. We are fortunate indeed to have had such a father and to have such memories, knowing as we do that although his life was short, he made the most of every moment. And although he died far too many years ago, his memory lives vibrantly in each of his children today.

✦ ✦ ✦

Some years after my father's death, in 1987, Serge and I bought an old stone house nestled among ancient trees and flowing meadows bordered by rich forest in Ulster County in upstate New York in the valley between the Catskills and the Shawangunks. Pioneers fleeing religious persecution in Europe built the house from fieldstone in 1756, exactly two centuries before my own life was disrupted and the events surrounding the Egyptian annexation of the Suez Canal in 1956 wrenched me from the house that my grandfather built and opened the pathway that led me to America. When I first opened the door of the old stone house and stepped into the living room, I knew the house had been waiting for me. In the dim light of a rainy spring afternoon, peace reached out to claim me, and I sank into its embrace and wanted never to leave.

From the kitchen windows I can see a small pond, which is fed by a secret spring, unseen, its workings mysterious. Without it, the pond would not exist. Although a stream also feeds into it, the stream sometimes rushes and tumbles over smooth stones in an exuberance of sparkling water and sometimes dries up and exposes its bare bones to the sky. The next rainfall polishes the stones to a dark gleam and snowmelt in the spring sets the water burbling again. But it is the spring in the pond itself, which we cannot see and often forget, that is the source of life for the pond, for the frogs, the dragonflies, the fish, and the snapping turtles, and the pond in turn attracts the deer, the flock of wild turkeys who drink from its waters, and the heron who comes to visit once or twice a year, elegant as a Japanese sculpture on his princely way to other destinations. The place fills me with wonder and repose and a sense of soul.

Cozy by the fireside, I expressed to Serge my profound sorrow that my father, who had so loved houses, would never see mine. That night I fell asleep in our big bedroom, awash with the pale light of a full moon, and I awoke to hear my father's voice calling. I got out of bed and went to the top of the stairs, and there he was in his old gray coat, smiling at me from the bottom of the stairs.

"Well," he said, "aren't you going to show me your house? You said you wanted to show me your house."

I ran down the stairs and showed him every room, pointing out the beauty of the countryside outside the windows, the oddity of the wide-board floors that gaped at the edges and allowed the light from below to peek through, the bathroom with the basin built for a giant, too high for comfort, but facing out onto moon-swept fields, each a study in grey and white bordered by the stark silhouettes of trees. He nodded and smiled with pleasure. In the morning I wept. It had been so real, but it was only a dream. He was gone.

⚜ ⚜ ⚜

Houses have always occupied a significant spot in the wanderings of my subconscious. Apartments lack the mystery, the possibility for hidden treasures, the ability to offer a reassuring bulk to shelter frailties of flesh and bone. I often returned in dreams to the house of my childhood, wandering into rooms that had never existed, searching in dusty chests for treasures I could not name and never found.

In the maisonette at 4 Spanish Place in London, the Tudor room where my brother slept had a narrow closet hidden behind the paneled walls, and it figured prominently in my dreams for many years after. I dreamed that it was large and long, and held racks upon racks of forgotten clothes that I needed to sort through and discard, or that it was somehow connected by dim and grimy passageways to the attics of the other houses along Spanish Place, and was filled to the rafters with secret hoards of dusty antique furniture that Miss Harper would invite me to wander through and select from. I have no idea why my dreams so often thrust me back into that pleasant little London house when I was living such a different life in America, but often at night, my children safely tucked up and fast asleep, the gentle rumble of my husband's measured breathing in my ear, I would close my eyes only to find myself back there, painstakingly going through the racks of clothing, trying dresses on for size, holding things up to the dim yellow light, driven by some inexplicable urgency and the need to winnow down the multitude of tightly packed racks to two or three.

It was always a slightly frightening experience, as if I had no business being there at all and needed to be careful not to be discovered. Sometimes the furniture beckoned me across the ocean, and I fumbled and stumbled my way between toppling oak wardrobes thick with dust, crowded chests of drawers with drawers locked shut, rickety chairs and sturdy tables, on and on through a labyrinth of attics until I forgot where I began and entered a nightmare world without landmarks and without end, calling for Miss Harper, who never answered, and finally grappling my way back into a New York morning.

I realize that my Smouha grandparents' rambling house in Alexandria where I was born, the majestic house my Mosseri grandfather built in Cairo where I grew up, the comfortable furnished maisonette on Spanish Place where I anchored myself for three years after leaving Egypt, and the old stone house in upstate

New York each has come to symbolize a significant period of my life. Each lives vividly in my imagination. Each has contributed to my knowledge of the world and of my place within it.

✦ ✦ ✦

Granny Smouha saw the deaths of her two youngest children and three of her sons-in-law in her latter years. It dimmed her *joie de vivre*, but living in her small house in Conches, outside Geneva, she continued to dispense counsel, love, and support to all of us until the fall of her eighty-ninth year.

The night of *Kol Nidrei* that year, walking home from services in New York City with the usual gaggle of East Siders who yearly brave the nighttime shadows of Central Park to walk the long way home from the Shearith Israel synagogue, I climbed eleven flights of stairs and fell exhausted into bed. I was soon asleep.

Next day, filled with a strange sense of peace, I told both my husband and my cousin Viviane of a particularly vivid dream that had illuminated my night. I had dreamed of a large and exquisite meadow filled with rich green grasses and bright flowers. I was crossing this meadow in the company of a tall personage whose face I never saw, and together we glided across the meadow toward a table with an umbrella in the center where two old ladies sat and chatted in the shadow of a mountain looming at their back. As we came closer, I saw that the women sitting there were my two grandmothers. I was startled, knowing somehow within the logic of my dream that Granny Mosseri had died many years earlier, yet there she was, serene and smiling in this idyllic setting. Granny Smouha got up from her chair, laughing and happy, and opened her arms to me. I started to run toward her but the personage at my side held me back, and Granny said, "Not yet, darling, you can't come yet." Looking back over my shoulder at these two beloved grandmothers, I was led away from them and out of the meadow. It was a beautiful, peaceful dream, a dream of love and golden happiness. I tried to convey this to Viviane as we sat side by side in the synagogue the next day.

At the end of the holiday we received phone messages that Granny Smouha had been rushed to the hospital. Shortly afterward, she died. To this day I believe that she visited me, and that the message she left me is one of love, hope, and continuity.

Jeff and I flew to Geneva from New York and joined our mother and Granny's other children and grandchildren at her funeral on a clear sunny day, the sky bright blue, the mountains sharp-edged in the distance as her coffin was carried to its resting place on the shoulders of her grieving grandsons, one from each family of her children. We were all devastated at the loss of a beloved grandmother, conscious that with her loss, we had lost a part of ourselves. We had lost the focal point and shared heart of a large and spreading family. Nothing would ever be the same again.

However hard my Smouha cousins and I try to maintain our strong connections to each other, time, age, geography, and the increasing tug and needs of our own separate families as they expand have diminished our opportunities to come together. But when we do find each other at one or another of the various occasions, happy and sad, that punctuate the passing of time in a sprawling yet close-knit family, the years dissolve in an instant. We listen to each other's grandparent tales and share our own, marveling that now, *we* are the grandparents. We catch resemblances among the younger generation, features and fleeting expressions that betray their shared heritage. We delight in the knowledge that so many of our children have bridged the great distances that now divide us and have become friends with each other, and that even the next generation, the great-great-grandchildren of Joseph and Rosa Smouha, know of the ties of love and blood that bind them into the future.

Grandpa Smouha built his family with the care he gave to his work, protective and inspired, creating an enduring family culture that has outlasted the immense fortune he made and lost and the lives of most of his children.

His first great-great-great-grandchild, the first of the newest generation, was born in September 2002. A boy, Jonathan Cohen, was born to Sara, eldest daughter of my cousin Patricia's eldest daughter, Rosalind, making Auntie Yvonne a great-great-grandmother in her eighty-ninth year.

⚜ ⚜ ⚜

After Granny Smouha's death, my mother, in her late sixties, made the difficult decision to move once again, this time to New York where two of her children were living. It must have been a hard transition, but she undertook it with the energy and positive drive that has characterized her response to challenge all her life. My father used to say that because she was the most fearful woman he knew, she was also the bravest.

She took calligraphy classes at a senior center as a weekend distraction. The senior center also offered art classes, and a few months later she enrolled herself in those. By her mid-seventies she had discovered the talent and passion that have illuminated her old age. Her vibrant paintings display the exuberance and vitality that are so much a part of her character and her charm.

Rich with color and variety, they are an outpouring of beauty and creativity that defies age, singing out her delight in nature, in the colors and fragrance of flowers, in snowstorms and mountain peaks and the singularity of the world and of life as she sees it.

*Painting by Joyce Mosseri in her eighties*

At ninety-one, she has shown her paintings in many public venues. They illuminate homes and offices, some have traveled to other lands, some enhance the living spaces of her children, grandchildren, and great-grandchildren as well as the homes of nieces, nephews, grand-nieces, and grand-nephews in the many countries where they reside.

Many have valued her work and paid tribute to it. Now in a venerable old age, saddened to be the last remaining child of her large family, she continues to celebrate the beauty in life with her

*Entrance to my grandfather's house*

creativity and her art. My grandchildren are the beneficiaries of her influence in their young lives. One morning, my grandson Justin was sitting with his father on the patio of the stone house in Ulster county. Both early risers, they sat in silent companionship, breathing in the crisp air of an exquisite early fall morning, watching the breeze stir the grass and the trees. After a while, six-year-old Justin sighed with pleasure.

"This is so beautiful," he said. "It makes me think of Gran-Gran's paintings."

Even in her nineties, she still plays the piano. She complains that her arthritis makes her fingers fumble and that she sometimes forgets what comes next. I hear only the extraordinary musicality and passion of her playing. It transcends any fumbles and cannot be learned. It is an intimate reflection of her profound relationship to the music itself and to the beauty in life. Her small great-grandson Yaniv, a solemn little fellow with the dark Cattaui eyes, was listening to a recorded Beethoven piano concerto played magnificently by Vladimir Horowitz on the car radio as we drove him home one day. Yaniv was then the youngest of four and heard piano practice every day, but this, he knew, was different. The position of his whole body proclaimed that he was listening intently. Then he sat back and looked at me. At two years old, he was a man of few words.

"Piano Gran-Gran," he said in the husky voice that characterizes him.

*Kasr el Nil Bridge in the 1930s*

# Return

*Serge and I* returned to Egypt for the first time with our grown children in 1990. After an absence of so many years, I anticipated a deep emotional resonance at finding myself once more in the world in which I had grown up. But that world had vanished along with my childhood. Nonetheless, my internal antennae began to vibrate at the airport, where the crowds, the shouting, the extravagant gesturing, and the sounds of Arabic, harsh with the urgency of travel and arrival, exploded around us. I expected to be plunged into the past on the long drive from the airport, along wide boulevards that I remembered led into the heart of town, a drive I had often experienced as a teenager returning home from boarding school. I looked out of the taxi windows with such urgency to reconnect with my childhood world that my head ached and my eyes stung. But I found nothing familiar on the drive from the airport to the hotel.

In the many intervening years, Cairo had evolved into a different city, one where monuments and museums had dwindled from their former majesty as new buildings towered above them, and where chaotic traffic and a seething mass of humanity and honking cars had invaded the open spaces I half-remembered. Where gracious villas had once nestled in expansive, extravagantly beautiful gardens rich with color, Zamalek had become a labyrinth of tightly packed buildings, jumbled apartment houses, a study in shades of gray, much of the green swallowed up into construction, flowers giving way to the press and hum of humanity. It was powerful and poignant to be in the city where I had spent so many childhood years, but the pleasure and interest I felt were anticipatory, intellectual, not springing from the heart or welling out of the subconscious.

We had somehow become the patrons of a charming and garrulous taxi driver who had established himself as our personal driver from the moment we arrived. We had an appointment the next day to visit the house that my grandfather built, so that first day in Cairo he took us to the *muski*, that wonderful Arab bazaar redolent with smells of meats grilling on open braziers, its narrow winding streets lined with cramped storefronts and crowded with leather goods, jewelry, polished wooden boxes, and small tables intricately inlaid with geometric patterns in mother-of-pearl and bone. Everywhere, craftsmen bent over small tables, focused and centered despite the chaos that surrounded them, decorating brass platters with intricate designs under an assortment of colorful merchandise hanging in haphazard fashion overhead. Music blared from each small storefront, dissonant, argumentative, a wailing rhythmic cacophony. Merchants bargained volubly and loudly over the price of carpets or copper pots, inlaid wooden boxes, or embroidered *galabyias* (caftans). We all tried our hands and our rusty Arabic at bargaining as we sifted through the overwhelming bombardment of unfamiliar sights, smells, and bright colors, edging our way past the men in white robes sipping tiny cups of Turkish coffee at an outdoor cafe, some hunched intently over backgammon boards while others puffed on a variety of elegant glass *houkas*. We tried not to lose sight of each other as the crowds pressed past us and the tempting profusion of goods drew us this way and that.

*(left to right) Jennifer, David, and Alan at the Pyramids, 1990*

Miraculously, our driver found us all at exactly the time we had planned and herded us carefully back to where he had parked his taxi. We had told him we lived in Egypt in the past and were now living in America, but not that we were Jews returning to visit our past in a land that had ejected us. No sooner were we wedged into the taxi and leaving the *muski* than he drove us up dusty streets, higher and higher. "Where are you taking us?" we asked. "To a very old synagogue," he answered. We were silent, wondering what had given us away and whether it mattered. We climbed a series of low marble steps as dusk began to fall, a brilliant pink and orange sunset spraying the sky with magic, and we found ourselves in a small, dark synagogue, its decrepit benches and dusty walls alternating with new wood and bright stained glass. It was clearly in the process of a major and lengthy renovation. "American money," said our taxi driver, grinning as he followed us up the steps. "This is very holy place."

Serge looked about him, taking in the ancient and the new. "I think I had my bar mitzvah here," he said slowly, in wonder. The children stared at him in disbelief, his connection to the rituals of religion having been more tenuous than mine or theirs. But indeed his bar mitzvah had taken place there, as we confirmed with his mother when next we saw her. This was the Moses synagogue where my father had prayed to be able to leave the country with his family the day before he received the visa that took us away from an Egypt we loved and feared into an unknown future. Now his descendants had returned, eager to connect with remnants of their history and their past. This synagogue contained the slab upon which Elena Cattaui Mosseri had been told to spend the night when my grandfather, my father's father, was a small boy. We had come upon it with no plan to visit it, and it had offered up the present, the past, and the distant past circling and repeating, touching at the edges.

The one certain thing in life is that time passes, and with the passing of time, a new memory of the stately house on the borders of the Nile has superimposed itself on those long-ago images of a forlorn girl taking her leave of her childhood and of the house that her grandfather built. It has replaced the angry turbulence of white-gowned crowds and harsh voices outside handsome wrought-iron gates. It has brought back the peace of cool marble floors, vast rooms, high ceilings, and light stippling like rich jewels through stained glass. Thinking that I would be gone from my home forever, I did not realize then that every moment is a forever and no sooner there than forever gone, past, present, and future merging indistinguishably.

This later memory concerns a middle-aged woman some thirty-three years later, her face alight with anticipation. She leans toward her husband and the three tall young people, who are her children. This is the life that has defined itself, far away in North America. They are all entering the closed compound that is now the Russian Ambassador's residence, bordering the Nile in Giza.

The graceful wrought-iron fence and gate that had once established a relationship between the house and garden and the world outside have been blocked in, preventing anyone from seeing in or out. The garden with its profusion of flowers has become a formal array of clipped grass and asphalt paths. I stop short and feel a rush of pain and fear as I step through a small iron gate next to the *boab's* empty gatehouse and step into the space beyond, a space filled with loss and remembering.

I cannot quite orient myself. Where is the archway? Where are the gravel paths? My feet hesitate on the asphalt driveway, searching for the texture of vanished gravel. There are still flowers to be seen, but they have been sternly disciplined and now sit in neat ranks where a rich medley of size and color reigned before. Palms still wave their fronds in the breeze from the Nile, but the huge old mango trees have disappeared. The synagogue that stood in one corner of the garden was deconsecrated and razed to the ground by my father before the Russians took possession of the house. Its absence is conspicuous, as is the absence of the vine-covered walkways that led to it and that shaded the outer perimeters of the gardens, but only to me.

We have formed a solemn procession as we walk slowly around the house. To the right a new, wide stone staircase descends from the sitting room terrace, closing off the iron gate that used to mark the garden entrance to the basement. I wonder silently what became of all the remnants of past lives that had lain in the basement gathering dust while a little girl circled but never touched the messages they held. Are my father's beloved lead soldiers marching to war in the room of a little Russian boy? A nameless anxiety floods my senses.

I glance up at the windows and I see that the house stands as it always did, a graceful red brick and cream-colored stone mansion. I can hardly breathe with anticipation as I climb the marble steps I clambered up so often as a child, led by a young Russian undersecretary and followed by my family. Slowly, with pain and reverence, I am reentering my childhood, paying my respects to the house my grandfather built. Tears sting in my eyes, but I blink them away, very conscious of our deferential young Russian host, who listens respectfully to my comments as I reach carefully into my past, trying to paint a word picture for them all about how it used to be, how and where it has changed, and how, nonetheless, it is still the same.

The Russians, quite excited by this visit, have prepared a feast of Russian delicacies in the corner room where my parents' grand piano once stood, the room that opened into the dining room on one side and the sitting room on the other. My mother's music lingers in the still air, unheard by anyone but me. The bones of the house are unchanged, but the aspect is different. The spirit of the past has left. The bottom half of the arched stained-glass doors at the head of the stairs at the mezzanine floor where Madame Marika used to sit is covered by a beige curtain, blocking the light and the jeweled colors of the glass. It serves as an office for the ambassador, who is currently out of town. We are not allowed to go upstairs. Those are the ambassadorial family's living quarters.

The dining room and sitting room furnishings lack the patina and majesty of age, and seem small in the space. The dining room chairs are contemporary, covered in a flowered chintz. The ornamented carved paneled doors are there, as is the rich and gleaming paneling on the walls, but the massive sideboard has gone, leaving the room with an apologetic unfinished look. The Russians' furniture in the sitting room echoes the placement of the furnishings I remember, but the elegant *Louis XV* carved armchairs and love-seats with their worn tapestry seats in muted pastel colors have given way to reproduction antiques, the gold glittering unabashedly, the upholstery a shiny blue damask. The same and not the same.

Overwhelmed at being there, I am too embarrassed to ask to see the library, and too afraid of what I might find. My children, awed to discover so much grandeur in their past, have found much to discuss with the Russian embassy staff who are hosting the tea that has been so thoughtfully laid out and who are eager to exchange views about the world with their American contemporaries. Serge lifts his movie camera and starts to take some film. My heart stops in fear, but it is *glasnost*, and the Russian Secretary takes the camera from his hands and arranges me with my family on the marble steps that lead upstairs, for a photo.

Surreal. I have found the house again, but I have not found myself in it. I wait for the moment to overtake me, but melancholy takes its place. As I stand grouped with my family on the stairs I had descended so many times as a child, my emotions in turbulence, it seems to me nonetheless that something significant has come full circle.

✦ ✦ ✦

We left the clamor of Cairo and journeyed up the Nile to visit the famous monuments of deep antiquity that none of us had ever seen before, the experiences and discovery of Egypt's extraordinary past bonding us in wonder. Serge's and my parents had visited the temples and monuments of ancient Egypt in their youth, doubtless planning to take us to Upper Egypt when school demands eased, but by then we were gone. We marveled at the gigantic scale of the temples and statues, the stylized detail of the hieroglyphs covering the walls.

But the small shocks of recognition of my own past continued to elude me.

After the exhilarating exhausting days of our cruise to Upper Egypt, we returned to the hotel in Luxor. That afternoon, I rested in my room while the others enjoyed the outdoor pool at the hotel, "gippy tummy" having caught up with me. As I lay there, the shutters half-closed and the window wide open, I heard the voices of the *suffragies* as they prepared for a gala event on the hotel lawn outside my window, setting up tables, covering them with billowing white cloths, laying out dishes and table settings, salt and pepper containers and bright flower arrangements. As they laughed softly and conversed among themselves about the tasks at hand, my childhood crept over me like a comforting blanket. I closed my eyes and listened deeply, with all my senses.

I was home at last.

And I realized that Arabic, the language I knew least, was what most defined my childhood self, just as my observation of certain holidays defined me to others as Jewish, or the boarding school years at Roedean School in Brighton England were defined by my British accent. In the Egypt of my childhood, I was not aware of being defined by my religion. I thought of myself as an Italian girl navigating happily in a rich sea of mingled cultures, of Greeks, Syrians, Armenians, Egyptians, Yugoslavs, French, British, and Sudanese. Social interaction cut across all of these cultures, the greatest divisions occurring around economic and class distinctions. But whatever language we spoke, and whatever origin each of us claimed, the subtext and the background music we all shared was the sound of Arabic, the household words and language that meant home to us all.

Endings are powerful moments, more compelling than beginnings. My life began to acknowledge the possibility of endings the day my eighteen-year-old self slumped in the soft Nile breeze and wept into the stone of the balustrade of the terrace outside my bedroom window, feeling both the retained warmth from the heat of the day and the dead cold underneath it. That day, preparing to move outward from the protection of my past, I tried to claim it, to imprint it on all my senses. That day I wondered how it would feel to be gone *forever*, the word echoing strangely in my heart.

Now I know better. The past is never gone. It is the foundation on which we build the present, every day of our lives.

Lorsque j'aurai ici exprimé ma tendresse,

Mes vœux pour que demain soit rempli d'allégresse

Et te comble, Chérie, de bonheurs infinis;

Encore me faudra-t-il, avant d'avoir fini,

Inclure dans mes souhaits celui que ta carrière

De poète et d'auteur progresse de manière

Et te donner un jour des satisfactions —

Que nous laisse à prévoir ta jeune inspiration —

Pour moi, qui entrevois l'avenir de ta plume,

J'ignore quelle prétention à te nuire assume

En exprimant la muse, scandant ces quelques vers.

Car, me faudra-t-il pas, plus tard, à l'Univers

Montrer que ton talent, ta verve littéraire,

Ont pris quelque origine à la plume de ton père?!

Le Caire, le 8 Janvier 1953.

(Avec mes baisers les plus
affectueux

...Daddy)

*The phone rings. A small voice pipes, "Granny?"*

*"Yes," I answer.*

*"It's Anna." Anna is my second son David's youngest daughter. She is three.*

*"Granny, can Sarah and me make* kaak *with you when we come to your apartment tomorrow?"*

*"Yes, darling," I say.*

*And I smile.*

*The Ben Ezra Synagogue in Old Cairo*

# Epilogue

*In writing* these pages I began to feel that this was perhaps the ultimate ego trip, a long study in self-indulgence. I began to question whether my memories, fragmented as they are, really made it significant to record a lost childhood, to gather stories about a family scattered by the winds of chances, to seek out the lives and loves of ancestors long gone.

But as I delved into fragments of my family's past and tried to find meaning in the movements of destiny in my own, I caught momentary intimations of the mysteries that shape our being. Instead of cobbling a path to the probable past, I observed the boundaries that separate past, present, and future dissolve into an infinite. Every memory that surfaced like a jewel from my past or my interpretation of the past of others led to more hidden doors opening, more windows clearing of dust, more tiny treasures excavated and saved from oblivion. I felt a little like an archaeologist, piecing together broken shards of disconnected memories in order to shape a coherent passage to the present.

I came at last to the conclusion that the precariousness that precedes the existence of any one human being makes the simple existence of each one of us the true miracle of life. I do not mean the kind of precariousness that attends the moment of conception or the moment of birth, or that directs our steps as we cross the road in the face of oncoming traffic, but an intricate, delicate tracery of disasters averted throughout past centuries, of adversities overcome, of ancestors granted life by a miracle, all leading to the momentary fragment of my own existence, and beyond mine, that of my children and theirs. If my mother's grandfather Ezekiel had not heard a voice urging him to leave an inn one night and had been murdered in his bed; if my father's Mosseri ancestors had not left Spain but had been trapped by the Inquisition and burnt at the stake or had become *conversos*; if my father, the unplanned child of his parents' middle age, had not been born; if my mother had contracted scarlet fever from her sister, Olga—if any one of these things had come to pass, I could so easily not have been.

We know so little of why the intricate spirals of this DNA rather than that one have been granted survival. The keys to existence lie in the places where our lives touch the lives of others, in the links that we forge with the world we know. I do not need an infinite map within which to measure the distances I have traveled. It is enough to have flared long enough perhaps to ignite others. I have here attempted to mark each small step remembered with crumbs of memories strewn along the path behind me for the unimagined future to retrace. I realize that I am a link in a chain that forms a pattern I cannot see. I know that the links that precede mine and those that follow have little knowledge of me. It only matters that by my existence I have held one arm out to the past and another to the future. The fact of my existence and the pattern of my choices have made it possible for my grandchildren to be. Perhaps their grandchildren or the great-grandchildren of their grandchildren will save a life, and by saving a life, save a world.

Behind me stretch survivors, their feet on untraveled trails, their eyes straining to catch the green flash of the sun before it sinks into the sea, their choices leading directly into my life. Their strength sustains me. Their courage grapples with my fears. Each of us is a world, and in each of us, the world is renewed. Each of us is a fragment in time.

# The family of Joseph and Rosa Smouha

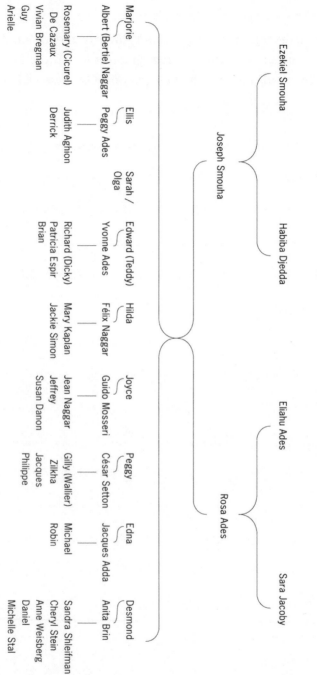

# The family of Joseph and Jeanne Mosseri

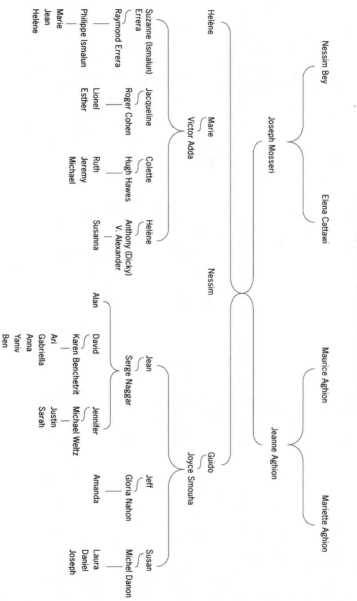

❦ ❦ ❦

# About the Author

*Photograph by Jessica Regel*

Jean Naggar was born in Alexandria, Egypt. She grew up in Cairo and attended the Gezira Preparatory School and the English School in Heliopolis before going to boarding school at Roedean School in Brighton, England. After her family left Egypt following the international Suez crisis, she attended Westfield College at London University and was awarded an honors degree from London University. She later married Serge Naggar and moved to New York City where she established the Jean V. Naggar Literary Agency, Inc. in 1978.

Her poetry has been featured in *The Listener* and *Athanor*. She has been published in the *New York Times*, the *Village Voice*, *Publishers Weekly*, the *Huffington Post*, and *Writer's Digest*. Jean is a member of the International Women's Forum, the Women's Media Group, PEN, and the AAR. She lives in Manhattan with her husband, Serge Naggar, and is the mother of three and grandmother of seven.

# A Readers' Guide

1) In the beginning of the book, Jean sees a black snake in the garden. What does the snake symbolize? How does the discovery of the snake affect the tone of the story?

2) Early on, Jean talks about her Auntie Helen and her ties to Israel and the Zionist movement. Though they lived in the same house, Jean was never aware of her aunt's Israeli connections until later. What does this reveal about Jean's childhood and her understanding of the larger forces around her?

3) Jean appears to be somewhat conflicted about marriage, as there are many instances in her family history of women who have been robbed of an education, and even a childhood, by marriage. Yet, as a teenage girl, she longs to get married and is distraught when she is told that she cannot marry her first love. How have the marriages of the women before her shaped Jean's understanding of the institution of marriage?

4) The narrator describes the celebration of Passover dinner in rich and abundant detail. Discuss the irony of celebrating the exodus of the Jews of Pharaoh's Egypt for this particular family, whose lives are torn apart by their own exodus during the Suez crisis. How does this represent the unease between Egypt and its Jewish population?

5) The theme of isolation comes up several times throughout the narrative. Jean and her siblings are isolated from the adult world in their nursery, and the family compound, complete with its own synagogue, isolates them from the rest of Cairo. How is this isolation a metaphor for the Jews' relationship with Egypt and the larger Arab world?

6) Though Jean considers Egypt to be her home, her parents send her to school in Britain and she grows up speaking English, French, and Italian. In light of Egypt's colonial past, how does her education affect her ties to her homeland? How do her schooling and her upbringing shape her later in life?

7) Several people in the memoir barely escape death: Jean's great-great grandfather Ezekiel leaves an inn in the middle of the night after hearing a voice in a dream and escapes a massacre; Bert, the driver, avoids a bombing when he brings cough medicine to Jean's Uncle Ellis; and Jean herself changes flights, thus avoiding being on a plane that crashes. Do you think this recurring theme of near-death suggests that the author believes she cheated death by getting out of Egypt?

8) How does personal spirituality, as opposed to religion, mold the lives of the Mosseri clan from both an ethnic and traditional standpoint? What other cultural influences play into the author's and her family's belief in fate, the power of prayer, and their various superstitions?

9) Jean describes her overprotective family as keeping her "in stasis, waiting for life to happen, sensing powerful darknesses around me but never touching them." Referring to the Suez crisis

that forced their exodus, she says, "The moment when my parents' world shattered was also the moment that set me free." How was she set free by leaving Egypt?

10) After Jean's family leaves Egypt, she moves to the UK and eventually to New York, where she goes on to have a successful career as a literary agent. How might her life have been different had she stayed in Egypt?

11) At the end of the book, Jean is talking to her grandchildren about making *kaak*, a traditional Arabic dish. How does food function in the book as a way to tie the present generations to the past?

12) What does the family's relationship with the Egyptian Muslim driver, Osta Hussein, whom Jean describes as "above suspicion" even at the height of the Suez crisis, represent? What does it reveal about personal loyalty versus loyalty to one's country or religion?

13) By the time she is writing this story, the author has close ties to Europe, the Arab world, and the United States. Discuss the ways in which she is influenced by all of these regions. In what ways is she a product of all three?

14) After the Suez crisis, tens of thousands of Egyptian Jews were forced to leave Egypt along with citizens of French and British descent. While the French and British citizens had countries to return to, the Jews, including Jean's family, were scattered across the globe. Discuss the implications of this difference, particularly with regard to Israel and the Jewish diaspora.

15) When Jean's mother marries her father, she goes to live in the family's compound with her husband's mother and sister instead of establishing a home of her own for her family. How is this a metaphor for the family's sense of displacement and greater search for a home?

16) In the book, Jean returns to Egypt one final time in 1990. So much has changed that she finds her homeland nearly unrecognizable. What do you think the author would make of the seismic changes in Egypt in 2011? Would she think it represented a true break from Egypt's troubled past or more of the same?

17) In this age of e-mail, there will be no handwritten letters lost in an attic to show future generations how we lived and who we really were. How does the personal exploration involved in writing a memoir affect the writer? Future generations? Is this just a matter of personal closure or an attempt to preserve the histories of individuals to add depth to the political overlay that dominates every "history"?

# Historical Timeline

1882: British troops take control of Egypt.

1896: The opening of the Suez Canal creates a direct passage between the Mediterranean Sea and the Indian Ocean, opening up a vital link between East and West.

1914: Egypt becomes a British protectorate, inaugurating the colonial era in Egypt.

1922: Fu'ad I becomes King of Egypt. Britain recognizes Egyptian independence.

1928: The Muslim Brotherhood is founded by Hasaan al-Banna. The Brotherhood will go on to become one of the largest and most influential Islamist parties in the world.

1936: After the death of his father Fu'ad I, sixteen-year-old Farouk takes the throne.

1939–1945: World War II. Although Egypt remains officially neutral until the final year of the war, King Farouk has close ties to both Germany and Italy.

1948: Egypt, Jordan, and Syria attack the new state of Israel one day after the United Nations' decision to partition Palestine.

1952: Gen.Gamal Abdel Nasser (also believed to be a Nazi sympathizer) overthrows King Farouk. Many believe that this act marks Egypt's true break from Britain.

July 1956: President Nasser nationalizes the Suez Canal.

October 1956: Israel, Britain, and France launch a joint attack on Egypt to protect international passage through the Suez Canal. As a result of tensions between Egypt and Israel, tens of thousands of Egyptian Jews are forced to flee Egypt.

1967: During the Six-Day War, Israel defeats Egypt, Jordan, and Syria and takes control of the West Bank, the Gaza Strip, East Jerusalem, Sinai, and the Golan Heights. The Suez Canal is closed.

1970: Nasser dies and is replaced by his vice president, Anwar al-Sadat.

1975: The Suez Canal is reopened.

1981: Anwar al-Sadat is assassinated and Hosni Mubarak assumes the presidency.

January 2011: Opposition protests calling for political change and the resignation of Mubarakerupt in Egypt.

February 2011: Under immense international pressure, President Mubarak steps down after nearly thirty years of rule and hands over power to Egypt's army council.

November 2011: Egypt holds its first parliamentary election. Turnout is unprecedented for an Arab nation.